SQUIRES
IN THE SLUMS

Settlements and Missions
in Late-Victorian London

Nigel Scotland

I.B. TAURIS

LONDON · NEW YORK

Published in 2007 by I.B.Tauris & Co Ltd
6 Salem Road, London W2 4BU
175 Fifth Avenue, New York NY 10010
www.ibtauris.com

In the United States of America and Canada distributed by Palgrave Macmillan
a division of St. Martin's Press, 175 Fifth Avenue, New York NY 10010

International Library of Historical Studies 45

ISBN: 978 1 84511 336 0

A full CIP record for this book is available from the British Library
A full CIP record is available from the Library of Congress

Library of Congress Catalog Card Number: available

Printed and bound in India by Replika Press Pvt. Ltd
From camera-ready copy edited and supplied by the author

CONTENTS

LIST OF ILLUSTRATIONS

ACKNOWLEDGEMENTS

My debts are many and various, but I would like to express my grateful thanks to a number of people who helped me at various points. In particular, Dr Kate Bradley, librarian and archivist at Toynbee Hall, guided me through Toynbee's documents and also pointed me to other valuable manuscript collections. The Rt. Revd Dr Geoffrey Rowell, Bishop of Gibraltar and Fellow of Keble College, kindly read the entire manuscript and provided me with constructive and helpful advice. The Revd Dr Jeremy Sheehy, Principal of St Stephen's House, also read the manuscript and made a number of helpful suggestions. The Revd Dr Alan Munden gave me useful information on a number of Victorian clergy.

Many college and school archivists and librarians also kindly made documents and facilities available to me: James Stickings, archivist of Bradfield College; Anne Wheeler, archivist at Charterhouse School; Jill Barlow, archivist at Cheltenham College; Rachel Roberts, archivist at Cheltenham Ladies College; Fiona Mackenzie, Library Director at Christ's Hospital; Elizabeth Stratton, archivist at Clare College; Robert Myers and Gill Cannell, archivists at Corpus Christi College, Cambridge; Dr J.R. Piggott, Keeper of the Archives at Dulwich College; P. Hadfield, archivist at Eton College; Victoria Sheppard, archivist at Haileybury School; Rita Boswell, archivist at Harrow School; David Tabraham-Palmer, archivist, and Yvonne Steward, librarian, at Highgate School; Norman Rosser, archivist at Malvern College; Dr T.E. Rogers, archivist at Marlborough College; Patricia Aske, librarian of Pembroke College, Cambridge; Clare Hopkins, archivist Trinity College, Oxford; Margaret Thompson, archivist of the United Reformed Church History Society; John Edwards, secretary of the Old Wellingtonian Society; Susanne Foster, deputy archivist at Winchester College; Harry Spry-Leverton, archivist at Uppingham School. In addition to the sources provided by these institutions, I also benefited from the Barnett Papers and a number

of other collections at the London Metropolitan Archives and at the
Bancroft Library in Bethnal Green.

I am very grateful to Accompli for compiling the index and preparing
the camera ready copy. I am also indebted to Dr Shelley Saguaro, Head of
the Department of Humanities in the University of Gloucestershire, for her
encouragement and support for this project.

Nigel Scotland
Cheltenham, 2007

PREFACE

The late Victorian years were a time when, on account of publications such as George Sims' *How the Poor Live* and Andrew Mearns' *Bitter Cry of Outcast London*, many in England were becoming acutely aware of the abject conditions of the poor in the nation's large towns and cities. At the same time, there was a growing concern among many of the privileged classes that the widening class gap needed to be bridged. Nowhere was this feeling more strongly felt than in the great public schools and university colleges. Indeed one observer noted that an increasing number of the sermons preached in the Oxford University Church of St Mary the Virgin in the 1880s were on social themes.

Coupled with this emerging social concern, there was an acute awareness that the Church, and the established Church in particular, had failed in its efforts to reach the working classes with the Christian message. By the 1870s there was a growing sense of duty towards those in need and it was this that caused a number of Anglican clergy to take on livings in London's East End. Among them were John Richard Green who worked in Stepney, Brooke Lambert who served as the incumbent of the parish of St Mark's Whitechapel, and Samuel Barnett who left a curacy at the fashionable church of St Mary's Bryanston Square to take on the parish of St Jude in Whitechapel.

In his early years at Whitechapel Barnett invited a number of Oxford students to come and spend part of their summer vacation living and working in his parish. Among those who came was Arnold Toynbee who was later to become a distinguished economic historian. It was the experience of having the assistance of these undergraduates that led Barnett to contemplate the idea of establishing a colony of university men in East London. The venture would not simply be staffed by undergraduates working in their holiday period but rather by those who had already graduated and were now working in one of the various professions and living in London's West End.

Barnett's vision was to build a hostel where a number of these university men could come and take up residence and share their breakfast and evening meals. In return they would agree to give several evenings each week and time at the weekends either to working in various clubs and activities or to become involved in local politics. Out of this vision Toynbee Hall was born, named after a celebrated historian who had earlier spent time in Whitechapel, and whose life had recently been cut short. Barnett's great emphasis was on the 'settlement' principle. As he saw it, the key factor was to be good neighbours and this meant to live among the poor and demonstrate neighbourliness in practical action.

Barnett's settlement plan hit the mood of the time and perhaps nowhere more so than in the University of Oxford where his vision was quickly taken up by others with Henry Scott Holland famously urging undergraduates of the time to 'Come and be Squires of East London'. It was because Toynbee Hall provided such a stimulus to others to get involved in this form of practical Christianity that it came to be referred to as 'The Mother of All Settlements'.

Barnett's institution didn't have a fixed religious agenda and some of his residents were not practising Christians. This was because he was solely intent on demonstrating the message by practical, educational and philanthropic activities. However, many Oxbridge colleges and public schools who embraced his settlement principle felt it was necessary to adopt a specifically Church or Christian agenda. Such was the case with Keble College's Oxford House Settlement in Bethnal Green. It set out with the combined objective of establishing a community that promoted social and philanthropic work and at the same time nurtured the Tractarian principles of the college founders. In this specifically Church commitment, Oxford House set the pattern for the great majority of settlements and mission settlements that were founded in the succeeding years.

By the end of the Victorian era there were in East and South London more than twenty University Mission Settlements and nearly thirty that were affiliated to the public schools. More were founded during the Edwardian years and the movement reached a high point shortly before the outbreak of the Great War. In the aftermath of the conflict it proved more difficult to recruit new residents and by the 1930s it became clear that local government and social services were providing many of the educational and recreational activities which had previously been organised by the settlers. In the light of this, some colleges and schools took the view that their institutions were no longer serving a useful purpose and closed down their premises. Others, however, were able to adapt or change their role and ethos, and a number of the original settlements, including Toynbee Hall and Oxford House, are still actively involved and serving the same local communities.

Although many of the settlements and missions barely survived the generation that founded them, they were a significant part of Christian mission in late Victorian London. They were a vibrant expression of practical Christianity and demonstrated what being a good neighbour entailed. In particular, their involvement in local government, educational work and management impacted many lives with Christian values. Additionally, the service of their residents as members of Boards of Guardians and sanitary committees and their active support for trade unions demonstrated their compassion and willingness to fight for justice.

It is not difficult to level accusations of condescension against the settlers but the 'Squires' brought an improved quality of life to several thousands of the working poor in East and South London. Whilst the number of settlements that remain today are relatively few, their residents set a pattern for philanthropic Church work and they were the pioneers of professional social work and social work training. The majority of settlers were motivated by a combination of Tractarian spirituality and the Christian Socialist stress on the doctrine of the incarnation which caused them to live among the poor and to demonstrate Christ's compassion by caring for the whole person.

1

LONDON'S DESPERATE NEED

In 1896 the future Bishop of London, Arthur Winnington-Ingram,[1] who knew more about the working poor of the city than most, famously said, 'It is not that the church of God has lost the great towns; it has never had them'.[2] The roots of this alienation in the nation's capital lay in the early years of the century when large numbers of people drifted from the Essex and Kent countryside into areas of North-East London and South of the Thames. Here they were joined in localities such as Bethnal Green, Shoreditch and Whitechapel by growing numbers of immigrants from France and other European countries. It was computed that in the closing years of the nineteenth century there were not less than 60,000 Jews in London.[3] In an effort to house them numerous sub-standard dwellings, often without careful planning, were run up in a very short space of time by speculative building contractors with little thought for the social or religious needs of the new communities. What at the beginning of the century were small villages clustered round a parish church on the outskirts of the city, suddenly in the space of a generation, became a sprawling mass of many thousands of people with no church and no priest to minister to them and offer any sort of Christian framework for their existence.

In 1890 William Booth, the founder of the Salvation Army, published his most celebrated book, *In Darkest England and the Way Out*. 'Darkest England', he asserted was to be found above all in London's East End, an area containing 980,000 men, women and children roughly equivalent to the entire population of Scotland.[4] Using statistics taken from Charles Booth's sociological survey, *Life and Labour in the East End of London*, he estimated that there were 17,000 inmates in workhouses, asylums and hospitals, 11,000 'loafers, casuals and Criminals', 74,000 'very poor' and 100,000 'starving'. These he called the 'Submerged Tenth' because across the nation as whole there were others in smaller towns and cities who were in comparable circumstances and together they represented a tenth of the total population.[5] Booth stated that if destitution existed everywhere in East London proportions, the country would have thirty-one times more starving people than there were in and around Bethnal Green.[6] Thomas Kelly has argued that John Ruskin's *Unto This Last*, which was published in 1862 and was the first of a series of trenchant attacks on the social and economic system of the time, also had a wide impact and greatly influenced those who later established settlements and missions.[7]

The truth of the matter was that the Church of England was essentially a rural Church whose structures were designed to fit the medieval village community with its squire, farmers and fixed hierarchy. It was in consequence ill-equipped to cope with the rapid growth of towns and cities which accompanied the industrial revolution. As *The Record* put it in January 1882, 'urgent reforms were required to re-locate the church's human, financial and physical resources to cope with changes in society, and to combat godlessness in the areas where Christianity was reported "not in possession"'.[8]

Inadequacy of the Parochial System

A major problem in the Church of England's organisation was its parochial system of small parishes dotted across the landscape. In a country where communities were relatively small, numbering anything from a few hundred to perhaps two or three thousand, the time-old system worked well enough. In a burgeoning urban sprawl, such as was emerging in London, it proved to be totally inadequate. In 1855 Lord Shaftesbury observed that the parochial system 'is no doubt, a beautiful thing in theory and ... of great value in small rural districts, but in large towns it is a mere shadow of a name'.[9] The Bishop of London, Archibald Campbell Tait, declared in his visitation address in December 1866 that 'the ordinary parochial machinery is quite inadequate to meet the needs of a dense population'.[10] Although many, including bishops such as John Ryle of Liverpool,[11] recognised the rightness of Shaftesbury's judgement, the problem was they were wedded to the past and could not envisage the national Church without its parishes and the status that it conferred on the local vicar or rector. A highly regarded clergyman who spoke at the Church Congress in 1881 declared that if the parochial system was brought to an end in large towns, 'we at once become Congregationalists'.[12] William Walsham How, who was to play a significant role in the emergence of Settlements and Missions in London, told a meeting at the Mansion House in 1880 that Churchmen 'could not set the parochial system aside if they would, and they would not if they could. (Hear, hear) Their plan was to supplement it'.[13] When it came down to it however, many clergy were unwilling to see their parish divided or supplemented. Working parties set up by the Convocations of Canterbury and York in 1889 and 1892 found that most of the clergy whom they interviewed were opposed to the division of parishes.[14] A further problem was that it was not always easy to create new parishes. Indeed until the 1843 Act of Parliament, new Church of England parishes could not be established without separate acts of Parliament. K.S. Inglis pointed out that from 1880 to 1900 the average annual number of new parishes was only 35.[15]

Lack of Church Accommodation

If the parish system was lacking so too was the amount of church accommodation and perhaps nowhere more so than in London. For example, in 1811, it was pointed out by the then Prime Minister, Spencer Perceval, that in St Pancras and St Marylebone there was church seating for only one-ninth of the population. In 1814 Dr William Howley was appointed Bishop of London and soon realised that there was church seating for only one-tenth of London's population. In 1815 Richard Yates published his damning pamphlet entitled *The Church in Danger* in which he stated that in London 953,000 souls were left without the possibility of parochial worship. Horace Mann, who reported on the findings of the 1851 Census of Religion, reached the conclusion that there were a million working people who could not have attended church even if they had wanted to. He speculated that a further 2,000 churches and chapels were needed in urban areas. Successive bishops did their best to plan and adopt strategies that would go some way towards meeting the crisis of reaching the capital's poor with the Christian message. In 1866 Archibald Tait, who was then Bishop of London, reported that the number of churches in the diocese had increased to 1,127 from 980 in 1862. But he went on to say that a further 194 were still needed, together with 325 new clergy and a proportionate staff of Scripture Readers.[16]

The paucity of Anglican church accommodation was further exacerbated by the pew system. This allowed families and individuals who could afford to do so to rent pews in their local Anglican church. Not only did this reduce the number of seats available, it also alienated the poor who were often relegated to rough benches at the back of the building. In his report Mann gave reasons why the labouring myriads absented themselves from public worship. One of these was that they disliked the social distinctions in churches, the division into respectable pews and free seats, and regarded religion as a middle-class luxury.[17] The other side of the issue was the fact that the more respectable found it difficult to sit at close quarters with the unwashed. A curate, who worked in Stepney and enjoyed good relations with the poor in his care, nevertheless opposed the abolition of the pew system: 'though it is a painful thing to mention, the dirt of some of the people, and the fleas that we see, would prevent many persons going'.[18] Strictly speaking pew rents were only supposed to be charged where Parliament specifically allowed them which usually meant those churches that were built after 1800.[19] The practice of pew rent, although in most instances illegal,[20] became widespread. St Philip's Clerkenwell became the first church in London to abandon the practice of renting pews.

In view of this state of affairs it was small wonder that church attendance in the metropolis was in decline. Charles Booth gave the following figures for church attendance in East London and Hackney in churches and chapels for Sunday 24 October 1892. Out of a total estimated population of 909,000, the attendances were Church of England 95,750, Congregational 20,000, Baptist 26,000, Wesleyan 19,100, Other Methodists 11,400, Presbyterian 4,000, Other denominations 7,500 and Roman Catholics 7,000.[21] Compared to the attendance for the country London's East End represented a bleak picture. In 1903 the *Daily News* published a census of London church attendance. It showed that attendance had fallen from 535,715 in 1886 to 396,196.[22]

Social Conditions

The social conditions of the poor in most of the parishes both in the East End and south of the river were harsh and unhealthy. It was well-known that the Christian Socialist novelist, Charles Dickens, often went to places such as Shoreditch in order to capture the atmosphere for his scenes of poverty. The author of an article in *The Illustrated London News* entitled 'Dwellings of the Poor in Bethnal Green' wrote that the condition of the poorer neighbourhoods of this wide and populous district have 'for years been subject to all the foulest influences which accompany a state of extreme filth and squalor'.[23] The same writer went on to state that Hollybush-place, Green Street, Pleasant Place and other neighbourhoods which 25 years previously had been a relatively healthy outlying village, 'now consist of ruinous tenements reeking with abominations'.[24] Commenting on the water supply of the area he wrote,

The water for some fourteen or fifteen houses is frequently supplied from one tap in a dirty corner, where it runs for only a short time every day; and the places are mostly undrained. Add to this the decay of vegetable matter, the occasional evidence of the presence of pigs from the adjacent houses which have back yards (these have none), and that sickly odour which belongs always to human beings living in such a state, and the result will represent a score of places extending over Bethnal Green parish for more than a mile in length and half a mile in breadth.[25]

The state of drinking water in south London was equally as bad. In 1849 Charles Kingsley recalled having gone down to the cholera districts of Bermondsey together with Frederick Denison Maurice and Charles Walsh. What they encountered he put in a letter to his wife.

I was yesterday ... over the cholera districts of Bermondsey; and, oh, God! what I saw! People having no water to drink- hundreds of them- but the water of the common sewer which stagnated, full of dead fish, cats and dogs, under their windows. At the time the cholera was raging Walsh saw them throwing untold horrors into the ditch, and then dipping out the water and drinking!! ... and mind these are not dirty, debauched Irish, but honest hard-working artisans. It is most pathetic, as Walsh says, it makes him literally want to cry-to see the poor souls struggle for cleanliness, to see how they scrub and polish their little scrap of pavement and then go through the house and see 'society' leaving at the back poisons and filth-such as would drive a lady mad, I think, with disgust in twenty four hours.[26]

Archibald Tait, who was Bishop of London from 1856–68, was well acquainted with the deprivation of the city's East End and, together with his wife, he regularly visited the cholera districts.[27] In 1866 when the River Lea was infected and 'conditions became very bad indeed', he called a meeting of the clergy of Bethnal Green, Stepney, and Spitalfields. Together they endeavoured to make a series of recommendations that would assist the sanitary authorities. Tait's wife, Catharine, later hired a house in Fulham in which to take care of some of the many orphaned girls from the area. The 'Home' later became established as St Peter's orphanage.[28]

Tait was also only too well aware of the problems associated with deprivation and squalor, and the ways in which they created a downward spiral of hopelessness, ignorance and a lack of self-respect. On one occasion he highlighted the issue in a graphic account of a conventional district in the East End of London, containing a population of 10,000 of whom 4,000 were Jews.

Not one in a hundred habitually attends a place of worship. Of 228 shops in the district, 212 are open on Sunday. About seventy, however, are closed on Saturday the Jewish Sabbath. Not half the Gentile adults can read. Half the women cannot handle a needle. Our mothers' meeting has seventy members, half of whom, though living with men and having families, are unmarried, and this is the proportion throughout the gentile district. Nine families out of ten have but one small room in which to live, eat and sleep. Not one family in six possesses a blanket or a change of clothing. Not one in four has any bedding beyond a sacking, containing a little flock or chopped straw (a miserable substitute for a mattress). Not one in twenty has a clock, – not one in ten a book. Many houses are in the most wretched condition of dirt and filth, walls, ceilings, floors and staircases broken and rotting. Drunkenness, brawling, blasphemy, and other sins are fearfully prevalent.[29]

The Challenge of *The Bitter Cry of Outcast London*

Sensational accounts of the horrors of inner-city life were not felt to be helpful by everyone who was engaged in working in the nation's slum areas. Nevertheless one such report stirred the churches of several denominations to action in a way that few had done before. This was a penny pamphlet entitled *The Bitter Cry of Outcast London: An Inquiry into the Condition of the Abject Poor* published in October 1883 by a Congregational minister, the Revd Andrew Mearns (1837–1925).[30] Mearns, who had been appointed secretary of the London Congregational Union in 1876, was deeply disturbed at the conditions in London's East End. *The Bitter Cry* was not altogether original since part of its evidence was taken from a more racily written tract produced by G.R. Sims entitled *How the Poor Live*.[31] In the preface to a later edition, Sims wrote, 'I have the permission of the author of *The Bitter Cry* to say that from these articles he derived the greatest assistance while compiling his famous pamphlet'. Mearns had no wish to undermine the existing efforts of the churches and the various home mission societies, he simply wished to highlight the ways in which the situation was becoming increasingly more desperate. He wrote,

> The Churches are making the discovery that seething in the very centre of our great cities, concealed by the thinnest crust of civilisation and decency, is a vast mass of moral corruption, of heart-breaking misery and absolute godlessness, and that scarcely anything has been done to take into this awful slough the only influences that can purify it.[32]

In addition to the writings of Sims and Mearns, some of those who became active in the Settlement Movement were impacted by John Ruskin's *Unto This Last*. First published in 1862, it was the first in a series of trenchant attacks on the social and economic system of the time.[33]

Mearns was under no illusions and made the point that while many had been engaged in building churches and dreaming of a coming millennium,

> the poor have been growing poorer, the wretched more miserable, and the immoral more corrupt; the gulf has been daily widening which separates the lowest classes of the community from our churches and chapels.[34]

He stated bluntly that we are living in a fool's paradise if we imagine that all the existing missions, temperance societies and other reformatory organisations are doing more than a thousandth part of what needs to be done. To reinforce his point, Mearns reported on the conditions of East London in stark detail, examining non-attendance at worship, living conditions, immorality, poverty and the heart-breaking misery of life in general. Reflecting on the non-attendance at worship he cited a number of neighbourhoods, among them an area of Bow Common. Here he observed that out of 2,290 persons living in consecutive houses, only 88 adults and 47 children were connected with a place of worship.[35] In one district of St George's-in-the-East only 39 persons out of 4,235 attended a place of worship.[36] In considering the conditions in which Londoners lived, Mearns was unwilling even to use the word 'homes' because compared with thousands of working-class dwellings 'the lair of a wild beast would be a comfortable and healthy spot'.[37] He went on to state that, 'Few who will read these pages have any conception of what these pestilential human rookeries are, where tens of thousands are crowded together amidst horrors which call to mind what we have heard of the middle passage of a slave ship'.[38] He continued,

> To get into them you have to penetrate courts reeking with poisonous and malodorous gases arising from accumulations of sewage and refuse scattered in all directions and often flowing beneath your feet; courts, many of them which the sun never penetrates, which are never visited by a breath of air, and which rarely know the virtues of cleansing water.[39]

Not only was the atmosphere supremely unhealthy, overcrowding was widespread. Every room in these rotten and reeking tenements', according to the pamphlet, 'houses a family or two' and 'in one cellar a sanitary inspector reported finding a father, mother, three children and four pigs!'[40] *The Bitter Cry* was given wide publicity by W.T. Stead in his *Pall Mall Gazette* and by the *Daily News* which highlighted 'the great dark region of poverty, misery, squalor and immorality'.[41]

Sims in *How the Poor Live* identified water as one of the greatest evils of overcrowded London'.[42] He noted that in many houses more water came through the roof than through the pipes which dripped foul-smelling liquid into tubs or butts in the backyard of the dwellings. As for water for sanitary purposes there was 'absolutely no provision for it in hundreds of the most densely-inhabited houses'.[43] Sims' conclusion was that 'the density of the population in certain districts, and the sanitary defects of the tenements, are at present absolute dangers to public health'.[44] On this ground alone, he urged agitation for reform.[45] For his part, Mearns saw only too clearly that the result of conditions such as these was immorality. His research soon led him to see that marriage as an institution was not fashionable in these districts of London. 'Ask if the men and women living together in these rookeries are married', he wrote, 'and your simplicity will cause a smile'.[46] He also observed that incest was common and that 'no form of vice and sensuality causes surprise or attracts attention'. Prostitution was widespread and 'many' of the girls involved were 'not more than 12 years of age'. In one street of 35 houses, 32 were known to be brothels.[47]

Poverty was deeply ingrained into the fabric of 'Outcast London' and due in large measure to 'wretched earnings'. A child of seven was capable of making 10s. 6d. a week thieving but to achieve the same in earnings he would have to make 56 gross of matchboxes a week or 1,296 a day. Women sewing the linings into trousers and stitching on buttons received two pence half-penny a pair and had to provide their own thread. For most engaged in the work it meant a day of 17 hours for a shilling.[48] The payment for other work done by men and women in East London, including sack making, babies' hoods and lawn tennis aprons, was little different. Two major factors served to increase the level of poverty; the cut taken by middle men and the cost of rent. One man Mearns visited stated that his master got a pound for the things he gave him but he received only three shillings in return.[49] Not only were these wages exceptionally low, half their total was spent on rent for their 'pestilential dens', leaving them little more than 4d. to 6d. a day for food, clothing and fire.[50] High rents had the effect of causing more and more people to crowd into small houses in an effort to reduce their costs but this overcrowding in turn caused greater squalor and the spread of disease.

The sum total of this state of affairs is heart-breaking misery. How these 'outcasts' could continue their labour at all was a marvel as far as Mearns was concerned. 'Although we cannot do all we wish', he went on to suggest some ways of remedying the situation. First, there must be State action in particular to provide better living conditions and to curb the high rents charged by landlords.[51] The Artisans' Dwellings Act had in some ways made the situation worse because although large spaces had been cleared of fever-ridden rookeries, the rents of the new habitations were beyond the reach of the abject poor. Second, the churches must be roused to undertake their share of the responsibility. Third, 'the Gospel of the love of Christ must be presented in its simplest form, and the one aim must be to rescue not proselytise'. Mission halls must be erected in each district and services of all kinds must be arranged and at the same time attempts must be made 'to relieve in some wise, though very limited way, the abounding misery, whilst care is taken to prevent the abuse of charity'.[52] Mearns issued a challenge to the churches to take some serious action. 'An exceeding bitter cry is that which goes up to heaven from the misery of London against the apathy of the Church. It is time that Christians opened their ears to it and let it sink down into their hearts'.[53]

New Mission Strategies

The full coverage given to Mearns' pamphlet struck deep into the hearts of all Christian denominations. W.T. Stead, who had just been appointed editor of the *Pall Mall Gazette,* took up *The Bitter Cry*'s agenda at the very moment when the nation had become concerned about the condition of the poor and their housing in particular. The main Nonconformist groups reacted in a united fashion and in 1884 the Wesleyans, Baptist, Presbyterians and Congregationalists organised a conference to consider the spiritual and social needs of London. In 1884 the Wesleyan Methodist Conference heard a paper from one of its delegates on 'Outcast London'[54] and later the same year the Wesleyan Conference minuted the fact that 'the temporal and spiritual interests of the dense populations of our large towns, more especially London, have excited much public attention through the year'. It also made a commitment to consider special methods for grappling with the problems of London. The following year the President of Conference took up the concerns of *The Bitter Cry* in his address and underlined the particular importance of London:

This great centre of national, imperial world-life is the prize, the citadel, for which the powers of light and darkness must contend ...

We can use no language strong enough to express our sense of the responsibility of English Christians in respect of the great city, its sin and sorrows.[55]

Dorothy Hughes recalled that her father spoke at a great meeting in response to *The Bitter Cry* at Exeter Hall that was chaired by Lord Shaftesbury. The immediate response among Hughes' fellow Wesleyans was that he should start a mission in East London and that he should be at liberty to stay there as many years as he was able to carry on the work. Sadly the suggestion aroused opposition which the disillusioned Hughes was unable to comprehend.[56]

The reaction of the Established Church was rather more piecemeal but in the end proved to be more substantial on the ground than the efforts of the Nonconformists. One important Anglican response was that of the Revd Brooke Lambert (1834–1901), the Vicar of Greenwich, who had formerly worked first as curate and then as Vicar of St Mark's Whitechapel, where he had set up a working men's club and a mutual improvement society and established a penny bank. He therefore knew the problems of the poor at first hand. Lambert wrote an article for *Contemporary Review*[57] entitled, 'The Outcast Poor- Esau's Cry'. Lambert saw clearly that London's poor, like Esau, had been deprived of their birthright 'and have no blessing'. The East London Esau may soon advance not with 400 but with 400,000 to meet us. They are men and women who live 'shut out from faith, hope and love'.[58] In a way not dissimilar to Mearns, Lambert went on in his essay to sketch some of the main features of what this meant in practical terms. First, there is the evil of bad houses the vast majority of which 'are constructed so as to last no longer than the duration of the lease, with inevitable discomfort to the inhabitants throughout the period'.[59] The large owners of 'horrible London' property make their living by exacting inequitable rents from those who can pay, when they can pay. In many instances the poor are unable to meet even minimal rent payments and this has meant that landlords have been unable to make the repairs or improvements requested by local boards.[60] Lambert followed Mearns in highlighting the evils of insufficient earnings. One of the root causes was competition of trade that makes large gains impossible, and reduces profits as it reduces wages. At this point Lambert commended trade unions as 'a way of preventing competition playing into the hands of unrighteous employers'.[61] His favoured solution also included cutting out the unscrupulous middle-men and a larger development of co-operatives. Underlying these particular evils was 'the misery in every form which reduces life into a struggle for bare existence'. Lambert proposed several remedies for the situation. On the matter of housing he favoured a solution based on Octavia Hill's scheme whereby property would be purchased by the rich and then put in the care of educated persons. There were, he suggested, thousands of women who might form a volunteer corps to carry out the scheme.[62] On the matter of poor wages there must be a mission not to the poor but to the manufacturer. Unlike Mearns, Lambert did not advocate the multiplication of mission halls, which he believed would only serve to alienate the poor further. His view was that the Christian Socialism of Maurice and Kingsley was 'a practicable system' that would be good news to the poor in ways that Mission Hall preaching would not. Lambert concluded, 'if we would win over Esau, whose bitter cry rings in our ears, we must first dispose of difficulties which our own carelessness and self-indulgence have allowed to become serious'.[63]

Lambert had earlier worked in a Whitechapel parish where he had formed several clubs and involved himself in local administration. His friend, the Revd John Richard Green (1837–83), did similar work in the parish of St Philip, Stepney. As early as 1869 the two men had met together at the request of John Ruskin to consider the possibility of setting up a colony of university men to expand and develop the kind of work both had been attempting in their respective parishes. They were both of the opinion that there was a need for educated men to take up residence in the poorer areas of London where they could assist in matters of local government and education. Nothing of these hopes materialised and Green became seriously ill and retired from the church's ministry. Lambert however remembered their earlier plan and in 1881 he addressed a group of undergraduates at Merton College, Oxford, and urged them to come down to Whitechapel and help in his parish during the vacation.[64] Samuel Barnett (1844–1913), who was to be the most influential figure in the Settlement Movement, had also begun what became a regular practice of inviting undergraduates to spend part of their vacation in the neighbourhood of St Jude's Whitechapel and to involve themselves in the work of the parish. Among those who came was the social historian, Arnold Toynbee, whose life was to become an inspiration to the Barnetts.[65]

Oxbridge Concern for the Poor

Through such visits to East London parishes undergraduates returned to their colleges with a growing concern about the conditions in which poor were living. Many became acutely conscious and worried about the widening class gap and resolved to do something to change the state of things.[66] There is no doubt, as Anne Ockwell and Harold Pollins argued, that the context of the Settlement Movement lay in the changing mood at Oxford in the second half of the nineteenth century. As early as 1850 senior academics were concerning themselves as to the role and responsibilities of the university to the nation as a whole. In 1850 William Sewell had mooted the idea of endowing professorial chairs at Birmingham and Manchester. Two decades later, Balliol and New College were prompted by John Percival, who was then headmaster of Clifton College, to give financial backing to University College Bristol.

A little later in 1877, partly as a result of Benjamin Jowett's influence, a committee was established to promote extension lectures in large cities. The first chairman, the philosopher, T.H. Green, who had already spent a good deal of pen and ink theorising on the nature of a just society, now had the opportunity to engage in some practical outworking. The committee became deeply concerned to promote educational reform and social justice. Their efforts, together with others who shared their vision, was later to bring about the *Workers' Educational Association*. Against this background, Ockwell and Pollins asserted that 'the universities settlement movement was based on the idea, not a new one, that the universities could help to revitalise the life of the great cities of the nation'.[67]

By the early 1880s the major national daily newspapers were regaling their readers with detailed descriptions of the miseries of East London life. Philip Littleton Gell noted that in consequence the first time university academics and students were startled into a feeling of responsibility for the working poor whose daily toil facilitated their privileged existence.[68] During 1883 and 1884 Oxford's interest in social problems reached a high point. Joseph Arch, the leader of the National Agricultural Labourers' Union (NALU), spoke at Oxford Town Hall in 1883 at a large meeting with several Oxford University fellows and professors on the platform. In October of the same year the Revd Dr Montagu Butler, Headmaster of Harrow, preached a university sermon on the text, 'Love the Brotherhood' in which he urged the members of the university to respond to *The Bitter Cry*.[69] The *Oxford Magazine* for December 1883 commented that 'above all it has been recognised … that Oxford has much to learn from the working classes as well as the working classes from Oxford'.[70] Among other radicals who spoke in Oxford were the American, Henry George and the Socialist, William Morris.[71] The same journal commented that 'the exceeding bitter cry of the outcast' had been ringing in Oxford's ears for the past year. Throughout 1884 there were reports on the work in East London.[72]

Settlements

In November the same year, Frederick Rogers, a working man of radical views from Whitechapel, gave a talk to more than fifty men in the rooms of Sidney Ball at St John's College. His address sparked a lively discussion that included the idea of establishing a settlement of university men in East London. Barnett who was present urged the assembled gathering to bring the life of the university to bear on the life of the poor. To his subsequent distress, opinion became sharply divided as to whether such an institution should be definitely committed to Church of England principles or seek to embrace a wider clientele.[73] Barnett spoke out strongly for the settlement idea rather than college missions which, he maintained, quickly developed into autonomous parishes. He was of the view that settlements would help to overcome the growing problem of class division.

Barnett's address was later published in 1894 as an essay in a volume entitled *Practical Socialism*. Here he underlined the fact that a mission is necessarily 'a churchman's effort'. His concern was rather that university men should not simply be satisfied with giving an annual guinea subscription to their college mission but rather that 'as university men they should themselves bear the burdens of the poor'.[74] The problem, as Barnett perceived it, was that university missions followed a pattern of erecting a district church or chapel and persuading a former graduate, now a young curate, to take on the work. So what does the university graduate find when he visits his college mission?

> He finds a church which is kept up at a cost of £150 a year. He finds a clergyman absorbed in holding together his congregation by means of meetings and treats, and almost broken down by the strain put upon him to keep his parochial organisation going. The clergyman is alone, his church work absorbs his power and attracts little outside help. What can he do to improve the dwellings and widen the lives of 4,000 persons?[75]

In the light of this, Barnett strongly advocated the settlement principle as a better way of influencing the lives of the poor. His strategy was that the place of the settlement must be chosen in some poor area but without a specific parochial district attached to it. A house must be taken with sufficiently large rooms to accommodate a warden and a number of residents. The man chosen to be the head of the settlement 'must have a good degree', be an educator in touch with local schools and be endowed with 'the enthusiasm of humanity'. Most importantly, he must be 'an encourager' whose duty it is 'to keep alive among his fellows the freshness of their purpose' and 'to recall the stragglers, refresh the out-worn, praise and re-inspire the brave'. A settlement that offered the opportunity for graduates and undergraduates to live and work together in East London, under the leadership of a clergyman, but without the restrictions of the parish system would, he asserted, be more appropriate for a university or a college.[76] It was this paper that led in 1884 to the founding of Toynbee Hall whose new buildings were opened on 10 January 1885. The broader concept of a Settlement was embraced by Nonconformists and the establishment of Toynbee led to a stream of Settlements, some of which were linked with Congregationalism and Methodism and some, such as Mary Ward House, had no orthodox religious basis at all. Barnett was in fact a strong critic of the established church's impotent structures and corruption. He fully realised that the situation in East London called for a new and radical approach. Commenting on the situation as he saw it, he wrote:

> As a "National Church", it is out of touch with the nation. There is no department in the state which can match the abuses connected with the sale of livings, with the common talk about preferment and promotion, with the irremovability of indolent, incapable and unworthy incumbents, with the restriction of worship to words which expressed the wants of another age, and with the use of tests to exclude from the ranks of ministers those called by God to teach in fresh forms the newest revelations of mankind.[77]

There was no place in Barnett's scheme of things for 'a church buttressed by party spirit', nor for a community founded on 'self-help respectability'.[78]

Barnett's paper at St John's sparked an ongoing debate among churchmen as to whether a settlement was preferable to a mission. In essence, missions were usually a small designated area taken out of a large parish which the incumbent selected with the agreement of the bishop. Most London clergy who worked in poor areas were more than happy to hand over a specific part of their charge to the care of a missioner whose salary was paid for by the school or university college concerned. Such missions usually built a church or chapel with halls where various clubs could be held and activities take place. Sometimes, if funds permitted, a gymnasium was added, and sporting and athletic pursuits were developed as an important means of reaching out to the younger age groups. Barnett's feeling about 'College Missions', as he called them, was that they tended to come to an end when they developed into parishes.

Barnett emphasised two key defining features of the settlement. First, that men and women came and 'settled' in the locality and second that they were not primarily established to proselytise. The settlement was a building in a poor district that served as an educational, social and sometimes religious centre. It included a hostel where graduates who had taken up work in the various professions in the nation's capital could come and live alongside the working classes. They would then devote several of their evenings to assisting in the various clubs or helping with one or more of the different activities. Some got involved in local politics, public health or gave support to trade union campaigns.

Education was central among the concerns of the settlements. As well as simple courses in reading and writing, lectures on a wide range of subjects were organised and in some cases there were university extension courses.

It was recognised by men such as Barnett that the poor were not only starved of many of the material necessities of life, they were also denied beautiful things. In this respect the settlements made a significant contribution by organising concerts, dancing and folk dancing, picture exhibitions, libraries and book clubs.

The settlers put the emphasis on being good neighbours by demonstrating practical care, improving the quality of people's living and so perhaps earning the right to speak of the Christian faith. In short, they saw their role as being a presence rather than preaching. In this agenda Barnett was inspired by Frederick Denison Maurice and the earlier Christian Socialists. Barnett's emphasis on the establishment of a residential hostel was the defining characteristic of the Settlement. As the author of the *Handbook of Settlements* in Great Britain put it:

Settlements vary in the aims and methods of work, but they have one thing in common, as their name implies: a number of men and women must have chosen to live in an industrial neighbourhood. They may live singly or in twos or threes, or they may live all together; they may live in private houses or in tenements, or they may live in a specially built hostel. The exact manner of residence is a detail, though an important one. The essential thing is that the residents should make themselves familiar with the district and should feel at home in it.[79]

The same writer went on to assert that the key test of a settlement's effectiveness is 'its ability to harness to the service of the neighbourhood those who in any case would be living and working in it'.[80]

Barnett's vision for settlements certainly caught the mood of Oxford at just the right moment. One student who signed himself 'C.G.L.', wrote to *The Oxford Magazine* in November 1883 as follows:

> Sir- It must surely be a general feeling that the scheme of University Settlements, sketched on Saturday by Mr Barnett of Whitechapel, affords one of the most practical outlets for that interest in social amelioration which is increasingly strong in oxford, owing greatly to the personal enthusiasm of such men as Arnold Toynbee, but which must lose much of its enthusiasm if it cannot find some practical sphere.[81]

Mission Settlements

Some time before Barnett had established Toynbee Hall a number of public school and university 'missions' were already in existence in parts of London. For example, Edward Thring, headmaster of Uppingham, had decided to start a school mission in the East End in 1869 and Winchester College established a mission at Bromley in 1876. Christ Church, Oxford had set up a college mission in Poplar in 1881. Such missions, which usually had specific religious agendas and were often linked to the Established Church. What was new was Barnett's concept of residence and the idea that the rich could also learn and gain from the experience of living among the poor. Barnett's view of the role of religion was altogether broader with much greater emphasis on the role of education, citizenship and practical care. It was not until after the arrival of Walsham How as bishop with responsibility for East London and Anthony Thorold as Bishop of Rochester, whose diocese included most of south London, that Missions began to be taken up with real understanding or enthusiasm. Indeed when Dr Ridding consulted the Bishop of London as to where the Winchester school mission should be started he was greeted with 'blank misunderstanding'.[82]

In the years after Barnett's founding of Toynbee, most of the missions, subsequently established by the universities and public schools in the East End and to the south of the Thames, built hostels and residences where graduates and undergraduates and past and present pupils were able to come and stay for varying periods of time. As well as enhancing the lives of Londoners, part of the aim was that public schoolboys and undergraduates would not be able to plead ignorance of the poor.

Both Thorold and How valued the parochial system but they both fully recognised that many London parishes were far too large for one incumbent to organise and care for. They both therefore came to the view that one obvious solution was to separate off sections of major parishes and designate them as mission areas. The great attraction of giving these 'mission' areas to public schools and university colleges was that these institutions had the capacity through their pupils and Old Boy networks to raise funds for buildings and salaries. Both Thorold and How put enormous energy into visiting both Oxford and Cambridge colleges and public schools, particularly those that were close to London. They gave chapel sermons in which they challenged their hearers to get involved with the needs of the poor and disadvantaged. They also spoke to undergraduates in their common rooms and made return visits as often as possible in an effort to keep the momentum and support going. On some occasions Thorold and How challenged and encouraged each other in the work. At other times they appeared to be rivalling one another in their efforts to get support either for East London or London south of the river.

Oxbridge Mission Settlements

Although many in Oxford and Cambridge were profoundly influenced by Barnett's brand of Christian Socialism the majority of the Oxbridge colleges were drawn to settlements with a more overt Christian agenda. Oxford House in Bethnal Green, which began in October 1884, was strongly identified with the Tractarians of Keble College. At a gathering called to inaugurate the venture, Walsham How was unequivocal that the purpose of their settlement was a missionary one. He was happy that the outcome of their work should be 'the true acceptance of the Incarnation, by which God and Man are brought together' but underlined the fact that 'the foundation of your work should be faith in our blessed Lord'.[83] Edward Talbot, the Warden of Keble, who chaired the meeting, underlined their Christian agenda in a fund-raising speech some years later. He said, 'one object animates the whole movement – the preparation of character for ... the reception of the religion of Christ, for the advancement of which Oxford House alone exists.'[84] One of the early heads of Oxford House, H. Hensley Henson, said that if the pagan East End of London was going to believe in the Christianity of a settlement then the settlers must show 'loyal intimacy' to the church in East London.[85] For this reason Oxford House shortly afterwards became formally associated with the parish of St Matthew's Bethnal Green. Significantly, one Toynbee member, Cosmo Lang, found the atmosphere there too intellectual and went across to Oxford House where he said 'they were rather loyally accepting something old and tried and sure and bringing it as a gospel, a good gift, to the people'.[86] Arthur Winnington-Ingram, who was Head of Oxford House from 1889–98 and later Bishop of London, was of the view that the very existence of a body of laymen working in the cause of Christianity for the people is a protest against the idea that it is only the clergy who believe in Christianity'.[87] The men of Oxford House gave Toynbee the credit for provoking them to action and relations between them were for the most part very amicable. However Henrietta Barnett did later reveal that her husband was distressed that another house had been founded for the reason that Toynbee was not in their opinion sufficiently religious. It was, she wrote, 'a deep, a very deep pain to Mr Barnett'.[88]

Significantly, of the university mission settlements that followed in the wake of Toynbee Hall and Oxford House, the majority adopted the ethos of the latter institution. Two other Oxford Colleges established their mission settlements in the East End. Trinity selected an area in Stratford close to the Great Eastern Railway works with a residence for the missioner in Romford Road.[89] The mission was formally opened on 13 January 1888 under the leadership of the Revd Charles Baumgarten. Christ Church established a similar venture in part of the parish of Christ Church, Poplar in 1892 under the inspirational leadership of Darell Tupper-Carey.[90]

While Oxford Colleges were drawn to the East End, Cambridge became strongly rooted in south London. St John's was the first college to establish a mission there and the work commenced in February 1884 under the leadership of the missioner, the Revd W.J. Phillips.[91] Trinity College, Cambridge established their mission in 1885 in the parish of St George's Camberwell with the Revd Norman Campbell becoming at the end of that year both vicar of the parish and Warden of the Mission. In 1887 a house for Cambridge residents was taken in Camberwell Road and renamed 'Trinity Court'. But a decade later in 1897 Trinity generously allowed the house and that part of their mission to become 'Cambridge House', a lay settlement with a clerical head but open to all Cambridge men.[92] Clare College Mission commenced in May 1885 in a district severed from the parish of All Saints Rotherhithe with a population of 5,000. The focus was strongly on religious work and the clergy were assisted by two Bible women, other lay helpers, and the sisters of the church.[93] Pembroke College commenced its mission at almost the same time. At a meeting held in the College library on 27 May the decision was taken to accept the offer made of part of the parish of All Saints Newington.[94] Corpus Christi College Mission was commenced in 1887 in a district taken from Christ Church Camberwell with a population of 8,000. For the first two years, services of worship were held in a temporary chapel in a railway arch. Gonville and Caius established their settlement in Battersea in 1887 in the district of Yelverton, which had been taken out of the parish of St Mary's Battersea.[95]

Queen's College began work in the parish of St Chrysostom's Peckham in October 1901 but this falls outside the time frame of this book.

Thorold, who was a pronounced Evangelical, was Bishop of Rochester from 1877–90. His diocese took in most of south-east London including Bermondsey and Southwark. Soon after his consecration, Thorold began to devise a strategy for London south of the river. He knew the benefits of the parish system first hand but recognised that it needed supplementing in various ways. His strategy was to create specific mission areas from the larger parishes containing some 3,000, 4,000 or 5,000 working people. In the midst of these areas he would put a young clergyman and hire for him a stable, a loft or even a cellar. He would encourage him to be diligent in visiting, teaching and praying, and by so doing to build up a congregation round him. In time this would develop into a mission hall and ultimately a new church. Thus J.W. Dickie observed that 'college missions were part of the church's attempt to make the parochial system work, by dividing unmanageable urban parishes into smaller units'.[96] Thorold's missioners were in one way close to Barnett's vision for they were not to take any part in the routine duties of the parish in whose bounds they lived.

William Walsham How (1823–97) became suffragan to Bishop Jackson in 1879. He was not a gifted preacher and so small of stature that vergers had to provide a platform so that congregations could see him. But in every other way he was the man for the hour, constantly involving himself in local affairs, holding meetings of the clergy and producing devotional literature for church workers.[97] Among other things he preached in the kitchen of a two-hundred-bed lodging-house and attended the Feast of Tabernacles in a large Jewish synagogue where he sat in one of the chief seats.[98] Bishop Jackson gave How more or less diocesan control over East London and never interfered with his decisions, an arrangement that continued until Frederick Temple succeeded Jackson in 1885. Temple, who had more decided views on diocesan policy, was unwilling to continue his predecessor's arrangements. However, in 1888 How accepted the new See of Wakefield.[99] How was recognised as 'a spiritual force' who was only too well aware that 'not all the funds in the world, nor all the clergy, nor all the lay workers, nor all the eloquence, nor all the tact, nor all the activity, nor all the organisation, can effect anything unless the motive power is "the promised power from on high", the power of the Holy Ghost'.[100] How is still remembered for his spirituality and his hymn, 'For all the saints'.

The state of things that confronted How on his arrival in London was well-recounted in an article in *The Worker* for July 1890.

A church cruelly under-manned, and struggling to provide the bread of life for 700,000 people, mostly poor ... The clergy were too few, and many of them were disheartened; jaded by the overstrain against too great odds; jaded by the unlovely pressure of their surroundings; jaded sometimes by illness, sometimes by old age. The endowments were sufficient for the incumbents in almost every case, but were not sufficient to provide assistant clergy, or lay workers, male or female. The paid church workers, therefore, like the clergy, were too few. In parish after parish the necessaries of Church life were lacking or inadequately provided. In the very corner of England, where the Church needed her fullest equipment, was that equipment utterly inadequate ...[101]

How's first concern was to fill up the gaps in both the clerical and lay ministry. 'A sufficient ministry', he argued, 'is the first thing needful for Church work'. In order to facilitate this the bishop founded the East London Church Fund at a meeting held at the Mansion House on 18 June 1880 with a council of clergy and laity formed to administer it.[102] The central focus of the fund was the provision of 'a sufficient staff of clerical and lay workers'. Money was also set aside so that 'incumbents who from old age or other adequate cause are unable to do their duty to their parishes, are able to retire'.[103]

Another major objective of the fund was to provide money to facilitate the formation of mission districts with mission clergy in large parishes where 'sub-division was considered expedient'. This initiative soon attracted further money and undoubtedly helped to inspire colleges and public schools to plan mission activities in London's East End.

A major aspect of Anthony Thorold's policy which made the diocese of Rochester 'one of the most active and energetic in England' was the setting up of the Rochester Diocesan Society. Its sole aim was 'to fashion new districts out of the overgrown parishes of metropolitan Kent and Surrey' by setting a clergyman down in rented accommodation in some back street, building him a mission-room and ultimately a church and parsonage house. The fund also provided money to send out Bible women and Scripture-readers 'to break up the fallow ground'.[104] In November 1878 Thorold appointed the Revd C.H. Grundy as organising secretary with the brief of supervising the diocesan missionaries, liasing with local clergy, preaching on behalf of the society and raising money. In the years that followed there was a constant stream of correspondence between the bishop and his mission lieutenant. On 22 November 1884 Thorold wrote, 'Sometimes you send three letters in one day, which is perhaps sufficient. Sometimes you don't write at all, which is insufficient when anything has been happening'.[105] Thorold was constantly pressing for action. To one incumbent he wrote in 1882 that the work of the Battersea mission chapels 'wants pushing' because every year of delay 'makes openings for Non-conformist zeal, gives the public houses and Bradlaughism a great vantage-ground, and justifies Salvation-Armyism'.[106] Thorold gave the credit to Toynbee Hall for having created the impulse that brought about so much concern for the poor on the part of so many Cambridge undergraduates. But he added that 'if it had not been Toynbee Hall anything else would have done equally well'.[107] Be that as it may Thorold's evangelical convictions led him in an altogether different direction to that of Toynbee. He favoured only distinctly church missions on parochial lines. A Cambridge undergraduate of the day recalled that a number of his contemporaries were attracted by the breadth and culture of Toynbee Hall but that in the end a good majority decided for the 'Old Church' and South London. According to his biographer, Charles Simpkinson,[108] Thorold regarded the introduction of college and school missions as one of the chief distinctions of his episcopate.[109] In the few months that remained after he had been offered the See of Winchester on 4 October 1890 and before his enthronement, he paid visits to all of them.

Public Schools Missions
Although the Oxbridge colleges established a significant presence in both the East End and in South London, the public schools also made a considerable impact. Whereas there were less than twenty university mission settlements active in London by 1900, there were more than twenty-five such public school missions,[110] well over half of which were located in the East End. Many public school headmasters were themselves clergy who were acutely aware of the needs of the poor and the way in which the established church of the nation was failing in its mission in the inner city areas. Edward Thring, the distinguished headmaster of Uppingham, spent his first years after leaving King's College, Cambridge, working as a curate in the new parish of St James, Gloucester. In this tough unhealthy environment of poor housing on the eastern side of the city where most worked as dockyard labourers or railway workers, Thring became acutely aware of the problems of the poor. Among other things he assisted his incumbent, Thomas Hedley, in the small three-roomed school alongside the church. There they did battle trying to teach the sons of poor 'the three Rs'. The challenge was how the Cambridge honours graduate, for Thring was no mean scholar, was to get into the minds of these young

disadvantaged children. But eventually he succeeded and there can be little doubt that St James' school was both the parent of Uppingham and the missions which were subsequently established in London. Years later Thring reflected in a sermon how much he also owed to Hedley. 'I remember the great man', he said, 'for he was a very great man, the quiet clergyman, under whom I had begun parish work, said in words I have never forgotten, "I never see a particularly disagreeable little boy come into my parish school without thinking here is someone I have to learn to love for Christ's sake"'.[111]

Many of the middle-class parents, who were sending their children to the newer public schools like Uppingham, shared the same concern about social deprivation, crime, squalor and immorality. They were more than happy to see that opportunities were being opened up to raise the quality of life of the disadvantaged sections of society and build bridges between classes. The establishment of missions would also help ensure that boys educated at public schools would not plead ignorance of the poor and would educate the nation's future rulers in their responsibilities to the working classes.

Among influential churchmen Walsham How proved to be a strong influence in persuading public schools to put down roots in East London. Not long after his consecration as bishop, he began visiting and addressing chapel services and offering definite districts that could be formed out of existing parishes. A number of schools were themselves acutely aware of the needs and invited priests who worked in slum areas to come and speak to masters, boys and old students. An 1887 issue of *The Berkhamstedian* captured the mood of the time. 'There is', it reported, 'a stronger spirit abroad and a greater desire to do something to benefit our fellow creatures'.[112] Of the 22 schools that established Mission Settlements, 15 did so in the 1880s and two others had been started before the decade began.

As with the majority of university establishments, almost all the public school missions had some kind of specifically Christian agenda in which they sought to make the local people members of the Anglican Church or at the very least to christianise the neighbourhood in some way. They also aimed to provide educational and life-skill opportunities as well as providing recreational, health and leisure opportunities. It is clear that the last two decades of the nineteenth century were the period of greatest enthusiasm for mission activity. By the time of the Edwardian years conditions were beginning to improve and the beginnings of the welfare state were taking over some of the social and practical caring work which settlers had previously been undertaking.

In all of these developments one thing was not in doubt and that was the impact of How and Thorold on the emerging university and public school mission settlements. How played the major role in establishing Oxford College and public school mission settlements in London's East End. Thorold, despite being an Oxford man himself, was responsible for bringing Cambridge to South London as well as encouraging a small number of public schools into that area of his diocese.

Tractarian Social Concern

The majority of Anglican, and indeed some Nonconformist settlement wardens, missioners and residents, were motivated and inspired by the social theology of the second generation of Tractarians. Their earlier predecessors, despite living in an intellectual environment that was dominated by empiricism, sought to declare the biblical creedal faith of the undivided early Catholic Church. Newman did constant battle with liberalism and used his intellectual capacity to undermine confidence in natural reason.

The younger Oxford Tractarians however began to recognise the validity of some at least of the findings of the scientists and biblical critics, and they began to look for ways to reconcile them with their Catholic faith. Two factors helped them in this process. First, they began to renew their confidence in the New Testament documents prompted by the work of Lightfoot and Westcott. Second, they found in the thinking and writing of T.H. Green, a philosophy that countered the rationalism of the earlier nineteenth century.

Thomas Hill Green (1836–82)[113] had been taught by Benjamin Jowett but went on to part company with much of orthodox Christian belief. That said, he was a spiritual man who valued Jesus' teaching and example of sacrificial service. Green was essentially an 'idealist' believing that ideas and ideals are products of the mind as compared with the world around us which is perceived through the senses. These ideals are therefore of a higher order of existence and linked with conscience, which Green regarded as the presence of God within man and therefore in the world. The true Christian, Green asserted, consults his conscience in order to discover the best way in which to know and honour God. Green believed that conscience, the spark of eternal consciousness, is present in everyone and, arising from it, each person is concerned to aspire to do good. This led him to stress the importance of conduct and in particular the duties of citizenship. In this he himself became a role model serving as a member of Oxford Town Council and President of the Oxford Band of Hope Temperance Union. It was this aspect of Green's life that led K.S. Inglis to comment that 'he deliberately set out to stir the civic consciousness of Oxford' and that 'his teaching and example helped to make Oxford men think about living in a Settlement'.[114]

The inner core of the second generation of Tractarians at Oxford included Charles Gore, a Fellow of Trinity, Edward Talbot, the Warden of Keble and Henry Scott Holland of Christ Church. Of these three it was Scott Holland who was most influenced by Green. Indeed he once remarked that Green 'gave us back the language of self-sacrifice and taught us how we belonged to one another in one's life of high idealism'. It was partly for this reason that Gore and J.R. Illingworth, another associate, came to focus on the incarnation. It was this doctrine more than any other that inspired the young men and women who took up the vision of Barnett and others to go and settle in the slum areas of the nation's capital in an attempt to incarnate the Christian gospel. J.W. Dickie noted that 'incarnational theology recognised the need for efficient sanitation and healthy amusements not merely as means to an end but as themselves expressions of Christian fellowship'.[115]

Methodist and Congregational Settlements and Missions

Although the Anglicans led the way in establishing mission settlements, the movement also impacted Nonconformists. Wesleyan Methodists established a settlement at Bermondsey in south London in 1891 under the leadership of John Scott Lidgett. Lidgett who came from the 'High Wesleyan' tradition went to Bermondsey following the Conference decision of that year to support the project. The main building, opened in January 1892, was to be the Warden's home for 59 years. Lidgett set out a list of aims for the settlement, one of which was 'to bring additional force and attractiveness to Christian work'.[116] Although public attention was still strongly focused on the East End of London following the publication of *The Bitter Cry*, Lidgett chose South London for his settlement because, in his own words, Bermondsey was 'at that time the most neglected neighbourhood of poorer London, as far as the purposes I had in contemplation were concerned'.[117] It had not, Lidgett observed, been 'written up' like the Mile End Road or the Ratcliffe Highway and 'offered no field for slumming by society women'.[118] Lidgett could doubtless have found people who would have supported him if he had been planning an evangelistic mission but his vision for Bermondsey was altogether larger. 'A settlement', he wrote, 'is or should be a community of social workers who come to a poor neighbourhood to assist by the methods of friendship and co-operation in building all that is essential to the well-being of the neighbourhood'.[119]

In 1895 the Congregationalists established both Browning Hall in Walworth and Mansfield House in Canning Town. The former institution came about during the long Walworth pastorate of P.J. Turquand

(1826–1902). There the chapel, which had been for that day exceptionally dark and ugly, was transformed into the light attractive structure and now worked as a Congregational Settlement under the name of Browning Hall.[120] Mansfield House was led by Percy Alden. Both institutions espoused Barnett's ideal of having residential helpers who would live in hostel accommodation and then devote their evenings and some of their spare time to clubs and other local community activities. In contrast to Toynbee, however, both Mansfield and Browning had rather more overt Christian agendas. Browning Hall was connected with a local Congregational Chapel and offered non-sectarian evangelical teaching.[121] An official account of Mansfield House stated that one of its key aims was 'to bring the teaching of Christ to bear on all the problems of a poor man's life'.[122] That said, it seems to have been the case that many of its residents were more concerned to engage in social action of various kinds rather than to try and convert the residents of Canning Town. The *British Weekly* kept a fairly tight watch over the two settlements in an effort to ensure that they didn't lapse into the 'creedlessness of Toynbee Hall'.[123] Notwithstanding both came to be strongly associated with social and political reform. One of the leaders at Mansfield wrote, 'To carry out Christ's teaching we felt that a vigorous attack must be made on the evil conditions of life in the district'. In order to support this, objective committees were established on public health, education, poor law and other matters. Browning declared their active support for the Labour Party and stated, 'We stand for the endeavour to gain for Labour not just the good things of life, but most of the best things of life. Come and join us in the service of Him who is the Lord of Labour and the soul of all social reform'.[124]

The Roman Catholic Church didn't stand aloof from the challenge of London's poor. Newman House in Southwark opened in 1891 and was in part a response to a call by James Britten to Catholic University undergraduates and public schoolboys to demonstrate a concern for the urban Catholic poor. St Philip's House in Mile End was the first Catholic settlement in East London, the project largely arising from Cardinal Vaughan's concern for the Catholic poor.[125] Several other Roman Catholic settlements were established in the 1890s.[126]

Settlers of More Radical Views
The later Victorian years bred an increasing number of individuals with radical and liberal views. Among those who were impacted by doubt and scepticism was Mary Augusta Ward better known as Mrs Humphry Ward. She was the granddaughter of Thomas Arnold and her father, also a

Thomas, was remembered by some for having twice converted to the Roman Catholic Church. She was of the opinion that Christianity could be made palatable by ridding it of its miraculous content and focusing on the practical social aspects of the faith. These ideas she also set out in her highly-successful novel *Robert Elsemere* which was published in 1888. Elsemere, a country parson, felt his Anglican faith undermined by the new science of biblical criticism and so gave up his living to take up work among the London poor. In 1890 Mrs Ward made her novel a reality when she was instrumental in establishing a non-sectarian settlement at University Hall in Gordon Square. It was based on a simplified ethical form of Christianity that emphasised social care. Mrs Ward said on one occasion that one aspect of University Hall was to show that the faith of T.H. Green, Martineau and Stopford Brook was viable.[127] Philip Wicksteed, a Unitarian minister, was the warden for a brief period but became disillusioned with the way in which the missionary and practical activities were segregated. After his resignation, the endeavour to nurture Unitarian religion was more or less given up. In 1898 Ward's organisation subsequently developed into the Passmore Edwards Settlement and largely concerned itself with social and educational work. Ward's later years were somewhat less radical as she opposed the suffrage movement and supported her son as a Conservative candidate for Parliament.[128]

2

SAMUEL BARNETT AND THE FOUNDING OF TOYNBEE HALL

'The Mother of All Settlements'[1]

Toynbee Hall, which adjoined St Jude's Vicarage, was opened in 1884 although its buildings were not completed until the following year. Charles Grinling[2] of Hertford College, one of the earliest residents, recalled there was still work to be done when he slept there for the first time on Christmas Eve 1884. Wadham House, named after Barnett's College, was opened in 1887 with accommodation for 18 men. Residents had three duties: to pursue some study, to consider other residents and every week 'to do something, however small, which will help the ignorant, the sad, or the sinning, remembering always that the true man is he that serveth'.[3] Balliol House, in honour of Benjamin Jowett, was completed in 1889 and had similar objectives to those of Wadham.[4] Barnett did not come to live in the Warden's Lodge until 1892.[5] It contained 30 private rooms for graduates and undergraduates of the university. Those who took up residence bound themselves to stay for a term of not less than three months. The premises also contained a dining-room, classrooms and five little halls for educational and entertainment purposes. In addition about a hundred non-residents at any one time were also involved in the work. The programme for a typical week in 1890 comprised of ten lectures, four of which were in conjunction with the University Extension Society, nine reading parties, the meetings of two literary societies, thirty-five classes of various kinds, a concert, a party for a particular group, a meeting of a pupil teachers' association and constant use of the library which contained over four thousand volumes.

As has already been noted Toynbee was the vision of the Revd Samuel Barnett, the Vicar of St Jude's Whitechapel. Samuel Barnett was made deacon at Her Majesty's Chapel Royal on 22 December 1867[6] and ordained

Early portrait of Samuel Barnett. By kind permission of Toynbee Hall.

priest by Archibald Campbell Tait on 20 December 1868.[7] Samuel had been curate in the fashionable London parish of St Mary's Bryanston Square under the Revd Honourable William H. Freemantle (b. 1831).[8] There he opened a Club Room for working men in Walmer Street, assisted in relief work, helped to found the first Charity Organisation Society and engaged in education and club work.[9] It was at St Mary's that he also had the opportunity of working closely with Octavia Hill who had opened a workroom for women. It was she, according to Barnett's wife, who gave him 'a new revelation of womanly potentialities, for which his dear mother and the women he had known at Bristol had given him no indication'.[10] Barnett rejected the easy option of becoming the incumbent of a safe parish in an affluent area. Instead he and his wife, Henrietta, whom he married in January 1871, chose to accept the offer of St Jude's Whitechapel in the East End of London which the Bishop of London described as 'the worst parish … inhabited mostly by a criminal population'.[11] He was inducted on 6 March 1873.[12] Here the Barnetts encountered a world of squalor and deprivation with slum dwellings, unsanitary conditions, poor health and all the problems associated with casual labour. Even at this early stage in his career, Octavia Hill was shrewd enough to recognise that he was destined to accomplish great things in his later life. In a letter dated 27 November which she penned to a Mrs Harris, she wrote:

I should not wonder if he becomes a great man, now he is simply a good man, a remarkable man, but not a great one .... This morning at Communion service, I heard in his voice a certain tenderness and depth of quiet feeling I have never perceived before. How thou would like his extreme truth, he cuts thro [sic] a lie as if he cd [sic] not help it.[13]

Barnett's wife, Henrietta, proved to be the perfect match. James Mallon (1874–1961),[14] one of Toynbee's later wardens described them as 'uniquely suited' and commented, 'For forty years they thought and worked together, stimulating, balancing and supplementing one another ... with the texture of their life so closely interwoven that their work and ideas belonged together'.[15] At Barnett's first Sunday service at St Jude's his congregation was 'six or seven old women, all expecting doles for attending'.[16] Happily the situation improved and by March the following year he was able to report 'about thirty in the mornings, and fifty to one hundred in the evenings'.[17] His aim which reflected the earlier Christian Socialist ideal was 'that everyone might know God as Father'.[18] Barnett had decided views as to why the poor absented themselves from traditional church. He soon began a service for children and went out visiting in 'lay headgear' and 'dressed as unlike a parson as he could well appear'.[19]

As the Barnetts sought to grapple with these problems they recognised that help was needed from outside the parish bounds. This led Samuel to experiment with the idea of inviting undergraduates from his university to come down to Whitechapel in their vacations and to give some of their time to helping with the parish organisations and clubs. Among the undergraduates who came to Whitechapel in the 1870s was Arnold Toynbee. Born on 23 August 1852 the son of Joseph Toynbee, the celebrated aurist, he passed his early years at Wimbledon. At an early point he had considered the possibility of entering the legal profession but his subsequent poor health meant that this was no longer an option. He prepared for university entrance by private study and, after a brief spell at Pembroke College, he entered Balliol in January 1875. He soon became an ardent follower of John Ruskin, the Slade Professor of Fine Arts, who championed the dignity of labour. Prompted by the high degree of philanthropic enthusiasm in the university and his contact with Edward Denison (1840–70),[20] Toynbee spent his summer vacation in Whitechapel. There he hired a sordid room in a poor lodging house in the noisy thoroughfare of Commercial Road and placed himself at Barnett's disposal. He became an active worker in the parish of St Jude's and familiarised himself with local political views by joining The Tower Hamlets Radical Club. On his return to Oxford it was clear that his health was weak and he was obliged to spend time in the quiet of the country. He did, however, make a number of shorter visits on other occasions and stayed with the Barnetts.[21]

On completing his degree Toynbee accepted the appointment of tutor to the Indian Civil Service students at the University. His marriage in 1879 renewed his vigour for a brief period and during the following year Arnold began a series of addresses to working men in Bradford. These lasted throughout the year and attracted large audiences. In consequence his energetic spirit was rapidly depleted and it became clear that he was suffering from an inflammation of the brain. He died after three weeks illness on 9 March 1883, Benjamin Jowett commenting that he 'was certainly one of the most promising of young Englishmen'.[22]

Toynbee, though dissatisfied with many of the teachings of the Church of England, believed that it could it could be reformed from within and might somehow be capable of raising the poor to a better quality of life. He clearly valued his Christian faith which was of a largely undogmatic kind and which he articulated in a letter written in August 1878 to his uncle, probably Captain Henry Toynbee.

My dear Uncle,
I do above all things desire to live a pure life, and I am sure no other desire, however much I may feel in realizing this, holds any permanent sway over me. With you I often feel a kind of despair at the perpetual failure of one's highest aspirations; but I take courage. Prayer to God is the greatest help I have; next to that, I think, the encouragement and example of holy people living and dead is my greatest assistance. May I say that the one thing that drew me first to the lady whom I am now engaged to, was the sense I felt in her presence of an appeal to the highest and noblest part of my nature.[23]

Toynbee wrote in another letter a few months before he died: 'You could I think consider me a Christian, though I do not hold a great many of the doctrines of Christian Theology'.[24]

His early death and his strenuous endeavours on behalf of the poor had a profound effect on his many friends and colleagues in the university and a fund called the Toynbee Trust was set up to provide a memorial in his name. The original hope was that it should have been devoted to a consideration of those economic problems that had occupied his academic studies. However, before any of this came to fruition, the revelations in the press regarding the needs and the suffering of the poor in the East End of

Toynbee Hall, Whitechapel. By kind permission of Toynbee Hall.

London led to a determination to attach his name to some sort of humanitarian scheme in that part of the world. Thus the name Toynbee Hall was given to Barnett's projected settlement which was planned to be built in Whitechapel on a site purchased for £6,250.[25] Henrietta Barnett later recalled how, as she sat in the chapel of Balliol College on Sunday 10 March 1884, 'the thought flashed to me, "Let us call the Settlement Toynbee Hall"'. Bolton King (1860–1937),[26] one of the students, had exactly the same thought and so the name was agreed.[27]

The objects of the institution were set out in a document entitled 'The Memorandum of Association'.

(a) To provide education and the means of recreation and enjoyment for the people of London and other great cities; to enquire into the condition of the poor and to consider and advance plans calculated to promote their welfare.

(b) To acquire by purchase or otherwise and to maintain a house or houses for the residence of persons engaged in or connected with philanthropic or educational work.

(c) To provide in whole or in part for the salary or maintenance of any person or persons engaged in promoting the aforesaid objects.

(d) To receive and apply donations and subscriptions from any
person desiring to promote the objects aforesaid or any of them
and to hold funds in trust for the same.[28]

As has been noted, in his approach to the problems of London's East End,
Barnett, wanted to avoid what he called 'the machinery of religious
missions'. In the words of Briggs and Macartney: 'His angle was very
different from that of the Evangelicals anxious to convert the poor or the
Tractarians calling them to worship. He wanted not only 'settlement', but
sharing of experience, 'not only contact but community'.[29] Barnett had no
wish to confine the project to Oxford undergraduates as was made clear by
the title of the newly formed association. Shortly after the project was
announced, The Committee for the Study of Social Questions in
Cambridge organised a meeting at the Guildhall and passed several
resolutions. Among them was: 'That this meeting of members of the
University of Cambridge desires to co-operate with the members of the
University of Oxford who are establishing a Settlement for university men
in East London'.[30] Barnett reported in a letter to the Council dated 31
March 1885 that a sketch of 'Toynbee Hall' has already been circulated at
the universities having been issued as a supplement to *The Oxford Magazine*
and *The Cambridge Review*.[31] The flow of young men from Oxford and
Cambridge never failed and among those who came were Arthur Sidgwick
and Henry Scott Holland.[32] By the following year it was already clear that
Barnett's scheme was having a positive impact on the local community.
Philip Littleton Gell, Chairman of Council, reported that Toynbee Hall 'is
rapidly being accepted as the visible embodiment of the almost legendary
life and culture of the old universities'. He went on to say that 'the Council
desire to join with the residents in expressing their deep sense of obligation
to Mr and Mrs Barnett for the measure of success attained'.[33]

As the years passed and the work expanded, more and more men were
needed and the Barnetts began to make regular termly visits to Oxford,
sometimes staying with the Master, Benjamin Jowett, and in later years
accepting hospitality from their former rector, Canon Freemantle, who
when out of residence at Canterbury acted as chaplain to the College.
Henrietta Barnett later reflected, 'It is not possible to exaggerate what the
hospitality of the Master of Balliol meant to us and through us to the
Settlement movement'.[34] In the early years of Toynbee, Jowett 'never failed'
to invite the Barnetts to spend a weekend with him and in later years when
they had their own accommodation he still frequently summoned them to
dine with him in the college. On one occasion during a walk after breakfast

in Balliol he admitted that he had initially been nervous about encouraging his students to go to London's East End. 'I used to be afraid of sending men to you, not knowing what you would do with them', he said, 'but now I safely send them, for you are ambitious for them'.[35]

Toynbee and Labour Concerns

Barnett was not one who could stand aside from the concerns of the working poor. Co-operation was the first working-class cause to appeal to Toynbee Hall and to be received with genuine concern and support. Benjamin Jones (1848–1947), the leading Co-operator, became a Toynbee Associate in 1886 and in 1889 a series of lectures on Co-operation was held at the Settlement. The October 1889 issue of *The Star* carried a report of a meeting addressed by Messrs Nash, Waggitt and Fuller on the subject of Co-operation. The correspondent went on to note that 'a co-operative movement is already on foot amongst a large section of stickmakers, and this section wants the Jews, who have recently formed a union to join with them'.[36]

Among other concerns Barnett was a vigorous opponent of the system of casual labour that operated in the docks and elsewhere. He described it as 'the hardest problem in east London'.[37] It was in his view the main reason why so many East-Enders were poor and in constant need of relief. Toynbee settlers shared his concern over this issue and gave their support to a number of other East London labour struggles. In fact from the earliest days Toynbee became the meeting place for a number of local trade unions. Prominent among them was the Dock Workers' Union. The residents became particularly concerned about the conditions in which their local neighbours lived and worked. In June 1885 for example, The Toynbee Hall Memorial Fund Committee resolved

> That it is desirable that a sum not exceeding £30 be paid to Mr J Bonar for the purpose of instituting inquiries into the condition of the Slopworkers (Tailors and Tailoresses) of the East End of London, on condition that Mr Bonar[38] is responsible for the inquiry and for drawing up a report thereon. Mr Milner to arrange the drawing up of the Report.[39]

They set up a committee to inquire into the terrible condition at Bryant and May[40] and in 1888 they interviewed the managers of the company. The situation worsened and eventually led to a strike of 400 match girls encouraged by Annie Besant. Vaughan Nash and Llewellyn Smith, who arrived at Toynbee in 1888, both devoted a great deal of time and effort into supporting trade and benefit societies in the local area.[41] Smith and two other residents, A.P. Laurie and A.G.L. Rogers,[42] not only supported the match girls in their struggle, they wrote to *The Times* on their behalf and expressed their concern at 'the want of sympathy which we have observed on the part of the directors, and the dislike and fear on the part of the girls'. They went on to state that the present strike offers unanswerable evidence of the deplorable conditions which exist in the factory'.[43] Barnett frequently intervened in trade disputes and one year did so on 14 separate occasions.[44] Toynbee's rooms were frequently lent for meetings to aggrieved employees.

A major industrial concern with which Toynbee concerned itself was the dock workers' dispute of 1889. On being informed of the outbreak of the strike, Barnett immediately returned home from his holiday in Switzerland in order to encourage the strikers in their demands 'for better organisation of unskilled labour, aiding by relief those who would have been without it, starved into unrighteous submission'.[45] The strike committee, which included Ben Tillett and Tom Mann, were entertained to supper on 21 September 1889. When the conflict was over the central strike committee were entertained to supper at Toynbee Hall on 21 September 1889.[46] Four days later he personally chaired the first meeting of the Trafalgar branch of The Riverside Labourers' Union. The meeting was held in one of the lecture halls and about two hundred labourers were reported to be in attendance.[47]

A month later, Barnett, accompanied by Ben Tillett, addressed a meeting at Oxford chaired by Charles Gore, Fellow of Trinity and Principal of Pusey House. Barnett, who was received 'amid immense enthusiasm', said that though 'the victory has been won, the crisis remains'. What he meant by this was that it remained to be seen whether or not those men who had joined the new organisation would be thrown out of work.[48] Ben Tillett who was also 'most enthusiastically received' concluded his address with some words specifically directed to the students. 'I ask you', he said, 'to come and live among us, and begin by raising our social position'.[49] At the conclusion of Tillett's speech, Professor Price rose and 'defended the position of the strikers from the political and economic point of view'.[50]

Even after the strike was well passed, Barnett was still emotionally captivated by the dock labourers and their concerns. On 16 November he wrote to his brother, Frank, from Hampsted:

> Your letters have been with me all during this week ... I wish I could be with the Dock leaders but I am bound hand and foot to serving tables. I should like to get hold of Mann and Tillett for with you I fear they are at a crisis ... At present we feel this world – our world – a lot too big and many things drift that ought to be guided.[51]

Tillett later claimed in his *Memoirs* 'that his inspirational leadership as a trade unionist owed much to a course of lectures he had heard at Toynbee by the future Archbishop Lang on "The Strategy and Tactics of Napoleon's Wars"'.[52] Following the end of the strike a number of Toynbee men joined the Dock Workers' Union and some took on official roles as branch officers. Thus as L. Smith observed, 'The Settlement was associated with the emergence of the New Unionism, which was attempting to organise the hitherto unorganised unskilled labourers and to extend unionism among the skilled and semi-skilled'.[53] The union continued its association with Toynbee with *The Manchester Guardian* reporting a quarterly Delegate Meeting at the Hall in April 1890 at which it was announced that the previous membership stood at 32,000 with the funds in hand amounting to £10,000.[54] In March 1891, *The Times* reported on a delegate meeting of the Dock, Wharf, Riverside and General Labourers' Union, which had been held at Toynbee Hall under the presidency of Mr Tom Mann.[55] In the same month Mr Peppin[56] of Toynbee organised a music concert the proceeds of

Samuel Barnett with a group of dockers, c. 1890.
By kind permission of Toynbee Hall.

which were used 'to improve the social conditions of members of the Dockers' Union living in the area and Wapping in particular'.[57]

The 1890 Annual Toynbee Report spoke highly of the value of trade unionism and stated that 'trades unionism appears to be an almost inevitable stage in the gradual evolution of a better industrial order'.[58] It noted that many of the new unions were holding their branch and business meetings on the premises. They included The Tailoresses Union, The Women Cigar Makers, The Stickmakers, The Tailors, Cutters and Pressers,[59] The Railway Servants, The Furriers, The Shop Assistants, The Fellowship of Porters and Dock Labourers', The Jewish Cabinet Makers and Jewish Bakers.[60] In the summer of 1890 The Amalgamated Society of Shipwrights held its annual conference at Toynbee Hall.[61]

Barnett often invited trade union leaders to Toynbee to discuss their aspirations as well as their grievances. He spoke in 1890 'of the many new friendships that have been made with officers and members of trade societies' and went on to remark that 'it is by the strength of these that the real value of a settlement in this and other relations must be tested'.[62] Significantly the first Chairman of the Labour Representation Committee that was set up in 1900 was Frederick Rogers, then a member of London County Council, who was one of the first Toynbee supporters.[63] Henrietta Barnett noted that 'from 1889 until 1906 when we left Whitechapel, my husband was often an invisible but a potent influence in labour disputes'.[64] Speaking at the eleventh anniversary of the founding of the Bedminster Co-operative Society, Barnett asserted, in what proved to be prophetically accurate words, that 'co-operation and trade-unionism are the two forces that will make the twentieth century. The twentieth century will be the working men's century, and they must take their place in it'.[65]

Toynbee was also active in supporting women's trade-union activities and a number of female trade unions held delegate and branch meetings at the settlement. Among those who found a supportive home base was The East London Tailoresses Society.[66] *The Women's Gazette* reported that The East London Tailoresses Society had held their annual meeting at Toynbee Hall on Friday 13 June 'in the charming drawing-room kindly lent for the occasion by Mr Barnett'. Short speeches were made and the evening concluded with music.[67]

All this involvement in trade-union activity and local politics led some observers to fear that Toynbee was developing into a hot bed of radicalism. Benjamin Jowett jotted down his impressions of the place in 1890 in one of his many notebooks. 'Toynbee', he wrote, 'seems to be gradually becoming a house of extreme socialists which it is very difficult to keep in

Some of the first 'squires' at Toynbee Hall.
By kind permission of Toynbee Hall.

order'. Jowett was evidently disturbed by the settlers' involvement in the dock workers' dispute for he went on to note that 'the young men kick over the traces and lately they made themselves rather ridiculous by taking part in the great strike as mediators'. Some of these feelings, Jowett stated, were prompted by things he had heard from Alfred Marshall (1842–1924), Fellow of St John's Cambridge and Professor of Political Economy, who regarded Toynbee as fostering revolutionary socialism.[68] The truth of the matter, however, was that Barnett was a Liberal as were the majority of those who worked with him. Barnett has often been described as a Christian Socialist but he himself was always concerned to point out that there was distinction to be drawn between 'theoretical socialism' and what he called 'practical socialism'.[69] As Briggs and Macartney observed, when Barnett's obituary notices were being written the nation would describe him as 'the most representative Liberal of his time'.[70]

Toynbee Social Concerns

Barnett was deeply concerned that Toynbee Hall should be a centre in which the Christian faith was expressed in terms of involvement in all aspects of the local community. In trying on one occasion to answer the question, 'What is Toynbee Hall?', Barnett concluded that, 'it is in a sense a club, the members of which devote themselves to the duties of citizenship in East London'.[71] Barnett was strongly of the view that Toynbee men should be active in local government and social administration. He believed that proper administration of the poor law was a vitally important way 'to instil principles of independence, habits of control, and knowledge of remunerative work'.[72] For those reasons he himself served as chairman of the Whitechapel Board of Guardians for a number of years and was later succeeded by another Toynbee man, James Brown.[73]

Barnett was an opponent of 'deterrence', the notion that the prospect of the workhouse would deter men from being lazy and cause them to actively seek work. 'It is not deterrence', he wrote, 'it is education or training which will make people work; and education, be it remembered, includes discipline. The first thing necessary, is to replace the workhouses and casual wards with what may be called "labour schools"'.[74] Such schools, he felt, should train men in whatever work interested them. Barnett was a strong campaigner for universal pensions of perhaps 8s. or 10s. to be given to every citizen who had kept himself until the age of 60 without workhouse aid.[75] Barnett also advocated the abolition of the property qualification for the Guardians, and that the meetings be held in the evenings so as to allow members of the industrial classes to serve in that capacity. In 1883 Barnett wrote an article in *The Nineteenth Century* advocating non-contributory old age pensions. His conviction was that pensions should be universal. S.C. Carpenter believed that Barnett was one of the earliest advocates of old age pensions.[76] A number of Toynbee residents and associates were elected to various offices on local borough councils, particularly Stepney.

Sanitary legislation was a key issue for Toynbee and courses of lectures were given on Sanitary Law to offer practical advice and help to local people. Toynbee established a Sanitary Aid Committee, which successfully achieved 'the removal of a number of specific nuisances'. A number of residents proved to be effective and vigilant sanitary inspectors helped to persuade both landlords and the local authorities to take greater note of the condition of tenement houses.[77] Barnett and others from the settlement were also actively involved in the Whitechapel Sanitary Aid Committee.[78] Barnett in fact served for a period as chairman. The committee's work appears to have made a considerable impact in the locality. Reviewing the work completed in 1894 Barnett showed that '31 cases out of a total of 72 defects had been completely remedied'. In addition out of a further 123 cases, 77 had been reported to the Sanitary Authority with 44 being considered too trivial to pass on.[79] Barnett, it should be said, was only too aware that no amount of new model dwellings would of themselves bring improvement 'unless', in his own words, 'the outcast are by friendly hands brought in one by one to habits of cleanliness and order, to thoughts of righteousness and peace'.[80]

In July 1896 there was a serious outbreak of diphtheria and scarlet fever. The main cause was found to be dirt brought about by the scarcity of running water. The Water Company claimed it was 'pumping oceans of water into East London'. The residents vehemently disagreed and a major conference was organised at Toynbee under Barnett's presidency with county councillors, health officers and members of Parliament participating. Resolutions were passed condemning The East London Water Works but still the company failed to respond. Finally Barnett led a delegation and the government intervened with the result that The New River Company began selling 3,000,000 gallons of water a day to its sister organisation. The Waterworks Company were very angry and turned on Barnett who responded with the following rejoinder in *The Times* dated 3 August 1896.

> SIR- The Company well knew – if by no other means, by the yearly increasing amounts paid to its collectors-that the population was increasing, and it ought, long before it did, to have applied for powers to give an increased supply of water .... The Company has, after pressure from the Home Secretary, made arrangements to buy water from the New River Company. It ought during the long droughts to have spontaneously made such arrangements before calling on people to give up baths and let their flowers die. The Company has seen its property doubled in value by the increase of value of the property on which it levies rates, and it ought out of its abundant profits to have made every possible provision before stopping the constant supply .... The fact is that the use of water is not sufficiently common, and many East Londoners welcome an excuse for not washing. It is certain, however, that a decreased use must mean greater liability to disease and a greater disposition to self-indulgence. I trust ... that by the purchase of water from other companies, East Londoners may have a constant supply to which they are used, and by which alone they will be helped to fight dirt and disease.
>
> Yours, etc., SAMUEL A. BARNETT.[81]

Toynbee's concern for local welfare even extended to combating street nuisance. Toynbee men first started to ascertain the facts in 1885. Their reports underlined a high level of disturbance which included, 'great noise from crowd' – 16 September, 'Three women knocking about a drunken man who had a nasty gash on the left eye' – 6 October, 'Woman's head badly cut by a man'– 9 October and 'Saw a woman dead drunk dragged along the length of the street'.[82] Following a major increase in crime, a Streets' Committee was organised in 1888 and the neighbouring part of Whitechapel was patrolled nightly for six months. After that a considerable improvement was observed and the committee only continued its work on the four noisier nights, Friday, Saturday, Sunday and Monday. After 13 weeks passed by in 1890 without a single disturbance being reported, the patrol was discontinued.[83] The Minute Book of Wadham House, one of the Toynbee residences, also contains a number of references to efforts on behalf of the settlers to bring peace and quiet to particular sections of the community. At their February meeting in 1901, a letter was read out to which Mr Canby was asked to write a reply 'strongly regretting the Council's inability to receive a deputation and also expressing surprise that the Council give no promise to take energetic action against the Costers as soon as the new streets are opened'.[84] In 1889 a Tenants' Rights Committee was formed with Samuel Barnett as chairman. About forty cases a week, mostly relating to lawless behaviour on the part of landlords were dealt with. Some of the tenants who suffered unjustly were Jews who spoke only Russian, Polish or German but Henrietta Barnett recalled, 'our Mr Lewis' managed to sort out a multitude of disputes.[85] Other activities that occupied Toynbee residents included helping immigrant Jews to fill in their Census Return forms.[86]

Barnett later wrote a chapter for Will Reason's book, *University and Social Settlements*, in which he claimed that Toynbee Hall had helped 'to inspire local government with a higher spirit'.[87] He went on to maintain that local government needed the presence of a few people who can formulate its mission and asserted that 'to some degree this had been done by the residents of Toynbee Hall'.[88] As examples of what they had achieved, he noted that Whitechapel now had a public library, that political parties in the area now had a social programme and that the local police were enforcing order on the streets.[89] Percy Alden, the first Warden of the Mansfield House Settlement, added his support to Barnett's testimony stating that 'Toynbee Hall has rendered valuable service to the work of local government through Mr Henry Ward, member of the LCC for Hoxton, who has for some years been working on that body as one who is specially interested'.[90]

Education at Toynbee

Barnett made education one of the central concerns of Toynbee's mission. Only by educating the poor would they be in a position to lift themselves out of their down-trodden situation. Barnett believed that University Extension lectures and courses would be a significant means of achieving this end and in 1884 the University Extension Society was welcomed into Toynbee Hall. In the St Jude's Report for 1885 Barnett reported: 'The University Extension Society has this year carried on its classes in Toynbee Hall. The number of students has risen to over 2,500 and a library of over 2,500 volumes has been formed'.[91] In the early days many of his friends and supporters were optimistic about the possibilities that lay ahead. The writer of an article in *The Scottish Leader* commented, 'The educational side of its [Toynbee Hall's] operations has developed in a most wonderful way since the institution was established as the first centre of the London University Extension Society'.[92] However, costs proved to be a major difficulty with Toynbee courses making a charge of £10 which was well beyond the reach of working men who earned little more than 20s. a week. In fact it soon became clear that many of the students were not from the working classes but came from other parts of the city.[93] Barnett himself came to see that University Extension education schemes were not sufficient to meet the needs of working-class students. 'The students', he said in 1887, 'must have not only the direction of a Professor, but the constant care of the tutor'.[94] In 1892 *The Toynbee Record* reported that 'University Extension has made rapid strides this autumn, with eight courses on hand'.[95]

By the end of the century when it was clear that the number of takers for the Extension classes was waning, Barnett used the situation to experiment and to try new approaches. In 1898, for example, a 'History School' was set up tutored by Robert E.S. Hart[96] and designed to give a guided course of study extending over a two-year period. Those who enrolled had to covenant to devote three or four hours to study each week and to produce written papers.[97] In 1900–1 the Extension Society agreed to provide three 'tutorial classes' – in literature, history and chemistry. These were designed to have far fewer students and provided more in-depth teaching and support than mere lecture courses. Briggs and Macartney observed that by 1902 extension lectures were not as successful as they had been during the 1880s but they continued to present what the Christian Socialist, F.D. Maurice, the founder of the Working Men's College in 1854, had called 'a union of "labour and learning"'.[98] In these developments Thomas Kelly has argued Toynbee Hall 'anticipated the later work of the Workers' Educational Association'.[99] Barnett and the many who were concerned with

Toynbee's educational work cherished the hope that it might one day achieve university status. Barnett in fact produced a leaflet that included the words, 'The ideal of many connected with Toynbee Hall undoubtedly takes the lead in the pre-eminence of its lectures'.[100]

Toynbee was concerned with education at all levels and its more popular and applied courses enjoyed much greater patronage and success. Henrietta Barnett gave a list of 134 different classes that were taught during her time at Toynbee. They included such practical classes as basket work, first aid, home hygiene, home nursing, human anatomy, life saving, sewing, shorthand and reading, writing and arithmetic.[101] One report in December 1891 asserted that better proof of the hold that Toynbee's education schemes had taken on East London could not be had than the fact that a thousand students were in weekly attendance at the classes, not to speak of the large number of people who took advantage of the library, lectures and miscellaneous meetings'.[102] The students were reported to be 'both male and female, old and young, and, instead of being well-to-do, are nearly all poor'.[103] The lectures, which were made as simple and practical as possible, were increasingly popular.

A number of Toynbee's members served on various school boards. All the teachers of these classes gave their time and effort entirely free of charge. The Annual Report for 1892 recorded that two of the settlement's oldest residents, Mr George Bruce[104] and Mr Cyril Jackson were elected as members for Tower Hamlets on the London School Board. It also noted that neither of the two gentlemen had stood as the nominee of any political party and that, while they differed in their views, both had come before the constituency as Toynbee men.[105]

Supporting local teachers was another of Toynbee's concerns. It gave Barnett great satisfaction to make Toynbee's facilities available to the School Board to be a part of Sir Edmund Currie's scheme to establish pupil-teacher centres. At the centre, which existed for many years, 'the teachers of the coming generation of Englishmen' were able to come together and find friendship and the freedom to broaden their horizons and open their minds to new ideas.[106] Samuel Barnett was strongly of the view that teachers need to be learners and to that end he formed a Scholarship Committee to send some of the ablest pupil teachers to the old universities.[107] The first group of men to gain Toynbee scholarships worked so well that when in 1886 they took their degrees, the majority of them achieved an honours classification. There were many more men wanting to go on to the university but money was proving to be the main obstacle. It was then the Drapers' Company stepped in and offered £500 a year, a sum which enabled 30 men to have a university education. Shortly afterwards a number of Oxford and Cambridge colleges took up the matter. Oxford, Balliol, Lincoln, and Brasenose offered respectively £50, £30, and £42. At Cambridge King's and Christ's Colleges each offered scholarships of £25 and Emmanuel £40.[108]

Similar work was also done among the female pupil teachers and a Girls' Pupil Teacher Association was formed at the same time as that of the boys. Mrs Fawcett was the first President but Henrietta Barnett succeeded her in 1891 and continued in the post until the Association became part of the London County Council some twenty years later. There were many activities for the girls at Toynbee. They learnt to swim; Mrs Barnett held a monthly Reading Club at which papers were read, poems recited and novels discussed. Barnett emerged as a strong advocate for women's education and for wider opportunities to be made available to them. The *Bristol Mercury* reported the following paragraphs from one of his lectures:

> The State should repeal all laws and abolish all customs which tempt men to lord it over women, or which interfere with the complete development of women's nature. In reply to a question as to whether the legal and clerical professions should be thrown open to women, the Canon said: 'I would abolish all laws which prevent women developing themselves as they choose. I do not think St Paul's prohibition of women speaking in the churches was intended to be a perpetual obligation.
>
> I am in favour of the removal of all legal restrictions on the occupations of women. They should have the same liberty as men to follow any calling and to vote at any election. Their present position of subordination develops the more brutal and selfish instincts of men, and at the same time provokes women to do acts and make claims which are unwomanly.[109]

Samuel Barnett's letters contain frequent mention of the Association's activities. In March 1885 he wrote, 'On Wednesday we had a party of girl pupil teachers. They are better stuff than the boys ...'. In July 1888, 'My wife is in Cambridge with a hundred pupil teachers'. To his brother Frank on another occasion in 1887, 'Dr Abbott dined with us and addressed 120 teachers'. Again to his brother the following year, 'On Tuesday we were overwhelmed by 300 teachers who came to an evening party in greater numbers than they had promised.[110] Henrietta Barnett made other major contributions in the field of education. Most significant was her service on the Board of Managers of the district schools at Forest Gate, a post she held for twenty years. She was entrusted with the task of selecting women officers who would have the responsibility of visiting schools. She visited schools at all hours and was very concerned at the ways in which children were 'petrified by discipline'. She fought with great vehemence against what in many cases were harsh regimes where children were sometimes brutally beaten or had their heads banged together.[111]

From the earliest days Henrietta recalled that despite her husband's colour blindness he had great love of the paintings of the old masters. She recalled that during their 40 years of married life 'we saw together the greatest pictures of all nations'.[112] It was therefore no surprise that one of Barnett's concerns was that the poor should have the opportunity to learn to appreciate art and so nurture the need of the human spirit for an aesthetic dimension to life. To this end each year he organised a major art exhibition in the church and persuaded wealthy individuals and artists to lend their pictures. Among those who did so were Archbishop Benson, who as the papers remarked thereby sanctioned the exhibition's Sunday opening, the Marquis of Ripon and Queen Victoria. A number of contemporary artists loaned some of their pictures, among whom were several of the Pre-Raphaelite School. Holman Hunt, Dante Rosetti, Sir John Millais and G.F Watts all lent various paintings over the years. Not only did many hundreds of local people come to enjoy and appreciate good paintings, the exhibitions had the added plus of bringing many prominent West-Enders to the East End for the first time. Barnett wrote to his brother in April 1885 full of enthusiasm at the successful conclusion of the annual event.

> This has been the event of the week. Day after day crowds have come. The spectators have learnt wonderfully during five years. They study the catalogues, remember the pictures of past years and compare their lessons. More and more am I convinced of this education which such an effort has accomplished. If preaching be any good – perhaps without life, it is more – this preaching had been of the best. We have sold 16,000 catalogues.[113]

In March 1890 *The Times* reported on the opening of the tenth annual Picture Exhibition in Whitechapel organised by the Revd S.A. Barnett and opened by the Duchess of Albany at St Jude's Church School House in Commercial Street. In an opening speech, following Barnett's introduction, Mr W.B. Richmond said that 'in earlier days art was the voice of the people; it was indissolubly connected with their religion; and beauty was held up as a divine essential to true life'.[114] In the week that followed 55,040 visited the Exhibition and 17,738 catalogues were sold.[115]

Barnett eventually raised enough money to build a permanent Whitechapel Gallery. Lord Peel laid the foundation stone in 1898 and the building was completed in March 1901. Barnett was also concerned that the poor who had little chance for relaxation during the week should have opportunity to enter galleries on Sundays. The result of this was that Toynbee entered into a controversy with the Lord's Day Observance Society over Sunday Art Exhibitions. Barnett wrote to the Bishop of London justifying Sunday opening.[116] 'The preaching of a Puritan Sunday', he wrote, 'will not touch them [the East-Enders] for God, while it may make them think that the clergy interfere with innocent pleasure for the sake of their own opinion'.[117] *The Handbook of Settlements of Great Britain* commented that,

> Those who live in poor districts of great cities do not go short of material things only; they starve for lack of beautiful things. On the aesthetic side the settlements have made a big contribution. Settlements organise concerts, dancing and folk dancing, picture exhibitions, Book Shops and have libraries.[118]

Whilst it is clear that Barnett was no sabbatarian he was a strong defender of Sunday as a day for worship and rest from work. 'Religion, it has rightly been said', he wrote, 'depends on the Sabbath. Unless that is people break off from work they will not think about God'. To his brother Frank he wrote in October 1885,

> As I get older, I think I see more and more the need of law ... Yes, if I were going with a Gospel through the land, it should be the gospel of a Sabbath, a day of quiet, a day set apart from the search after health and wealth, a day devoted to meditation and communion with the unseen.[119]

Barnett was for a number of years a active supporter of The Sunday Society and in 1895 he became its President. In his inaugural address he pointed out that a committee of Convocation had reported that 'The cause of Christ has nothing to fear from reasonable and careful extension of the principle of Sunday opening'.[120] On the one hand Barnett was adamant that 'Sunday must be protected from the demon of greed, which would fill its hours with the noise of strife and strain'. On the other side he was of the view that Sunday opening 'should be allowed for all places of recreation and culture which are under national or municipal control' and that 'private places for the same objects at which money is taken should be opened under licence from the local authority'.[121]

Barnett recognised the great importance of providing books for the poor who had little opportunity to read or sufficient resources to purchase any literature of their own. When he first arrived in Whitechapel there was no public library and the equipping of Toynbee's library therefore became a major priority. Despite the lack of grant aid, the library continued to grow every year. In 1888 there were 3,878 volumes, in 1890, 5,216 volumes and in 1900, 7,449 volumes. The daily average number of readers in 1892 was 55 on weekdays and 74 on Sundays, which meant that the total attendance for the year was over 21,000.[122] A 1d. tract was produced by Mr S. Hales, the Toynbee librarian, which aimed at persuading local working men to make more of library facilities. At the same time the residents of the hall were also hard at work sounding out the opinion of local ratepayers regarding the building of a local library.[123] Barnett noted in a letter to Mr Harry Lawson MP in March 1890 that more people used the library at Toynbee Hall on Sunday than on any other day, 'yet everything was quiet and orderly'.[124]

Eventually the pressure of Toynbee's campaigns came to fruition with the opening of the Whitechapel Public Library in 1892.[125] The formal opening ceremony was performed by Lord Rosebery and Samuel Barnett who had been responsible for raising the necessary funds, gave an address entitled, 'Books and their Uses' in which he stated that the uses of books were innumerable, but their chief use was to be our friends. He went on in his talk to underline the fact that 'Books sometimes made the turning-point in a man's life'. 'Books were', he said, 'friends which inspired and rebuked and never wearied, which never sulked and never had any moods; they were friends which gave and took, for there must be reciprocity in true friendship'.[126] Barnett served as a Commissioner on the governing body of the Whitechapel Free Library for a number of years and watched with interest as the number of readers continued to rise. Barnett who was a strong advocate of formal training for librarians had proved to be a significant influence in the development of public libraries. Mr A. Cawthorne, the Chief Librarian and Supervisor of Museums for the Metropolitan Borough of Stepney, later penned this tribute:

> Early in his career he formed parish and students' libraries which prepared the way ... educated public opinion, and brought about the adoption of the Public Libraries Act. The successful establishment of a public library and museum in Whitechapel was achieved mainly by

his energetic action, and it has the distinction of being the pioneer of its kind in the East End.[127]

Frequent conferences were held at Toynbee on a wide variety of topics. Subjects included, The Essentials of a Good Friendly Society, Co-operative Credit Banks, Co-operative Difficulties, The Possibilities of Extending Trade Unions, Labour Farms, New Openings for Co-operation, The Unemployed and The Utility of Strikes.[128] The pages of *The Toynbee Record* capture the wide range of activities that took place in the settlement. The edition of April 1898 for example, included details of the following: Whitechapel Picture Gallery, A New Opening for Co-Operators, a Conference on Labour Homes, the Children's Holiday Fund, Election of Pupil Teachers' Scholarships, Guardians' Election, Saturday Evening Lectures, Sunday Afternoon Concerts, A Chat about Pictures, Millais, University Extension Centre at Woolwich, Toynbee Literary Association, Toynbee Natural History Society, Toynbee Travellers' Club, Toynbee Nursing Guild, Nursing Classes, Toynbee Football Club, Toynbee Swimming and Lifesaving Club, Occasional Notes on Visitors to the Picture Show, Summer Plans, Donation of Jewish Teachers to the Picture Show, The Students' Library, The Students' Union Summer Programme.[129] Henrietta Barnett listed 38 of the most important activities and noted that in 1886 Mr George Bruce's Natural History Society had 192 members. The largest of Toynbee's societies proved to be the Travellers' Club, which became fully active in 1892.[130] Although the membership of this club was largely confined to Toynbee residents and representatives of the middle-classes, a number of more obviously local people took advantage of the opportunities to travel to destinations such as Florence, Spain and Switzerland.[131] At the beginning of the new century it was felt important to encourage specifically labouring classes to travel and The Toynbee Workmens' Travelling Club was founded.[132] Writing in 1898, Will Reason summed this part of Toynbee's role in the following paragraph:

Toynbee is far ahead of all other Settlements in this respect. It may be likened to a People's University. There are classes (including Hebrew) and Modern languages, in languages themselves; in different branches of natural science; in history; in economics; in ethics; in such technical subjects as shorthand, book-keeping, friendly society finance, drawing, ambulance, nursing, swimming etc. There are also ... afternoon classes for girls in subjects ranging from domestic economy to hygiene, through ordinary class subjects to such things as musical drill, wood-carving and swimming.[133]

Country Holidays

A growing concern which was shared by most settlers with many churches
and organisations during the later Victorian years was the Children's
Country Holiday Movement which aimed to give as many poor urban
children as possible one or two weeks away in the country. In order to
facilitate this objective, The Children's Holiday Fund was inaugurated as a
national organisation. The way in which the scheme worked was that local
branches persuaded parents to contribute a very small sum each week and
then the local branch met the difference, usually paying the remaining half.
Barnett soon realised the great value of the project and later served for a
period as chairman of the Fund.[134] The importance of 'sending children
away for a breath of country air' was highlighted in the 1889 Annual
Report and Toynbee became closely associated with the Whitechapel and
Stepney Committees of the Country Holiday Fund. It was reported that of
17,600 children sent away in 1888, 1,600 were sponsored by the
Whitechapel and Stepney Committees.[135] In 1898 Barnett, together with
his Vice-Chairman, wrote a letter to *The Times* appealing for more funds.
An addition of the *Toynbee Record* in spring 1898 noted that 31,513
children had been sent away for a fortnight in the country in 1897.[136]

Religion at Toynbee

As a young man Samuel Barnett wrote a short paper in which he set forth
his religious ideals. They reflect a kind of religious idealism that was popular
among liberals in the mid-Victorian era.

When I calmly think what is best in life, I see goodness; that which I
feel to be good, which means restraint from spite, impurity or greed,
and which manifests itself in love. Goodness is more desirable than
power. I set myself to gain goodness. I check all emotions towards the
opposite, and ... I try to find what that is of which I feel my
impressions of goodness to be but a shadow. There is somewhere
Perfect Goodness. I commune with ideas of goodness which is
equivalent to praying to God. Across my vision passes a figure of
perfect Man. I am seized, borne by Jesu Christ. In communing with
Him I find the greatest help to reaching goodness. I pray to Jesus
Christ and through Him come to the Father.

Why, though, stand alone, why dissociate myself from the body of
worshippers I find in my country? All their forms express a conviction
of the greatness of goodness. So, I worship God. So, I worship Jesus
Christ. So, I worship with my fellows, using their forms as being the

ancient expressions of aspirations like my own. Then I think of what is the object of my life. I see it must be to do good, to improve the condition of the people.[137]

Barnett kept a regular practice of private devotion and regular reading throughout his life.[138] Theologically, he identified with the Broad Church views of the earlier Christian Socialists. Among his close associates were Henry Scott Holland and Benjamin Jowett. When it came to the needs of the inner-city poor he was convinced that neither the Evangelicals nor the Tractarian approaches had the answer. Of the latter he wrote, 'I more and more feel the day of ritualism is over and when the revival comes it will be swept off'.[139] In an essay entitled, *Settlements of University Men in Great Towns*, Barnett wrote, 'Many have been the schemes of reform I have known, but out of eleven years' experience, I would say that none touches the root of the evil which does not bring helper and helped into friendly relations'.[140] In his Annual Report for 1890 Barnett stressed that Toynbee was non-sectarian in its ethos. He wrote that 'among the residents of Toynbee have been found Churchmen, Nonconformists, Roman Catholics, Jews and unsectarians ... No man can say that Toynbee Hall has any narrow aim; it does not exist to increase any party, or bring honour to anybody'.[141] That said, Barnett was clearly aware that as a clergyman of the Established Church he had a responsibility to provide Christian spiritual care for those in his charge. 'Naturally', he wrote on one occasion, 'as a minister of Christ, I am concerned before all things for the growth of true religion in East London'.[142] However, following the earlier Christian Socialist leaders such as Maurice and Kingsley, Barnett was of the view that 'traditional methods and common teaching fail to commend religion'. As he saw it the Christian message needed to be embodied in service and doing good.[143] Barnett nevertheless made every effort to convey the truths of the Christian faith as he understood them in as lively and attractive ways as he was able. A visitor from America recorded his impressions in the following lines:

We went into St Jude's Church – probably the most highly coloured sacred edifice in London ... everywhere red and green and blue paint to which full justice is done by abundance of gas, and on every pillar hangs a picture, a copy of some great work, by which the vicar hopes to teach something to his congregation. For those whose wandering attention cannot be arrested during an ordinary service, there is a "Worship Hour" every Sunday evening – something short and specially attractive –at half past eight. It had need to be specially attractive, for there are street rows always happening somewhere near, and we know the charm of a row. There are public houses – full of welcome – at every few yards.[144]

Every morning there were prayers held in the settlement drawing room for all who wished to join in. Samuel Barnett 'did not rush through a set of prayers as some clergy do', nor did he 'gabble over a whole chapter of the Bible regardless of its length'. His practice was to select a short passage and comment on it. This was followed by prayers and a hymn, which were carefully chosen.[145] Among the Toynbee residents however religion was very much an open question. Any one who wished to connect himself to a church or chapel was free to do so and indeed to work with its religious organisations with the aim of drawing them into the social and educational life of the settlement and its work within the community. Many men were 'strong denominationalists' but some belonged to other faiths or had no formal religious affiliations.

Notwithstanding his liberal views and broad theological sympathies, Barnett was distressed when a group of men from Keble College felt it necessary to establish a Church settlement. That others should have felt it important to establish a rival institution because, in their view, Toynbee's religious convictions were too vague, was a source of 'very deep pain to him'.[146] Barnett wrote in March 1884, 'The Keble people are very vigorous and it will strain one's charity to be in spirit their fellow-workers. I must begin by quenching the desire to say what I think. Words do a great deal to give form to thought'.[147] He was also hurt when Octavia Hill, with whom he had worked so closely as a friend and colleague at Bryanston Square, went to Oxford and spoke at one of the 'Oxford House' meetings without consulting either him or his wife.[148] However with the passing of time Barnett overcame the wounds inflicted by rivalry and in the years that lay ahead he gave much time to encouraging the founding and promoting the growth of other settlements. Among those to whom he gave advice and support were Caius House in 1887, St Hilda's for women in 1889, Mansfield House in 1890, Bermondsey Settlement in 1891, Canning Town in 1892, Browning Hall in 1895, Cambridge House in 1896, Passmore Edwards in 1896 and Plain House in Bristol. The Christian element at Toynbee was certainly a marked feature in the early years but its place later became less apparent with the passing of time. In the first 10 years, 16 out of Toynbee's 80 residents went into the church's ordained ministry. Thereafter the number declined.[149]

Some of the early residents of Toynbee Hall with Samuel and
Henrietta Barnett. By kind permission of Toynbee Hall.

The Achievements of Toynbee

Henrietta Barnett was the perfect match for Samuel. The achievements of
Toynbee was in almost every sense a joint affair. Some time in 1872 before
they were married he wrote to her that he could not conceive of there being
another woman in the world 'who will so meet my wants and stimulate my
powers'. At a later point long after his death when she had completed his
biography, she could write, 'I have loved living with my husband's spirit as
I wrote his life and painted his character'.[150] T.E. Harvey, Barnett's
successor as warden, wrote of Henrietta that 'her will-power harnessed men
and women to tasks which would otherwise have been untouched that
needed doing'.[151]

Barnett was constantly active in recruiting new residents. On 9 May he
wrote to his brother Frank, 'Oxford was good. On Sunday we had a
meeting at Balliol. I once more fiddled on the Settlement string and found
the men as ready as ever to dance. In fact the men altogether are as
responsive as ever and put us in good heart'. He went on to state that one
really positive outcome of their stay was the relationship they formed with
the Bishop of Ripon. Samuel noted that he understood 'that high class men
require intelligence rather than dogmas' and need to value rightness of life
more than rightness of views.[152]

In December 1887 Benjamin Jowett, the Master of Balliol, wrote in a
letter to Florence Nightingale, 'The Barnetts came to see me since I saw

you. They seem to be very happy and are very useful at the East End of London'.[153] Six years later in another letter to Nightingale he wrote, 'Let me tell you of two preferments which have given me great pleasure; Mr Barnett's appointment to the Canonry at Bristol ...'[154]

There was a decided middle-classness about Toynbee Hall. It was noted that a characteristic of Toynbee tea was 'one in which the maid brought in a trolley laiden with buttered muffins and assorted cakes'.[155] Visitors to Toynbee felt it to represent too much of the ethos of a University College tucked away in East London. A visitor noted the comfort of the drawing room with many easy chairs and hung with excellent portraits of great men such as Browning, Matthew Arnold and Lord Shaftesbury. The dining-room, he noted, 'is rather sombre, with the arms of the Oxford and Cambridge Colleges decorating the walls'.[156] A past resident wrote:

> To old public-school and university men, Toynbee Hall, with its collegiate atmosphere, had a familiar feeling. There was the society of contemporaries, there was the kindly guidance and supervision of an elder man, there were the meals in common and community life.[157]

All of this was deliberate policy on Barnett's part since he wanted the men who resided with him to experience something of the atmosphere and security that they had known at Oxford.

Notwithstanding these comments there can be no doubt that Barnett was not only the pioneer but the inspirer of settlements. Toynbee Hall was indeed in the words of Will Reason, 'The mother of all Settlements'. By this statement of course Reason referred to the fact that Toynbee became the model for almost all the differing settlements and mission settlements that followed in the years immediately after 1884. Barnett unselfishly gave of his time to tell the Toynbee story in schools and colleges who were interested to take up his vision. Whilst it is true that many of them differed in regards to some of their specific objectives or the place and role of religion, Barnett's perspectives and influence is clearly visible in them all. There can be no doubt that in this and a number of other spheres he was a minor national figure. He gave a major encouragement to university extension education, he played a significant part in supporting trades unions in the East End of London and, perhaps above all, he demonstrated the ways in which the National Church could and should be involved in championing the cause of the inner city poor. It was for these contributions that he was honoured with a memorial tablet designed by Sir George Frampton RA on the north wall of Westminster Abbey. The inscription read:

Canon of Westminster Abbey 1906–1913 and Sub-Dean Designate
Founder and Warden of the First University Settlement Toynbee Hall
Whitechapel 1884–1906 Canon of Bristol Cathedral 1892–1906
Vicar of St Jude's Whitechapel 1872–1893

The Westminster Gazette reflected that Canon Barnett 'who founded the first University Settlement, was the adviser and prompter of statesmen and practical men in the field of social reform, who looked undismayed at the problem of poverty, and was fertile in ideas for its amelioration'.[158] When Father James Adderley, who was the second warden of Oxford House, reflected on Barnett's death, he wrote: 'I am convinced that in the death of Canon Barnett the Church has lost one of the very few prophets that we have had in our midst for a hundred years'.[159]

3

OXFORD COLLEGES IN THE EAST END

'Come and be Squires of East London' – Henry Scott Holland[1]

At the time Samuel Barnett was sharing his plan for a settlement in Whitechapel, a group of High Churchmen at Keble College, Oxford were of the opinion that his vision was altogether too secular in its aims and objectives. Roused by the appeals of Bishop Walsham How and Octavia Hill[2] and led by their warden, Edward Talbot (1844–1934), later to be Bishop successively of Rochester, Southwark and Winchester, they drew up proposals for a community that firmly focused on creedal Christianity. Talbot summed up its major objective as 'the preparation of character for ... the reception of the religion of Christ'.[3] On 2 April 1884 he announced that the Vicar of St Andrew's Bethnal Green, had made a commitment to start a settlement in his parish. This decision was taken at the suggestion made to the committee by Walsham How.[4] The first premises were the disused school building of St Andrew's which was described as 'neither handsome or commodious'.[5] Talbot was not only the inspiration behind the founding of Oxford House, he was Chairman of the Executive Committee in Oxford and acted as a major link with the university. When he left Oxford in 1888 to become Vicar of Leeds, it was stated that his contribution to the House had been 'simply invaluable, both as its earliest promoter and as the most constant and devoted of its friends'. It was further said that 'the success of Oxford House had been largely due to his wise council and unfailing sympathy'.[6]

Bethnal Green was widely recognised as one of the poorest districts in London. In 1879 an Anglican priest had written of it as 'a howling wilderness; alleys; pauperism rampant; religion nil'.[7] This lack of interest in religion surprised Arthur Winnington-Ingram, one of Oxford House's early wardens, because it was not long since that Bishop Blomfield of London had built, at great cost, 12 churches in Bethnal Green named after the 12 apostles'.[8] Some time later, however, Ingram got a more personal taste of East London's cynicism regarding religion as he walked in a procession to St Faith's Stepney. He heard a bystander remark in an audible voice, 'Look at them there, prostituting their intellects'.[9] Osborne Jay, another clergyman, who went to work in the 'Nichol', wrote of the

> squalid degradation, the abject despair, the criminal activity of this, its saddest and most desperate quarter ... women, sodden with drink, fighting and struggling like wild creatures; men bruised and battered, with all the marks and none of the pleasures of vice upon them; outcasts, abject and despairing, without food and shelter.[10]

Once the home of literally thousands of silk weavers the industry had long since declined as a result of the mechanised looms in the north of the country and imports from foreign parts. The housing conditions of the locality were notoriously bad and a government inquiry into 'The Sanitary Conditions of Bethnal Green' was launched in 1887.

Oxford House

The founders of Oxford House shared Samuel Barnett's view that the clergy could not cope on their own and that the laymen of the universities must come down and get to know the poor. On 8 September 1884, Oxford House opened its doors two months before Toynbee Hall with just three residents,[11] two of whom were William Campion and Winfred Burrows. At that time the house could only accommodate five men so that others who came had to find lodgings in Bethnal Green. As James Adderley saw it, a resident had no need of any particular skills:

> For if he cannot preach in the streets, he may be able to play football on a Saturday afternoon; while if he cannot give a scientific lecture or sing a song, he can at any rate make himself agreeable at one of the clubs, by talking to the men, and getting to know and like them as friends.[12]

Jimmy Adderley whose congenial leadership style was valued by those who worked with him did not remain in post for long. 'I could never have settled down as a conventional parson at the Head of a University Settlement. I wanted more independence. Socialism was in the air'.[13] The aims of the Settlement were stated as follows:

The first Oxford House.

The Oxford House in Bethnal Green is established in order that Oxford men may take part in the social and religious work of the Church in East London; that they may learn something of the life of the poor; may try to better the condition of the working classes as regards health and recreation, mental culture and spiritual teaching; and may offer an example, so far as in them lies, of a simple religious life.[14]

The last objective was one of Oxford House's hall marks. Hensley Henson in his 1886 Annual Report made the point that the settlement existed to provide opportunities for university men who wanted to understand the real condition of the poor and artisans of the East End of London and 'who are prepared to take part in the furtherance of Christianity and education, and the bettering of the moral and sanitary condition of the various neighbourhoods'.[15] James Adderley was of the view that 'Church and Settlement should be directly associated'.[16] The religious emphasis continued to be marked under Ingram's leadership. The report at the end of his first year as warden stressed that the principles of Oxford House 'are and will continue to be first and foremost the belief in Christianity as the true starting point of all civilizing effort, and secondly the recognition of the

power and efficiency of community work under religious sanctions.'[17] This
was clear for example, at the 1894 London Annual Meeting in support of
the Settlement when the chairman, Lord Wantage, reviewed the work of the
House and laid stress on its mission 'to forward the teaching of the Christian
religion, as taught by the Church of England, as a means of bridging the gulf
between the classes'.[18] An article in *The Oxford House Chronicle* the
following year gave an indication of the way in which the religious impact
was being extended. It reported that 60 or 70 boys were voluntarily
attending Bible class every Sunday and that there were 'always 200 or more
at the Sunday night Club Service'. Alongside these was a growing body of
Club Communicants every Sunday night. All this, the article stated,
encourages us to believe that the Clubs when originally planned by the
founders of Oxford House 'were planned on the right lines'.[19]

The programme included similar sorts of activity to those promoted by
Toynbee. There was a boys' club, gym, library, Sunday afternoon lectures and
'Sunday evenings with a smoke or talk'. With the passing of the years the
programme expanded to include Bible classes, debates, concerts and the
establishment of a mutual loan society. Additionally, a labour registry was
started to help those out of work. One of James Adderley's contributions was
to set up together with Mr Harold Buchanan, The Federation of Working
Men's Social Clubs. This organisation eventually spread all over London and
by 1894 there were some 60 clubs with a membership of 6,000.[20]

Education

Oxford House, like Toynbee, soon became active in a wide variety of
educational activities. In 1886 the House became a centre of the London
Society for the Extension of University Teaching. The lectures attracted
students, 'mainly of the working classes' from all the surrounding districts,
from Dalston, Hackney, Stoke Newington, Haggerston, Stepney,
Whitechapel, Bow, Clapton and Shoreditch, as well as from Bethnal Green
itself. By mid-1890s some sixty gentlemen were giving lectures in
conjunction with the House in addition to the staff who carry on the
Sunday lectures. There were libraries in all the clubs. Among other groups
who made regular use of the premises were The Christian Social Union and
The Church Reading Union.[21] Some of the lectures included Christian
Apologetics. For example, the Revd L.E. Shelford lectured in November
1894 on 'The Origin of Our Gospels and the External Evidence for their
Authenticity'. In December the same year Lord Hugh Cecil lectured on St
Paul who he said was 'a great organiser' and 'a strong Churchman'.[22] In
April 1894 the Revd J.E.C. Welldon, Headmaster of Harrow School,

lectured on 'the great subject of the Resurrection' and dealt with the evidence that supported it.[23]

There was an important Pupil Teachers' Centre close to Oxford House in Abbey Street and the residents did a good deal to entertain and encourage the male students. In 1886 Hensley Henson taught them Constitutional History and Dr Berdoe of Oxford House taught English literature to a class of eighteen pupil teachers. A Music Society, Debating Society and a Dramatic Society were also organised for them. Forty male and female pupil teachers enjoyed rehearsing together in the latter society to produce an entertainment.

During its first four years the House was led in quick succession by three heads. The first was the Revd W.E. Jackson, who had the title 'Secretary'. He was succeeded in 1886 by the Hon. James G. Adderley, 'an aristocratic product of Eton and Christ Church'.[24] He in turn was followed by Herbert Hensley Henson (1863–1947), a future Bishop of Hereford and Durham.[25] In his early days his sympathies were with the Tractarians though James Adderley later recalled that 'he never held the Tractarian view of apostolic succession'.[26] With the passing of the years his theological opinions became increasingly liberal such that his consecration to Hereford was opposed by Anglo-Catholics. Henson, 'a regular tornado', stamped his impress on the Bethnal Green community in the vigorous debates which he had with local secularists. However he lost confidence in the settlement ideal and moved on after only a year to become Vicar of Barking. 'The Oxford House', he declared, 'is an impossible scheme, and must in the end fail'.[27]

A report of the House in those early years described it in expansive tones as 'a headquarters for those who are anxious to understand the real condition of the labouring classes in East London … and who are prepared to take part in the furtherance of Christianity and education, and the bettering of the neighbourhood'.[28] The overt religious commitment was made plain in the words of one of the early residents who said, 'We wanted to get a footing in the place, and we found that the best way was to start a club and provide a place to spend the evening in without politics or drink … And in Sunday lectures we showed that we were Christians out for the conversion of souls'.[29]

A.F. Winnington-Ingram

When Henson left office, Henry Bromby, son of the Bishop of Lichfield, to whom Ingram was chaplain, said on hearing of the vacancy: 'Ingram is the man to succeed him'.[30] Bromby who had been appointed Vicar of St John's Bethnal Green in 1885 became involved in a number of aspects of the work of Oxford House. In 1889 the Ladies Settlement from Cheltenham was established at Mayfield House under the leadership of Miss Newman, an old friend. Bromby had known Dorothea Beale (1831–1906), the Principal of Cheltenham Ladies College, from his early days in that town. It was largely his invitation that determined her decision to establish the school settlement in Bethnal Green.[31] In 1888 Bromby, who had departed from the plain evangelical views of his father, pledged himself before Bishop Walsham How to a simple life of regularity. He wrote that 'Mr Adderley, who was Head of Oxford House; has come to live with me. We live under a Simple Rule and we hope that it may be the beginning of a Community of Mission priests'.[32]

It was the Revd Arthur Winnington-Ingram, the fourth head of House and later Bishop of London, who stayed in office for nine years, who really put Oxford House on the map and made it a significant part of the life of Bethnal Green. Ingram, a former graduate of Keble, had been chaplain to the Bishop of Lichfield. He embarked on the task of warden of Oxford House never having visited East London. He left nine years later to become the Bishop of Stepney. His predecessor, James Adderley, wrote that he left Oxford House 'almost the most important factor in the ecclesiastical life of East London'.[33] He was an athletic man with a love of sports and strong straight-forward orthodox Christian faith. In consequence men of sporting prowess were soon attracted to the work. Among those who came early on were Hewitt, a rowing blue from University College and Cross, an excellent runner from New College.

From time to time Ingram visited Oxford recruiting new residents. By 1890 his enthusiasm was captivating more undergraduates than could be adequately accommodated. Ingram commented in his report for that year that 'out of seventeen residents there is only room for three, in addition to the Head, in the House itself. The rest have had to be placed here and there, in adjoining or distant lodgings, wherever a sleeping place could be found'.[34] The Annual Report of 1892 listed 28 residents and workers of whom 22 were Oxford graduates.[35] Ingram, who was a man of vision, saw clearly that if the work was to fully develop new premises were a necessity. Prompted by his enthusiasm an appeal was signed in March 1890 by the Bishop of London as President and by the Warden of All Souls College as Chairman of the Executive Committee asking for the sum of £12,000 for building purposes. Of this sum £2,000 was required for the purchase of the freehold site in Mape Street close to the Bethnal Green Road, and about a hundred yards from the existing premises. Plans were prepared for a house to hold 20 residents, a Lecture Room with some extra buildings and over it and the Club Buildings.[36] For the next two years Ingram was tireless in his endeavour to raise the necessary funds for the project.

New Buildings for the House

His campaign began in January 1891 when 'an influential meeting' was held at the Mansion House to appeal for funds. The Lord Mayor of London took the chair for the first part of the meeting and the Bishop of Bedford took over for the latter half of the proceedings. The treasurer stated that something like £5,000 out of the total of £12,000 had so far been subscribed to the project. In the course of his address the Lord Mayor stated that 'the large population of the east end had grown to such an enormous extent that it was impossible for the clergy who ministered there to cope with the numbers that were put under their spiritual charge'. As he saw it, 'the only practical way of awakening interest and showing the Church's sympathy with the working population was by having Mission-houses fixed and settled in the East of London'. He went on to say how glad he was that 'many colleges of both the Universities of Oxford and Cambridge, and some public schools, had adopted that mode of working, and with good effect'.[37]

Lord Brassey proposed the first resolution which was: 'That this meeting cordially approves of the principles upon which Oxford House in Bethnal Green was founded, and of the work accomplished by it in the East End of London during the past five years'. During the course of his speech he said that 'from personal observation made within the walls of Oxford House, he could say that a better work could not have been established'.[38] Sir Edmund Brassey proposed the next motion, 'That this meeting pledges itself to use every endeavour to raise the necessary funds for providing a permanent and suitable house for those engaged in this work'.[39] In the course of his remarks he said that 'they wanted not one Oxford House, but several. If the members of Oxford House could only appeal personally to the Oxford men who are working in Lombard-street, he believed they would get the money in a week'.[40]

Canon Henry Scott Holland, who seconded the resolution, was of the view that there was the problem of the surplus of educated gentlemen. In a somewhat humorous speech that caused a good deal of laughter, he asked, 'What was to be done with them?'. The problem was, 'They had a way of accumulating in congested districts, and of swarming together in shoals like herrings. One of the districts where they accumulated, and which was terribly congested, was the West End, round about Piccadilly'. Here, according to the Canon, they who were 'the cream' of Oxford 'sat idly in their clubs or mooned and cadged up and down Piccadilly'. He went on to say that such cream was of no use unless there were cats to lick it up. 'So', the solution to the problem, he suggested, was 'the labour refuges or shelters for congested gentlemen that had been established at the East End. One was Toynbee Hall, another was Oxford House'.[41] It was unnatural that 'all the people who made jam should live, say in Hackney, and all those who ate jam should live in the Cromwell Road'. So they would 'bring these poor unfortunate gentlemen under the healthy influence of contact with working men and the poor of Bethnal Green and other places, and they would be surprised to see how it would improve their moral tone'. [42]

An entry in *The Oxford House Chronicle* in February 1894 noted that 'the Head of House 'goes to Oxford for a fortnight's campaign in the Colleges' and was due to preach in the chapel of Merton College on 18 February 18.[43] He was resolved that Oxford House should have its own purpose-built premises and put a great deal of his energy raising the necessary funds. 'I put it to all Oxford men', he said, 'that if they would not come to Bethnal Green, they must at least supply a house for those who would'.[44] In addition to his own efforts, Ingram set up a council to oversee the building and the management of the community. Just five years later in 1892 the new impressive complex in red brick was opened on a site that lay between the Bethnal Green Road and the main railway line from Liverpool Street Station. Both Archbishops and six other bishops were present together with the Duke of Connaught for the inaugural ceremony.[45]

Perhaps more significant was the presence of local 'Bethnal Greeners' with their own banner in which they had sought to depict the scope of the Settlement's work. It carried the words 'Education; Temperance; Religion; Equality; Fraternity; Success to Oxford House'.[46] The new buildings which were designed by Sir Arthur Blomfield, the architect of Selwyn College, Cambridge, were described as 'solid and handsome: a fit home for the workers of the settlement, a fit centre for its manifold work'.[47] By the time of his departure from Oxford House in 1897 to be the Bishop of Stepney, Winnington-Ingram had established the organisation and framework that was to function in the community until the middle years of the twentieth century. From the day that the new building was opened until the day he left Bethnal Green, Ingram recalled, 'we never had less than thirty men there, and we had established ourselves as a permanent fixture'.[48]

Ingram was described as 'entirely devoid of either Oxford or clerical mannerisms', 'incapable of patronising anyone' and 'as much at home in a slum as in a palace'.[49] He was an outgoing personality who was confident in himself and secure in his faith. He was at ease in public speaking and for a number of years was the chief lecturer in the local park and during his

Sunday talks spoke to many thousands. When he finally left the area he received a touching testimonial in the form of a beautiful cabinet made in Bethnal Green by a man who was converted by the Sunday lectures, and which was subscribed for by the rest of the audience.[50] In all the activities of the House Winnington-Ingram always kept his sights on the unchurched. 'You must remember', he said, 'we were out all the time to supplement and not supplant the work of the parish clergy, and therefore made for outsiders'.[51]

Parochial Involvement

From the very beginning it had been part of Oxford House's vision not to be confined to the activities of the house but to be involved in the work and ministry of the parish of Bethnal Green. The warden reported in 1886 that members had been visiting in St Andrew's parish in the Mape Street district and the immediate neighbourhood in which the house is situated.[52] By 1895 this work had extended to the parishes of St Bartholomew's and St John's and in addition work was being carried out in St Paul's by Mr Bonham Carter and in St Anthony's by Mr Campion who had been enrolled as a Church worker.[53] 1895 was brought to a close with the Head of House leading a ten-day mission in Hackney Wick assisted by the greater part of the Oxford House staff.[54]

Ingram seemed to have enormous energy and in the summer of 1895 he was appointed Rector of St Matthew's Bethnal Green 'at the Bishop of London's special request', in addition to his responsibilities as Head of House. The Bishop's view was that 'the House will help the parish, and the parish will help the House'.[55] Ingram continued to live at the House but had five curates who lived at the rectory and thirty laymen in the Oxford House. In addition, he had ten lady workers from St Margaret's House, which by this time had been started in Bethnal Green. He commented that, 'it was rather like turning a pack of hounds into a cover. The people were astonished to see this charming crowd running up every staircase and knocking at every door'.[56] Oxford House came to see this joint enterprise as being of great benefit to the parish. St Matthew's benefited with increased numbers of communicants and more and more club members finding a spiritual home in the Church. Additionally it was reported that, 'the parish still feels and expresses, the beneficial experience of being visited and looked after by the residents of the Oxford and St Margaret's Houses'.[57]

Ingram's departure from Oxford House was a terrible blow. Percy Coulton, Ingram's biographer, later recorded, 'He found it a small, struggling institution fighting for its life amid hostile surroundings ... He left it as ... one of the greatest influences for good in England and flourishing like a green bay tree'.[58] The year after Ingram had left, the Senior Resident at the House reflected on his work. He wrote: 'Notwithstanding the withdrawal of his personal presence from the House, the spirit in which his work was done permeated all departments of the House and of the Parish, and everything during the inter-regnum went on much as before. It is not all work that can stand that test'.[59] When Ingram left for Stepney, his successor, Bernard Wilson,[60] also took on the role as rector of St Matthew's.[61] Under his direction the involvement in parish work not only continued but steps were taken to widen the scope of this aspect of the work with residents working in some of the surrounding Bethnal Green parishes.[62]

Clubs and Activities

In its several buildings Oxford House provided a varied programme of social, athletic and life-enhancing activities. Most of these came under the umbrellas of one of the three main clubs: The Oxford House Club for Clerks and Skilled Artisans, The University Club for Unskilled Working Men and The Webbe Institute. The latter was named after the cricketer and philanthropist, Herbert Webbe of New College, and founded by his family in 1888 in his memory. It provided activities for boys up to the age of eighteen. The Webbe Institute, which was originally located at 457 Bethnal Green Road, was reckoned to be one of the most important contributions of Hensley Henson's brief tenure as warden. In 1889 the Institute occupied new premises in Hare Street which had been generously funded by friends and family members of Herbert Webbe.

The work also produced encouraging spiritual results with a steady attendance at the monthly club service and smaller numbers at the weekly Bible class. By 1895, it was reported, 'we find 60 or 70 boys coming voluntarily to Bible Classes every week' and 'a full Mission Service on Sunday night' and 'always 200 or more men at Club Service, and a small but growing body of Club Communicants meeting in the Oxford House Chapel every Saturday night'.[63] Additionally, some thirty members of the club formed the choir of the Oxford Hall Mission service and six lads from the club were confirmed in October 1889.[64] The Annual report for that year ended by emphasising the Christian objectives of the club.

> Meanwhile, in the midst of all this recreation and instruction we are not forgetful that the ultimate aim and object of the Institute is, like all the other work of the House, Christian, and we have before us, both

literally in a beautiful photograph, and still more, morally, the character and life of Mr Herbert Webbe, in whose memory it is founded.[65]

These clubs provided an enormous range of facilities that included 'dispensaries, co-operatives, workshops for making boots and shoes and the 'poor man's lawyer' who offered free legal advice to members long before the days of legal aid and neighbourhood law centres'.[66] The Oxford House Club was a flourishing concern from the very beginning though membership tended to fluctuate in the early days. Adderley stated in his Annual Report of 1886 that 'altogether 320' had been on the books during the year. He also stressed the fact that as the club occupied the ground floor of Oxford House it afforded the residents 'every opportunity for associating with typical specimens of the upper grades of East End Society'.[67] The membership continued to grow thanks to the widening range of activities.

One of Adderley's most important contributions during his wardenship was the formation of The Federation of Working Men's Clubs, which he founded in 1886. This umbrella organization had three specific objectives:

> To unite into one organization those Working Men's Clubs which have no political character or aim. (ii) To further the establishment of good Clubs, where opportunities shall be afforded for recreation, education, and non-intoxicant refreshment. (iii) To establish a central management for the extension of educational and recreative advantages to the Federated Clubs.[68]

Many of the working men's clubs formed by other university colleges and public schools joined the Federation and were able to share in events, concerts, entertainments and other activities organised by them.

James Adderley was also responsible for initiating the publication of *The Oxford House Chronicle* in 1887. It was published monthly priced at 1s. and 6d. and gave accounts of the various branches of the Federation's work. It could be ordered from Mowbrays book shop in St Aldates in Oxford and this helped to keep undergraduates and others in the colleges up to date with events and needs.

The opportunities for recreation and sporting activities provided by Oxford House were considerably extended when the Goldsmith's Company made a generous grant that enabled the House to purchase 22 acres of land as a recreation ground for club members. Winnington-Ingram was profoundly convinced of the positive influence of Christians in sport. On one occasion, he retorted:

I must say that I do believe it was the sight of those young athletes, whom I subsequently was able to bring up from Oxford, going to church and even Communion, which did more than any sermons to convince Bethnal Green that there was something in religion after all.[69]

Ingram himself set great store by the Sunday Mission services in the University Hall which were informal in style with 'simple hymns' and 'a straightforward gospel preached'. It amused him that this service was popularly called 'going to Ingram's Hall'.[70] Oxford House was actively involved in the Children's Country Holiday Fund. 755 children were sent away for a week or two weeks during the 1888 Board School holiday period as compared with 337 in 1887.[71]

Politics and Social Concerns

The political affiliations of Oxford House residents were diverse but they were all agreed that no one was attempting to bias them in any particular direction. Winnington-Ingram later wrote that 'The House had no politics and backed up eagerly all the good efforts for social betterment ... As a matter of fact, during my nine years as Head, I was sometimes fighting with the Radicals against the Conservatives, and sometimes the other way about'.[72]

Much of the important education achieved by Oxford House was at a personal level and conveyed through individual relationships and example. James Adderley for instance, noted that many 'Bethnal Greeners' needed to be taught the virtues of thrift and prudence and singled out the need for adequate instruction regarding marriage. 'The levity with which lads and girls enter matrimony without any adequate provision', he wrote in one of his reports, 'can only be met by convincing them that prudence in this matter is a duty which is as fully recognised in other grades of society and it is ignored by themselves'.[73]

Residents actively involved themselves in a range of neighbourhood social and governmental concerns and served on local Guardians and School Boards.[74] They energetically concerned themselves with the major issues of the locality, one of which was the issue of sanitation. As early as 1886 it was reported that 'various members of Oxford House have acted in succession as Secretary to the Bethnal Green Sanitary Aid Committee'.[75] The Committee had during that year 'been of great use' in alerting the Nuisance Authorities to their responsibilities and thereby getting some of the worst places visited and satisfactorily amended.[76] More important still was the fact that the Bethnal Green Committee had been able to make strong recommendations to the Central Committee of the Mansion House.

In June 1887, Harold Hodge[77] of Oxford House took on the task of secretary to the Bethnal Green Sanitary Committee and, largely as a result of his work, a government inquiry into the sanitary conditions of Bethnal Green was set up. Its findings demonstrated that there were 'a very large number of houses which from age or defective construction are objectionable from a sanitary point of view'.[78] The Bethnal Green Committee sent out circulars advising of the dangers of scarlet fever. The Oxford House Annual Report reminded readers that 'there is a great deal of sanitary work which can only be done by local effort' and that no effort, and no organisation, no secretary's zeal, no effort of the Central Mansion House Committee can avail, unless the people of Bethnal Green will stir themselves and give all the help that lies in their power'.[79]

In January 1894, a two-day conference was held in the Oxford House Lecture Hall on 'Sanitary Reform in Bethnal Green'. The meeting was chaired by the Head of House and it was unanimously agreed that a deputation headed by Mr Ingram,

> should wait upon the Vestry on March 1st, to press upon that body the need of at least two additional Inspectors to carry out the Sanitary Acts in Bethnal Green; and to assure them, that in taking such a step, they will be backed up by public opinion, so far as it was represented by the very representative Conference.[80]

Oxford House made it a particular concern to ensure that local residents were aware of their responsibilities to keep the properties they rented in good order. They were reminded that they 'must take proper care of the sanitary fittings' in the rooms in which they lived. Individuals 'must avoid for instance, choking the sinks, or 'cutting the pipes and selling them as lead' and 'whenever they think something is wrong, they must write to the Sanitary Inspector'.[81] They must 'keep the house clean' and 'avoid overcrowding'. At a meeting in June 1895 it was reported that a number of members were elected to the Local School Board and to The Board of Guardians by good majorities.[82]

Another important social aspect of Oxford House's work was The House of Shelter, which opened to the public in February 1887.[83] Its aim was to try to help those who were on the verge of sinking into the 'Casual' or workhouse class who were absolutely desolate and so unable to pay for a night's lodging. The residents who organised the venture found that their main and difficult task was that of attempting to identify those who were capable of getting back into employment and then searching on their behalf for suitable work. In the first seven years of its existence 'thirteen thousand destitute people' entered the shelter's doors. During the period 1 November 1888 to 29 April 1889 the shelter took in 1,806 people. Of these, 278 found work and 29 were assisted to emigrate. 43 individuals had received assistance to emigrate in the previous year.[84]

Residents became concerned by the general scarcity of work in the Bethnal Green area and in September 1887 they set up The Oxford House Labour Association. Its main object was to keep a register for men out of work and to ascertain what skills they had with a view to assisting them to find suitable employment. The Association was able in some circumstances to advance money for the purchase of tools or other necessary items. Membership was confined to members of the Bethnal Green Clubs. By the end of the year there had been 37 applicants, 28 of whom had been helped to find new work. £27 2s. 0d. was expended in order to make 14 loans of sums varying from 6d. to £3 15s. 0d.

Co-operatives

In 1888 a significant step was taken when the University Club formed The University Club Industrial Co-operative Society. It was registered as a co-operative society on 13 June with the object of carrying on a general business. Management meetings were held quarterly. The venture proved to be immensely popular and about 1,000 customers personally purchased goods at the stores every Saturday. In October 1889 the Co-operative moved to new buildings which had been left vacant on Victoria Park Square. Sales rose steadily during the course of 1889 and a dividend of 1s. 6d. in the £ was paid to members.[85] However there was set-back in 1891 when their progress was reported to be hindered by 'quarrels among the members'.[86]

In August 1889 The University Club Boot and Shoe Manufacturing Society was launched with the objective of manufacturing boots in Bethnal Green on the principles of productive co-operation. The society, which had 420 shares, set up its factory in Bethnal Green Road and its shop in the Arcade of the University Club. The Boot and Shoe Manufacturing Co-operative was short-lived and had to be closed in 1891 since it was not paying its way. Its failure was put down to the fact that its boots were of too good a quality and could not cope in the cheap market.[87] *The Productive Co-operative Cabinet Makers' Society Limited* was also registered in February 1889. It was originally located at 479 Bethnal Green Road but moved later the same year to the Arcade of the University Club. *The Annual Report* of 1889 stated that its great need was 'to obtain an increase of custom'.[88] The Workmen's Co-operative Association Ltd had also been started in 1887 for tailoresses and afterwards for shirt-makers. By 1889 it had a capital of £1,000 and 140 workers. The Co-operative also opened a retail shop in the Arcade of the University Club.[89]

Religion

The atmosphere of the House remained distinctively 'churchy'. One of the residents, Ernest Bramwell described an early visit to the House:

> My first impressions were what a nice house, what splendid clubs etc. for working men, and how fresh fish smelt. In the House were Oxford and many Cambridge men, and they all had different jobs assigned to them, they were all full of the Head's enthusiasm, and there was a delightful spirit of friendship and welcome. Religion, of course, there was. It was as natural with the Head to go to Chapel first thing as it was to have breakfast. Nobody was pressed to attend but everybody did.[90]

Percy Colton in his biography of Winnington-Ingram wrote that Oxford House emerged from a new school, which was a continuation of the Tractarian Movement combined with the Christian Socialism of Frederick Denison Maurice and Charles Kingsley. It was largely the same group who in 1889 produced the epoch-making essays of *Lux Mundi* that started Oxford House in 1884.[91] Ingram remained true to the Tractarian principles that he had learned at Keble College and his life, work and spirituality were nurtured and sustained by sacramental and devotional principles. He was not however an extreme ritualist and, like John Keble himself, he did all things well, 'even the trivial round and the common task'.[92] That said, Ingram also had the heart of 'a fervent Evangelical'[93] and desired above all that Oxford House and its residents should bring men and women, boys and girls to a personal faith in Christ. It was for this reason that local Nonconformists were not alienated from the activities of the residents despite their 'definite Church principles'. Indeed several members of the local chapels were also members of the Oxford House Home Reading Group for the study of literature.[94]

Christ Church and Trinity

Two other Oxford Colleges took up the challenge of East London, Christ Church in 1881 and Trinity in 1888. Both were influenced by the ethos and personnel of Oxford House, this despite the fact that the Christ Church Mission was founded several years earlier. Indeed *The East End News* later described the priests who formed the staff of the Christ Church

Mission as 'a body of clergy, associated with what is known as the Oxford House Movement.[95] The idea of a Christ Church Mission was conceived at a general college meeting in the Hilary Term and was partly inspired by the example of the Eton College Mission which had been founded during the previous year at Hackney Wick. A committee was appointed to deal with the proposal. It consisted of Dr H.G. Liddell, then Dean of Christ Church, Dr Edward King who was later to become Bishop of Lincoln, the Revd H. Scott-Holland, Mr J.G. Talbot, brother of the Warden of Keble, and some junior members of the college. Bishop Walsham How was then approached and asked to provide a suitable sphere of work for the new venture. He reacted warmly to the proposal and offered a small but thickly populated district of 7,000 souls in the parishes of St Michael's Bromley by Bow and All Hallows East India Docks. A magazine article written at the close of the nineteenth century stated that the inhabitants 'were not only the victims of poverty, but for the most part depraved and brutal, caring for nothing beyond the things of the moment, … living practically as heathens, their conditions and lives being little above those of the mere animal'.[96] In the words of one early mission report, it was 'a compact mass of heathens'.[97] One of the first wardens stated that,

A group of men from Trinity, Oxford, at Stratford in East London on the occasion of their visit to the college in 1892. Some of the 'squires' can be seen sitting above the door. By kind permission of Trinity College, Oxford.

There were a large number of dock labourers employed from day to day who seldom did a day's work ... There was a good deal of noise and drinking and occasional fights. Yet the people were cheerful, warm-hearted and affectionate, – and ... richly gifted with broad caustic humour.[98]

Luke Paget,[99] the first missioner, later reflected in 1931 as Bishop of Chester, that people desperately wanted a mission chapel that they could call their own 'so we secured No 14 Lodore St., where our first altar stood, and which is really the cradle of the Mission'.[100] The two ground-floor rooms were knocked into one to create a hall that was 20 feet long by 12 feet wide and a small red lamp announcing 'Christ Church Mission' was put up. A curtain concealed the altar and the room served as Sunday School, Mothers' Meeting place and Lads'Club.[101] The first service was held on 27 November 1881. Holy Communion was celebrated at 8.00 a.m. and there was an evening service at 7.00 p.m.

Paget was described by James Adderley as 'a most delightful combination of the cultured and the humorous, the busy and the devout'.[102] It was therefore no surprise that within a short while his services began to attract large numbers. Paget long remembered how one old caretaker told him with pride that the building was full and 'all highly respectable'.[103] The first man to come down from Christ Church was Victor Seymour[104] who took up residence with Paget at 399 East India Dock Road and spent a lot of time visiting up and down the streets. Paget recalled that on one occasion when he knocked on a door, the child who answered yelled upstairs, 'Mother, here's religion'.[105] On Sundays, Seymour's duty was to keep the door and act as 'chucker out'.[106] Other helpers soon followed including the Revd Edward McClaughlin in 1882 as a deacon and the Revd Tufnell Barrett, a priest from St James' Plymouth in 1884. Bishop Walsham How took a constant and active interest in the Christ Church Mission and gave much encouragement. In a letter that he wrote in April 1883 which revealed his distaste for William Booth's activities in the area he expressed his delight at churchy atmosphere of the premises.

Perhaps you will like to hear that I visited the Christ Church Mission on Easter Tuesday, taking part in the evening service in the new Mission Room. I was greatly pleased with the service, and all the arrangements, and the Mission Room was made very nice and 'church like'. But best of all, there was a room full of the right kind of people, most of them unmistakably working-classes. I do earnestly trust that

Christ Church will help to rescue the poor, ignorant people around their Mission from the indifference and infidelity which are so prevalent, and, no less, from the unworthy conception of Christianity presented to them by such bodies as the Salvation Army.[107]

Paget was a man of great energy and within a year an appeal was sent out to all Christ Church men inviting them to subscribe to a fund for the erection of new and more permanent premises. The new building was opened on Easter Saturday, 1882 and provided facilities for a large clubroom.[108]

In 1886 Paget moved on to become Vicar of St Ives in Huntingdonshire and was succeeded by the Revd the Hon. Reginald Adderley, a former Christ Church student who had been working in Stoke-on-Trent and at All Hallows, Barking. In two short years before he was offered and accepted the valuable living of Chesterfield, he pushed forward the building of the new mission church. The foundation stone was laid on 6 July 1889 by the Duchess of Albany, a daughter-in-law of Queen Victoria. It was dedicated to 'St Frideswide, Virgin and Abbess'. St Frideswide, it was pointed out, founded a small religious community some 1,200 years ago on the site where Christ Church Oxford now stands. The new church, which held 550, was dedicated by the Bishop of London on 15 July 1890 and Dr Scott Holland preached the sermon.

The Trinity Mission House was founded in 1888 in a district carved out of the parish of St John's East Stratford. The mission buildings comprised a church that seated about 400, a large hall, a club and rooms for the missioners. The mission house was completed in 1893 with rooms for three residents.[109] A branch of St Margaret's House Bethnal Green was formed in 1896 largely through the efforts of Mr Roxburgh. It was situated at 93 The Grove and functioned as an affiliated settlement and was under the leadership of a Mrs Crossley.[110] During the course of 1897 there were eight permanent residents and a further eight or nine occasional residents.[111] The new premises were opened by the Duchess of Albany.[112] Harold Legge in his account of the early years of the mission wrote that,

Few other missions could boast of such buildings, and in all sixty clubs of the Oxford House Federation, with a membership of some 6,000 working men in all parts of London, not one could boast of finer premises than those of the Trinity College Mission.[113]

Interior of Christ Church, Oxford, St Frideswide Mission in Poplar.
By kind permission of the Bancroft Library, Bethnal Green.

Aims and Ethos

The primary aim of both the Christ Church and Trinity Missions was to bring about religious commitment, albeit Tractarian in character. The Revd Darell Tupper-Carey (b. 1866)[114] who had been a curate at Leeds parish church, took on the wardenship of the Christ Church Mission in 1898 made it his first business to convert the people. What struck him was 'the tiny proportion of professing Christians to the vast mass of pagans' and this in spite of the fact that in his time at any rate three-quarters of the population had attended Sunday School in their youth.[115] 'Tupper,' as he was affectionately known, was always on the look out for those who were outside the Christian community. He once advised one of his curates that when they were visiting they should 'always call on two fresh people every day'. 'It is fatally easy', he said, 'to spend all one's time on the sick or on people who are already attached. They must not be neglected but the faithful priest will also never cease from his efforts to bring new fish into his net and reclaim the lost sheep'.[116]

Tupper in fact revived the practice of his earlier predecessor, James Adderley, of open-air preaching. Sometimes he would start out from church on a Sunday morning with the choir in procession and make his way to a house and, having previously obtained permission, address the gathering crowd from an upstairs window. This somewhat unusual pulpit never failed to captivate the curious and pull in the people.[117] On Good Friday and Easter Sunday Tupper's plans were more ambitious and elaborate. He went out into the streets with the clergy, choir-boys carrying bunches of primroses, with banners, their bearers dressed in red cassocks, preceded by a crucifer carrying a processional cross, and followed by a considerable proportion of the congregation. The whole processions were sometimes a hundred yards long. Tupper was of the view that 'these out-door services were the most successful means of evangelisation we tried'.[118] In the church itself Tupper aimed to give Sunday Evensong as evangelistic a character as possible. His custom was to have four well-known hymns at each service, prayers said audibly and sermons that would appeal to the unconverted. He also found a children's service organised by his helpers in the Mission Room on Sunday evenings was a popular draw, especially with children who were not in the habit of attending Sunday School.[119] Charles Clarke,[120] who was one of Tupper's colleagues, later reflected that one of his weaknesses was that having brought people into the fold, he was inclined to 'leave them to other people to look after while he was busy casting his net for more'.[121]

Trinity's Mission in Stratford began in 1888 largely through the initiative of Bishop Thomas Claughton of St Albans.[122] In a letter dated December 1887, H.G. Woods, the President of Trinity, announced the College's proposal to open a Mission at the Great Eastern Railway Works at Stratford in the East End of London, the intention being 'to bridge over the gulf which separates class from class in London, and in particular to benefit the men employed at the large Great Eastern Railway Works at Stratford'.[123] The letter went on to state that the Revd Charles Baumgarten,[124] has been appointed missioner, and a hall, which is also licensed for Divine Service, placed at the disposal of the mission. Woods also announced that past and present members of the college had raised a fund that would guarantee the sum of £200 for five years.[125] With the passing of the years the Christian focus of the mission was maintained. Thus in his Annual Report for 1897–8, the Revd H. Mosley, announced the arrival of two Church Army officers who had come in response to the previous year's report 'that something more must be done to reach the very poor of the district'. Captain Mantey's work was to consist in visiting and open-air preaching in the Tenby Road and the district round Cullum Street, which is one of the worst slums in Stratford'.[126] Reflecting on the year 1899–1900 Mosley wrote that 'while we recognise that spiritual needs must come first, the needs of the other parts of man's nature must not be beneath the care of the Church'.[127]

Both the Christ Church and Trinity Missions were influenced by Oxford House and the ethos and convictions of the Tractarians. This is immediately apparent on account of those who were appointed to the post of missioner. The first man to be appointed to the Christ Church Mission was the Revd Henry Luke Paget (1853–1938) who was afterwards, Bishop of Chester. He left after five years of strenuous work and was succeeded by the Revd and Hon. Reginald Adderley. He in his turn was followed in 1888 by his brother, the Revd and Hon. James Adderley, who had been Head of Oxford House from 1886–7. It was Adderley who built the Mission Church of St Frideswide, which seated more than 500 people. He persuaded Miss Catherine Mary Phillimore who had met the cost of the church[128] to further pay for the building of a Mission House to accommodate the Clewer Sisters who were working in the Mission.[129] The new mission church with its elevated chancel and sanctuary giving uninterrupted views of the high altar was clearly designed to facilitate Tractarian ritualistic worship. Indeed newspaper reports of the opening ceremony noted that money still had to be raised in order to purchase various vestments and ecclesiastical furnishings that were necessary aspects of Tractarian worship. These included a pendant cross, Sanctuary lamps, white and red chalice veils and burses, and white and red eucharistic stoles.[130]

The opening of St Frideswide Mission House some two years later was preceded by a procession from the church headed by the Revd J. Hewlett bearing a cross and followed by the choir singing a hymn 'Oh, what joy!'. Immediately following were some 26 sisters belonging to the House of Mercy at Clewer, who were working in different parts of London. They were followed by the Mother Superior of the Order and Sister Constance who was in charge of the Mission at Poplar. After them came Mrs Gladstone who performed the opening ceremony and the Revd and Hon. James Adderley and the Revd William Vaillant (b. 1864), followed by Canon Carter, the warden of Clewer, who was clad in a handsome yellow cope.[131] In 1893 Adderley was succeeded as warden by the Revd William Carroll[132] who remained in the post until 1898 at which point the Dean of Christ Church visited Darell Tupper-Carey and persuaded him to take over.

Tupper-Carey, who had been curate at Leeds for eight years, was a pronounced ritualist who instantly found himself at home at St Frideswide, which was described by the *East End News* as having been 'always ritualistic'.[133] 'Tupper', as he was affectionately known, proved to be a real go-getter. He found that few undergraduates had ever heard of the Mission and so he made it his business to inform them. His custom was to go knocking on the doors of undergraduate students and then to ask them if they knew anything about the Christ Church Mission. Almost always the response was, 'No, I am afraid not'. To this Tupper's invariable reply was, 'I thought you wouldn't: I will tell you about it'. He then proceeded to regale them with details about the work in Stratford in the most captivating way. He was the best of company and always full of good stories with the result that he never lacked for hospitality. His Annual Mission meeting at Christ Church was sometimes attended by over a hundred undergraduates.[134]

Trinity Mission also developed links with Oxford House. In February 1893 for instance, they reported their joy at having Winnington-Ingram among them and stated that 'we are determined to cement our connection with the House'.[135] One of those who worked at the Mission under the leadership of the Revd J.W. Roxburgh (b. 1865), was Frank Weston (1871–1924). He was a Trinity graduate who worked first as a layman and then as an ordained assistant missioner at the Trinity Mission. A passionate Anglo-Catholic controversialist, Weston subsequently became Bishop of Zanzibar in 1907. Roxburgh's successor at Stratford was the Revd Henry Mosley (b. 1868) who had acquired a wide experience of the East End working under Winnington-Ingram.[136]

The demands on missioners and their families, particularly those with young children, were many and it is no surprise that most didn't stay in East London for very long. A five-year span in office seems to have been about average. The Revd Charles Baumgarten began to suffer considerable ill-health after only four years in Stratford. In a letter penned to the President of Trinity in July 1890 he wrote of 'my health giving away altogether' and of the doctor's advice that 'I am on the verge of breakdown in my lungs and my only hope is to go abroad immediately for 2 or 3 months'.[137]

Social and Educational Activities

Alongside their religious missionary endeavours both Christ Church and Trinity developed a broad range of social and educational activities. In addition to promoting the Christian faith the Trinity Mission aimed 'to bridge over the gulf which separates class from class in London, and in particular to benefit the men employed at the large Great Eastern Railway Works at Stratford'.[138] In this objective they appear to have had a measure of success. Amongst the Trinity College Mission papers and photographs is a beautifully written letter dated 23 September 1891 from G. Williams who signs himself 'G. Williams over 40 years a servant of G.E.R'. He wrote:

Looking at the portraits of the "fifty men good and true'" from the GER Works who had the honour of being entertained by yourself and some of the students of Trinity College last Whitsuntide reminds me of a neglect of duty on my part in not thanking you all before this for the kindness and hospitality received by me a mere cipher and a small one at that of the above party. Such actions as the above as carried out by you gentlemen ... serve to bridge over the gulf that as [sic] too long existed in this country between the professional and mechanical worker by bringing us together which I believe result in showing us our interests are not antagonistic but identical.[139]

Such visits by members of the missions to the school or college who ran them became commonplace.

For all his active religious concern the Revd Henry Mosley was quick to point out that such things as clubs and gymnasiums 'are not to be regarded as merely means to a higher end, but rather a response to man's social needs'. 'Our great aim in the Mission', he said, 'is to do what we can to raise the conditions, whether social or physical, under which so many are forced to live'.[140]

The Trinity Mission established a wide range of clubs and activities. They included a 'Nigger troupe', Bands of Hope, a men's club and a newspaper club. There were biscuits and ginger pop for refreshment and a variety of games including billiards. Billiards also proved particularly popular with the men of the Christ Church Mission. Indeed on one occasion Tupper received a cheque for £50 'on condition it was used for the bodies and not for the souls of people in Poplar'. Tupper purchased a billiard table with the money remarking that 'he had never heard of anyone being converted by billiards'.[141] Tupper was particularly gifted with the men and he not only enlarged the premises he quadrupled the membership so that it became one of the largest clubs in the Oxford House Federation of Working Men's Clubs.[142] Tupper was of the view that one of the significant causes of poverty among working men was drink and he was a warm advocate of The Church of England Temperance Society. He felt however that the more rigid Tee-Totallers were inclined to be self-righteous. He once shocked the Sisters by commenting that one of his more self-righteous communicants needed 'to get drunk occasionally. It would teach him humility!'[143]

Both Christ Church and Trinity were concerned for the needs of the children in their respective mission communities. Trinity had a Church Lads' Brigade and a growing work among the girls that was carried out by the women from St Helen's House whose helpers were reported to be 'invaluable to us'.[144] The month-long great dock strike of 1889 inevitably brought huge distress to the community and people of Poplar because there was no organisation to look after people in such a crisis situation. Reginald Adderley devoted long hours to collecting a large fund out of which he was able to help hundreds of dockers' families who would otherwise have been in a state of destitution.

Politics

As was the case with other missions and settlements it was inevitable that both Christ Church and Trinity would become involved in local politics and that the eyebrows of some of their supporters would be raised as had happened at Oxford House. In February 1894 President Woods received a letter of complaint from a Mr Stevens who professed himself to be 'uneasy about the general drift of things at the Mission'. His concern was focused on the range of speakers being invited to address the Trinity Mission community: 'They have Earnest Gray, the Conservative candidate ... coming to preach on a Sunday evening service in the Mission Church and ... an avowed secularist to speak on education a little later'. As Stevens saw it, Roxburgh and Weston, 'both good fellows' didn't appear to realise these speakers were securing a platform for their own ends.[145] Trinity's sympathies clearly leaned in the direction of social justice and in 1893 they established a branch of the Christian Social Union which began with two meetings that discussed the issue of land ownership and rent.[146]

Clearly all three Oxford College Missions, Keble, Christ Church and Trinity, were impacted by a combination of both Tractarian worship and doctrine together with the ideals of Christian Socialism. The latter aspect showed itself both in their practical concerns as they sought to incarnate the Christian message through education, clubs and involvement in local governmental issues. A more specific link with F.D. Maurice was apparent in their concern to promote self-help among the working poor. This was seen not only in their range of educational and practical activities which were similar to those at the Working Men's College, but also in their support for trade unions and the their establishment of co-operatives.

4

CAMBRIDGE
SOUTH OF THE THAMES

While the Oxford Colleges, inspired largely by the influence of Toynbee Hall and Samuel Barnett's frequent visits to the university, focused their energies in the East End of London, Cambridge recognised there was an untouched mission field south of the Thames. In the Victorian years seven settlements connected with the university were established across the river.[1] They were prompted to take up the cause partly through the influence of Toynbee but also from concerned individuals among their fellows and other senior academics.

The first of the Cambridge Colleges to establish a mission was St John's. Undergraduates and Fellows were inspired as they listened to a sermon in the college chapel on Sexagesima Sunday 28 January 1883 by the Revd W. Allen Whitworth (1840–1905), Fellow of St John's, and Vicar of St John's Hammersmith. He suggested that they 'should support a Mission in some neglected district of London'.[2] Members of the College were aware that Christ Church and some public schools 'have already undertaken similar work' and it was felt that such a venture would be in the spirit of foundress, Lady Margaret' and 'would serve as a bond of union between rich and poor, educated and ignorant, and generally between class and class'.[3] As a result a meeting was held in the College Hall, on Tuesday 8 May 1883 with the Master in the chair, to which all members of the College were invited. Numerous letters from non-residents expressing support and offering financial contributions were read out. There were a number of speeches including one from the Bishop of Bedford and Archdeacon Cheetham on behalf of the Bishop of Rochester. The Following resolution was adopted: 'That a Mission be undertaken in London. That funds be raised from members of College, and that such provision be made for maintaining a direct interest in the working of the Mission as shall from time to time seem advisable'.[4] The first mission service was held on the same Sunday a year later in the Mission Church in Salisbury Avenue, Walworth.[5] Although the direct inspiration for the St John's mission settlement appears to have come from the Revd Allen Whitworth's sermon, the college became 'closely connected with Toynbee'.[6] The college magazine, *The Eagle*, reported in December 1885 that three Johnians had lectured at Toynbee Hall during the autumn and that their lectures had been 'warmly appreciated by East End audiences'.[7] In the spring of the following year 'a meeting was held in connexion with the Toynbee Hall Movement' at which 'Mr Henry Rawson, a resident of Toynbee, gave a very interesting account of the work which was being carried out by the residents and others'.[8]

The idea of forming a mission in London was first discussed by members of Clare College in the spring of 1884 when a circular was sent to all old Clare men whose names could be found to test their feeling on the matter. It became clear from their responses that there was definite support for the venture and a guaranteed fund of nearly £200 per annum for three years was promised. After some consultations with the Bishops of Rochester and Bedford, it was clear that South London was in greater need of help than East London. It was in consequence eventually decided to establish a mission in a district of some four thousand people in the Parish of All Saints, Rotherhithe.

The movement to found a Trinity Mission was first mooted at an informal gathering in Lent, 1884 after which the Revd Vincent Stanton, the Senior Dean, was commissioned to visit the Bishop of Bedford during the Easter vacation to ascertain whether he would assign them a sphere of work somewhere in the East End of London. No immediate answer was forthcoming from the bishop and they then became involved for a brief period with Toynbee Hall but last term they were led once again to reconsider the idea of a College Mission.[9] By this time it had become clear that the Bishop of Bedford did not wish to make any further subdivisions of East London parishes and this had led them to contact the Revd Charles Grundy, the Bishop of Rochester's Wilberforce missioner,[10] who recommended St George's Camberwell. This in turn led on to a large meeting of members of College being held in the main hall on 18 May 1885. On this occasion, Stanton moved the resolution, 'That a College Mission be established in the parish of St George, Camberwell'. This district contained some 6,000 people and was at the greatest distance from the parish church. Stanton stated that 'he did not know who it was that first started the idea of some definite piece of work being connected with a school or college, but it seemed to him to be an extremely happy idea'. He felt that the idea of a college mission did 'not need much justification' and was of the view that they should have embarked on the venture before the present time.[11] The resolution was adopted, the *Daily News* reporting that some of the younger spirits of Trinity College 'were fired with the desire to do something of what Trinity Hall has so successfully done for the East'.[12]

The origins of Pembroke's Mission can be traced to a meeting held in the College Reading Room on 5 March 1885 when an address was given by a delegate from the Universities' Settlement in East London. Following this a committee was appointed to ascertain whether the College should support the work at Toynbee or establish a work of its own. During the Easter vacation they visited Toynbee Hall, the Harrow, Eton and St John's College Missions and were taken over some of the lowest districts of East and South London. A great deal of information was collected and presented in a report to a meeting of undergraduates, which was held on 30 April. On the previous day at another meeting, Charles Grundy, had made the point that the needs of South London were far greater than those of the East End. Bishop Walsham How had also unselfishly recommended South London. It was therefore agreed that the Pembroke Mission should be located south of the river and a part of the parish of All Saints Stoke Newington was selected. On Sunday 14 November 1885 the Bishop of Rochester preached a stirring sermon in Pembroke College Chapel based on the text of Romans chapter 1 verse 14, 'I am debtor' stressing 'the debt we were under to God, to our neighbours, and ourselves'. In the evening of the same day the Bishop gave an account of South London and its great needs and described some of sorts of people who lived in the mission district. He also introduced Mr Sturgess who had been chosen as the first missioner and he briefly outlined his plans for working the mission.[13]

Corpus Christi's Mission was largely prompted by the example of St John's and Clare who had already started their work. The undergraduates were the first to promote the idea and they succeeded in winning over the Revd Charles Pollock (1858–1944), one of the Fellows, to their cause.[14] A meeting was held in November 1885 when the Revd F.S. Coleman, a former Corpus student working in South London, came down to offer encouragement to the plan. Following this as many former members of the college as possible were approached and it was clear that there was enthusiastic support for the venture. The mission was launched in a section of the parish of Christ Church, Camberwell in 1887. [15]

The Gonville and Caius Mission commenced in the Yelverton district of St Mary's Battersea in 1892. The seeds of the idea were first sown by Canon Clarke, Vicar of Battersea, who invited the college to come and work in his huge parish. One of his staff at Battersea, the Revd Francis W. Pawson (d. 1921), was a former soccer blue and member of Gonville and Caius and so provided the link between the college and the parish. Canon Clarke generously placed at the college's disposal, the old Battersea Vicarage, a substantial building close to the Thames and known as the Vicarage House. It stood in large gardens and had a mission-room attached. The house, which was formally renamed 'Caius House', was able to accommodate between six and eight residents or 'settlers'. It was used by Caius men from December 1887.[16] A printed circular letter dated August 1888 stated that 'every settler will interest himself in some aspect of the work as is the case of 'institutions such as Toynbee Hall'.[17]

Caius House. By permission of the Master and Fellows of Gonville and Caius College, Cambridge.

Cambridge House originally opened as a lay house with a clerical head and was established as a part of the Trinity Mission. It began in 1887 after two Trinity Bachelors of Arts, Messrs T. Dalton, who was later to become Mayor of Cambridge, and Henry Torr (1865–98) a London solicitor, initiated moves that resulted in the leasing of 131 Camberwell Road, on the edge of St George's parish. The settlement which was named Trinity Court was never limited to Trinity men and nor were the residents' activities restricted to St George's parish. Dalton became its first head and under his leadership adjoining properties were leased and a large hall with additional rooms was built.[18] Then almost a decade later in 1896 the new Bishop of Rochester, Edward Stuart Talbot, expressed his hope that there should be 'a Cambridge something' in South London which could claim the support of the whole of the university. Largely through the influence of Bishop Selwyn this led to a meeting in the Cambridge Guildhall in November 1886 presided over by the Vice-Chancellor. There were addresses from the Bishops of Durham and Rochester, the Right Hon. Alfred Lyttleton, Bishop Selwyn, the Provost of King's College, and others. The following resolution was unanimously passed: 'That in response to the appeal of the Bishop of Rochester a Cambridge House be founded in South London'.[19] At this point Trinity College's generous offer of Trinity Court to be the base of the newly formed Cambridge House was gratefully accepted.

Settlement Areas

The areas in which the Cambridge Colleges set up their mission settlements were among the poorest in South London. St John's College Mission was located in Walworth, half a mile from the Elephant and Castle. In 1887 the Revd Frank Francis,[20] the assistant missioner, spoke of the area in the following terms:

Outside the houses looked very respectable. When you went inside you found two families on every floor; the rooms were very dirty, no nice ornaments or pictures. The people were all distinctly poor. He hardly knew of one who earned £2 a week. The wages were generally between 20s and 30s but sometimes below 20s.[21]

Clare College's Mission was located in the Dilston Grove district of the Parish of All Saints, Rotherhithe. It was described by the missioner in 1885 as 'over-built', 'containing upwards of 4,000 people', 'inhabited solely by poor people' and 'cut off from the rest of the parish by Southwark Park'.[22] Trinity's Mission was established in two separate districts divided by the

Grand Surrey Canal and taken out of St George's Camberwell, 'a great parish of 20,000 souls'. The people were described as 'composed almost entirely of the working classes and small shop-keepers, with a considerable number of the very poor'.[23] The housing included 'four huge blocks of model lodging-houses, containing many artisans and their families to the number of about 1,600'.[24] There were some 3,000 destitute poor, so that all those problems they were most longing to solve, would meet them there'.[25]

Pembroke Mission was set up in an area adjoining the St John's Mission that consisted of about twelve acres in the parish of Newington and about half a mile South East of Elephant and Castle and close to the Old Kent Road. It contained seven public houses, one common lodging house and a police station. The people of the district were described as 'very poor', the majority living on what they were able to earn from day to day.[26] The Revd Charles Andrews (b. 1871)[27] who became the missioner in 1896 wrote that the Mission district was 'crowded with costermongers and casual dock labourers, who are amongst the poorest and most neglected of London's poor'.[28] He recalled[29] that the area was marked heavily all over in blue colour in Charles Booth's descriptive map of London's poverty. This meant that 'it was not only full of poverty but crime also'.[30] Andrews noted that owing to a lack of employment and enfeebled health, 'it was a common experience for whole families to sink down to the extreme verge of hunger bordering on starvation'.[31]

The Corpus Mission was located in the parish of Christ Church, Old Kent Road. It had a population of some 8,000, mostly working people, employed on the railways, in the gas-works and building trade and there were a small proportion of costermongers.[32] Drink was reported to be a major problem in the area 'with a very large proportion of our poverty, disease and crime traced to this cause'.[33] Gonville and Caius established their mission in the Yelverton district of Battersea. A mission pamphlet dated 1888 stated that it contained a population of 'about 6,000 of the very poor, who are chiefly employed in the adjacent factories' and that 'there are also a large number of those who are called *In Darkest England*, "the submerged tenth"'.[34]

Aims and Objectives

Speaking at a meeting to raise funds for the Trinity Mission on 6 June 1891 Mr R. Strong, who was formerly MP for Camberwell, 'declared himself unable as an outsider to distinguish between the Mission and the Settlement'.[35] In truth the Cambridge College Missions in South London combined the two concepts. They followed the earlier Victorian missions in that they all had specifically Church of England religious agendas but they also adopted the Toynbee Settlement principles, whereby men took up residence in the district and aimed to build bridges through practical involvement in the local communities and by being good neighbours. The very fact that most of the Cambridge Colleges adopted the title 'Mission' rather than 'Hall' and referred to their leaders as 'missioners' was indicative of their desire to be a little more up-front about their distinctive Christian agendas. The St Johns' College Mission, for example, was quite specific that, 'Christianity had been the basis of their work, and from this they had worked outwards, trying to get hold of individuals and to bring them to Christ, rather than to attract a large number of insincere and nominal believers'.[36] Despite the advice of local clergy that Prayer Book services would prove ineffective in an area populated by so many poor and uneducated the St John's Mission found that their endeavours 'had surpassed even their expectations'.[37]

The Clare Mission had similar objectives to those of St John's. Their first missioner, the Revd Alfred King (1857–1948) who was in charge from 1885–9, stated emphatically in his 1887 Annual Report that, 'The spiritual part of our work is, however, kept in the front, and all social and secular work is subordinate, and used only as a means to an end'.[38] Such an agenda stood in clear distinction from that of Toynbee where all social work was done without any strings attached and was seen simply as an act of love for one's neighbour. Rule 1 of the Clare Mission when it was first set up, was: 'That the Mission be called "The Clare College Mission" and have for its object the Christianising of some spiritually destitute district'.[39] Some years later the Revd Andrew Amos (1846–1931) who was missioner from 1898–1907, wrote in his Annual Report, 'I think there is every reason to thank God that the Gospel of Christ has gone home to many hearts, and that the Mission has been effective in leading many to a very real and very earnest interest in the message of God'.[40] Amos illustrated the point by observing that the holiday school which he had helped to organise in the August vacation period was for the purpose of 'giving definite religious teaching to the children attending neighbouring schools'.[41]

When Trinity's mission was set up there was a specific department for evangelistic work.[42] Its main objective was 'to assist generally in the work of the parish and in the support of its institutions as far as shall prove possible'.[43] In 1888 the missioner, with the full consent of the Master of Trinity, invited the Sisters of St James Holme, Kilkhampton in Cornwall to assist in the work. They clearly shared his overt Christian agenda and John Tetley Rowe (1860–1915)[44] wrote to the Master 'that the object in view is that the sisters would aid me in the first place in the spiritual work of my district'. More specifically he went on to state that 'they would be making by God's grace a Personal Saviour known to those whom they visit'.[45] Cambridge House, which was originally part of Trinity, also had a specifically Christian focus. By its articles of association the settlement was formed 'to provide, promote, assist, or encourage religious, social, educational and benevolent work and means of recreation for the people of the Southern parts of London and elsewhere'.[46] It was stated in a piece entitled 'Cambridge House in Camberwell' that its function was 'to provide a centre … where by the Grace of God and in the name of Christ, men may carry forward to success anything that is for the spiritual, moral, and physical benefit of their fellow-men'.[47]

Pembroke's Mission aimed in much the same way as Trinity to bring the people of the mission district into a personal relationship with God. A brief synopsis of the mission included a section entitled, 'The Lines on which the Mission is being worked'. It begins with a frequently asked question, 'Is this Movement of yours a Social or a Religious one?'. Our answer, the writer continued, 'would be that the first and foremost object of the Mission is to bring people to feel and recognise their relations to God, and to accept Salvation through Jesus Christ with all its attendant blessings here and hereafter'.[48] Having made this point clear, the pamphlet goes on to state that 'we are bound to acknowledge that their bodies want caring for as well as their souls, especially when we see what terrible privation, misery and want have in steeling a man's heart against good influences'. For this reason the mission aimed 'to combine practice with preaching' thereby enabling people to see that there is something practical in the Gospel we preach'.[49] At a meeting held in the Jerusalem Chamber, Westminster, to give 'Old Pembroke Men' the opportunity to hear about the mission, Bishop Thorold of Rochester endorsed this understanding of the College's Mission. One of its objects, he said, was to bridge over the chasm between class and class 'based on Christian truth'.[50]

The aim of the Corpus Christi Mission was very much on the same lines. Its constitution stated that: '2. The object of this Society is to further Christianity in connection with the Church of England and to promote the work of the Church among the poor resident in the Metropolis'.[51] Gonville and Caius Mission similarly stated clearly that 'the work aims to be religious, educational and social'.[52] Shortly after the new building had been dedicated the Warden recorded that so far as the religious work was concerned 'we are gradually gathering round us a congregation who worship at the Caius Mission Church, and hardly any of whom have darkened a church door before'.[53] The College Magazine reported in 1901 that, 'As to the distinct spiritual work of the Mission things do not move very quickly .... We are thankful for the progress the Mission has made, but we need, and I hope we have, the prayers of all those who care for the spiritual work of the Mission that it may go forward'.[54]

The Missioners

Whenever they could, the Colleges tried to appoint one of their own former graduates to the post of warden or missioner. On the few occasions when this proved not to be possible, the appointing committee looked for the most suitable candidate from elsewhere or left the choice to the bishop. The majority of the missioners appear to have been High Churchmen with Tractarian sympathies who sought to bring the people of their districts into a personal relationship with God through Christ. Only a few of their number had any sympathy with advanced ritualists. One reason for this was that Anthony Thorold, the Evangelical Bishop of Rochester from 1877 until 1891, who was their chief encourager and mentor, refused to tolerate ritual excess. Two of the six Cambridge College Missions, those of Trinity and Clare, showed their Tractarian convictions by inviting nuns to assist in their work.

The Revd William Phillips (1853–1934) was appointed the first Head of the St John's Mission in 1883 and remained in office for 15 years. He was a man of great energy and dedication whose labours 'were untiring'.[55] He began with only a small mission room but was able to inspire the building of a large well-furnished church, vicarage, parish room, clubroom and hostel. In his first years as missioner he found that 'the work was slow and on a small scale' but was nevertheless able to record that 'the Church and Christianity had certainly changed the district'.[56] Such was the progress of Phillips' labours that it became possible at the close of 1885 to announce the appointment of a former graduate, Frank Francis, as assistant missioner. Francis[57] trained at the Leeds Clergy School and was made deacon by the Bishop of Rochester shortly before Christmas 1886. He was 'a zealous supporter of the Mission scheme when it was first started' and it was said 'no member of the College is better known at Walworth'. In his work, Phillips was wholly supported by his wife. A report in *The Eagle* noted that over a period of 14 years successive generations of Johnians 'experienced and appreciated her kindness and hospitality whilst staying in Walworth'.[58] When Mrs Phillips died in 1899 the same magazine stated that 'all connected with the College Mission whether in the College or Walworth or elsewhere, have suffered a very sad and painful loss by the death of Mrs

Phillips'.[59] Later that same year when Phillips retired to take up the Crown living of Stonehouse near Gloucester, it was reported that he 'has won for himself a lasting place in the affections of the people of Walworth'.[60]

The first 'Mission curate' appointed by Clare College was 'an old Clare man', the Revd Edmund King.[61] He soon proved himself to be 'thoroughly earnest and conscientious in his work' and it was therefore no surprise that he 'succeeded in winning the confidence, and rousing the interest of large numbers in this hitherto neglected district'. The 'bright, hearty and entirely unsensational' services, which King organised in the Mission Room, were reported to be 'well-attended, sometimes even to overflowing'.[62] When the Bishop of Rochester attended an open meeting for all interested in the Clare Mission, he pointed out that there was much cause for giving thanks to God for the way in which the mission had so far been blessed. He went on to say 'how thankful he was that we had such a good and devoted man as missioner in the person of Mr King'. 'The Clare College Mission', he continued, 'was the only one in his diocese that possessed a building of its own'.[63] King, who married in 1889 and accepted the incumbency of St Phillips Sydenham, was succeeded by the Revd Andrew Amos.

On his arrival, Amos spoke with great enthusiasm of the condition in which he found all departments of the mission'.[64] Bishop Thorold was evidently impressed by Amos's ministry and when he visited the mission in 1893, 'he expressed himself as extremely pleased with what he had seen, and was particularly emphatic in his praise for those who are working in the district'.[65] In his annual report for 1894 Amos wrote, 'I think there is every reason to thank God that the Gospel of His Christ has gone home to many hearts, and that the Mission has been effective in leading many to the very real and very earnest interest in the message of God'.[66] Two years later Amos was able to record 'his profound conviction that in all cases the Holy Spirit has been working with us'. He went on to say that though there were no startling results nevertheless during the past twelve years forces had been at work 'which in time will revolutionise the district'.[67] In 1898 Amos, who had always been of the opinion that it was not desirable that the post should be occupied by the same person longer than ten years, left the Mission to become rector of Datchworth.[68] He was succeeded by the Revd James Pridie (d. 1943) who remained in the post until 1901. Both Amos and Phillips of St John's had remained in office for a substantial period of time and witnessed considerable progress in both the religious and social activities of their respective missions. Amos for example, reported large numbers being confirmed in 1895[69] and in the following year it was noted that 'the various Associations for mutual improvement, edification, thrift and recreation ... continue to be successful and well-supported'.[70]

Trinity College's first missioner, the Revd Norman Campbell (1854–1915), was appointed as both Vicar of St George's Camberwell and 'Warden' of the Mission and remained in office from 1886–94. He was to have the general oversight of the mission so long as he continued to be vicar.[71] In order to help him with the work he was to have one or more 'Mission Curates'.[72] Campbell's ministry soon made a very positive impression and Mr Sedley Taylor, one of the Committee members, who visited the Mission during the Easter vacation of 1886, reported 'the great satisfaction it had given him to see Mr Campbell's work'.[73] Campbell's High Church convictions were evident when in 1888 he invited the Sisters of St James Holme, Kilkhampton in Cornwall to establish a centre at the mission for women's work.[74] There were initial fears among some of the Executive Committee that this might lead to ritual excesses but these were laid to rest when a letter was read from Sister Mary Clara. She wrote, 'I am no ritualist, if I were I should not come to Camberwell! If Canon Thynne sends us he will I know expect us to work faithfully for, and under Mr Campbell'.[75] Campbell remained in office until 1894 at which point he was forced to resign through ill health. In a letter to the Master he wrote, 'I send you formal notice of my resignation as Warden ... You are aware I am acting under medical advice and I assure you that I do so with much regret'.[76] The following year, the Revd J. Tetley Rowe, who had been Campbell's assistant missioner since 1886, also took his leave after having been offered the rectory of St Mary's Chatham.[77] Norman Campbell was succeeded in 1894 by Richard Appleton, a former Fellow and Tutor of Trinity, who was Vicar of St George's for nine years and later became Master of Selwyn.[78] In the same year the Revd R.H. Grubbe was appointed as 'missioner' with responsibility for the Trinity Settlement.[79]

When Pembroke first formed their mission they were unable to find one of their own graduates and so they asked Bishop Thorold of Rochester to recommend a suitable candidate and he chose the Revd M.C. Sturgess (1859–1939).[80] Bishop Thorold visited the College on Sunday 14 November 1885 to preach in the chapel and in the evening of the same day, he introduced 'with one of his bright and earnest speeches', the newly appointed missioner.[81] Sturgess, who came from Cavendish College, Cambridge, soon endeared himself to the Pembroke community and after he had only been at the helm for six months they reported, 'We can fully endorse the Bishop's recommendation'. The account of his work continued,

If you want to know what he is like you cannot do better than to go down and spend a day or two with him, and you will be surprised to see what he has done in the time, how he has won the affection of the people round him, and with what courage he faces single-handed the great difficulties of his post.[82]

Sturgess was particularly effective with the young lads of 14–18 years of age. Many who had first 'insulted him in the streets' now greeted him with a 'Hullo Mr Sturgess'. About 35 of their number attended his Bible class on Friday evenings.[83] The older men Sturgess found an altogether different proposition. They were 'extremely difficult' to bring to services. Some are 'avowed atheists' and 'many seem quite hardened by the fashion of indifference against religious influence'. Others, he reported, 'feel that their lives are inconsistent with the smallest profession of religion; and some are kept away by fear of ridicule and abuse with which they would be abundantly visited, if they attended our worship'.[84]

One of Sturgess's successors as Pembroke missioner was the Revd Charles Andrews[85] whose autobiography gives many insights into the district, its people and the nature of the work. Andrews typified many of the early missioners in that he came from an Anglo Catholic tradition but had a profoundly personal faith in Christ. In his early years he was nurtured by his parents' deep Christian commitment and in particular by his mother. Andrews related that *The Book of Common Prayer* was part of her daily devotions and that she attended the sacrament whenever she could. The letters she wrote to him in his teenage years were often inscribed with verses from Keble's *Christian Year*.[86] In view of this it was perhaps not surprising that Andrews should have had a deep personal encounter with God. It happened one day shortly before he went up to Pembroke. He was alone in his room and 'had knelt down for a few moments at the bedside to say my evening prayer'. He recounted his experience in the following lines:

Then without warning, the strong conviction of sin and impurity came upon me with such over powering strength that every shred of false convention was torn aside, and I knew myself as I really was. To describe the sudden agony which followed is completely beyond my powers. It broke me down completely. There had been nothing during the day to lead up to this: and in church, where I had attended, there had been no stress laid upon 'conversion' as a necessary religious step in Christian progress. It was agonising, alarming, and unexpected, breaking in upon me like thunder, leaving at first nothing but black darkness behind it. I buried my head in my hands and knelt there, alone with God, in anguish of spirit that blotted out everything else and left me groping for the light ... So the struggle went on, long into the night. At last a new and wonderful sense of peace and forgiveness came stealing into my life at its very centre, and tears rushed out, bringing infinite relief. I dare not venture to explain further the process of the change that was wrought in me ... but I knew at that time that Christ was my Saviour and my Redeemer, and that His love had won my heart for ever. The chain of evil habit was broken, and its hold over me had vanished.[87]

Pembroke Mission was Andrews' first charge. Despite the 'mean streets and low quarters' a happier crowd, in Andrews' view, could hardly be imagined: 'Their good humour was constantly bubbling over, making life full of merriment' and 'the way in which they went through their troubles with a brave smile always did one good to witness'.[88] The house Andrews lived in at the centre of the Pembroke Mission was almost a night and day clubroom. Boys and girls wandered in and out under the motherly care of Miss Goss and Lizzie Middlemiss who had come with Andrews to share in the work. It was small wonder, he reflected, 'that his predecessors Mr and Mrs Simpson, had retired through ill health resulting from the strain of the work'. Years afterwards, Andrews still had vivid memories of undergraduates from the college descending on them at all hours to 'join us in our daily work and amusement'. Sometimes there were as many as 15 sleeping on camp beds crammed into the small mission house. The mission church was a multi-purpose building and when services were not being held the chancel was shut off with a screen and the rest of the building became a club in which all manner of games and activities took place. Children were by far the most frequent occupants of the premises. Each evening they would arrive from five o'clock onwards and many of them stayed until nearly midnight. Later in the evenings the men came in from their day's work and sat around by a blazing fire 'smoking tobacco till the air was almost too thick to breathe'.[89] In the midst of such friendly and loving people Andrews found it a constant struggle to attain a clear vision of Christ. At times he was also plagued by doubts on certain points of doctrine and was always anxious when the time came around to recite the vengeful Psalms in public worship.[90] Yet as he partook of the early morning sacrament of Communion and saw individuals transformed by Christ's presence he found the strength to carry on the work. Eventually the continual strain of the ministry and grappling with his doubts at the same time proved to be too much and his health broke down. While holidaying in Yorkshire with Bishop Westcott, it became clear that he must obey his doctor's instructions and leave the work he loved. After a period of rest, his health recovered and 'the presence of Christ became real to me in a way I had never known before'. Indeed, he wrote, 'Christ was now all in all to me'. Prompted by Dr Herbert Ryle, one of his oldest friends in Cambridge, he left for missionary work in India in February 1904.[91]

The first Corpus Christi missioner was the Revd William Woodcock Hough (1859–1934).[92] He began his ministry in 1887 and remained in the work until 1900 when, like so many others, he was forced to retire through ill health. Hough began his work in the most restricted circumstances, his first church being an 'inherited undenominational chapel under a railway arch' the dirt of which was 'appalling'.[93] The early days were particularly difficult as on occasion he encountered unruly youths throwing hassocks and general stubborn indifference. However, throughout his years in Camberwell he was ably supported by his wife who became very active in the Sunday school work which, at its height, attracted between 1,200 and 1,300 children.[94] A new church was dedicated by Bishop Thorold of Rochester on 25 October 1890. Sometime later the lease on a piece of adjoining land was secured and a Men's Club and Classrooms were erected and later dedicated by the Master of the College in October 1897. Here Hough was able to start 'on a proper scale a Men's Institute where, night by night, men and boys, tired from their work of the day, could restore their exhausted energies in the many pleasures of the various clubs'.[95] Despite having to leave the work on account of his broken health, Hough subsequently recovered and in later years became Bishop of Woolwich.

The Revd William Hopkins (1862–1917), described as the son of a valued former member of the College, was appointed first warden of Caius House and missioner in 1891 and continued in the work until 1899.[96] He was succeeded after only three years by the Revd Arthur Shillito (1873–1947),[97] who was gradually able to gather together a congregation, hardly any of whom had previously darkened a church door. Under his inspiration an appeal was launched for a new mission church which was completed in 1898.[98] Shillito was a particularly effective communicator and his Friday evening lantern services were often packed to the doors. The services consisted of hymns and parts of the service thrown by the lantern on to the screen. These were followed by a series of pictures illustrating the address. *The Caian* commented, 'it is a sight not easily forgotten to see in the dim light three or four hundred small people whose eyes are all riveted on one spot'.[99] In 1900, *The Caian* reported that during the winter 25 lantern services had been held with a total attendance of 10,000.[100]

Activities

Aside from their religious activities, the central focus of which was organising mission services and a range of confirmation, Bible classes and Sunday school activities, the remainder of the wardens' and missioners' time was taken up with promoting and sustaining a wide range of social and educational clubs, classes and other facilities. Gonville and Caius Missions for example, reported in 1893 that 'at the present time there is an attendance of at least 1,000 every week at the various meetings'.[101] These included ambulance lectures, a nursing class, a monthly jumble sale, and 'A Club Smoker'.[102] *The Battersea Caian and Yelverton Magazine*, 'a monthly record of the work in connection with Gonville and Caius College Cambridge Mission Settlement', was packed with details of past and present activities. The issue for February 1892, for example, carried details of the 'Sunday Sacred Music Evenings', 'The Annual Supper of the Yelverton Working Men's Club', 'A Course of Four Lectures on Political Economy', 'A Series of Popular Lectures illustrated by Lime Light Lantern', 'Miss L Simpson's New Year's Day Tea for Fathers and Mothers', 'Smoking Concerts', 'the Bagatelle Handicap', 'the Men's Meeting to discuss "The Parable of Creation"' and 'the Annual Meeting of the "flourishing" Yelverton Cricket Club'. Libraries played an important social and educational role in the life of the settlements. Clare for example had a Penny library and in 1884 the St John's put out an urgent plea for more books for their library.[103]

In the Eighth Annual Report of the Clare Mission, the assistant missioner, the Revd Thodore Gobat (d. 1937), responded to those critics who felt they were too deeply involved in social action of various kinds. He contended that a 'few weeks spent at Rotherhithe would convince anyone that we should be neglecting an obvious duty if we did not try to promote that feeling of kindness and brotherhood which the present day conditions of life do so much to destroy, or at least downgrade'.[104] For this reason Clare and some of the other college missions engaged in providing for the destitute and the very poor. The Revd Andrew Amos, the Clare missioner, was acutely aware that the loss of income when men were sick was a frequent problem. He recorded that during the course of 1897 their Penny Bank, Provident Club and Sick Benefit Society had paid out in many directions more than £730 in total.[105] Clare also set up a soup kitchen, managed by a Miss Perham, at which about 25 gallons of soup made of good meat stock, peas and vegetables were sold daily to ticket holders for a half-penny a pint.[106] A similar work was established by Caius College Mission when they first established their settlement in Battersea. They set up a cheap eating house where meals could be obtained for as little as a half-penny for a basin of soup to 6d. for a dinner consisting of soup, joint and pudding'.[107]

The St John's missioner worked as far as possible with The Charity Organisation Society and relief was given in money when safe, but more especially in orders for groceries, bread and coal. St John's also ran a soup kitchen during the winter months.[108] The Eagle reported in 1887 that 'the soup kitchen has been a very welcome help to the poor, as also the blankets lent during the cold weather'.[109] St John's also opened a dispensary, regarded as 'a valuable auxiliary to the Mission in many ways'.[110] Activities at the Pembroke Mission included a mothers' meeting, a 'Happy Evening' for boys 9–13 years of age, boys' club for 14–18 years and a penny bank (Saturdays). Between 8 May and 30 September 1886, 227 deposits were made at the Bank totalling £17 17s. 0d.[111] The following year the missioner reported that 180 new accounts had been opened.[112] He also noted that the sick and poor fund provided 'small quantities of nourishment and necessaries for the sick, and bread, tea and sugar for those who are starving' since 'it is hard to be ill and be without such things as beef-tea and milk'.[113] The Corpus Christi Mission established a similar range of activities and clubs as their fellow Cambridge Missions but found that alcoholic drink 'is a major problem in our area' causing 'a very large proportion of our poverty, disease and crime'.[114] In an attempt to counteract the problem Amos established a Total Abstinence Society and a Band of Hope. Trinity College Mission also found drink to be the root cause of social and domestic problems in their district. In consequence in January 1887 their Executive Committee proposed that the Men's Club be conducted on Temperance principles.[115]

All those who worked among London's poor were acutely aware of the polluted atmosphere and of the damage this caused to the health of children. For this reason support for The Country Holiday Fund was an important aspect of Mission work among children and young people. The Clare College missioner reported in 1887 that a total of 30 children had been sent into the country during the summer by means of The Country Holiday Fund.[116] The Gonville and Caius missioner reported in 1900 that the Children's Country Holidays took up much time on the part of the Mission staff and that eventually they succeeded in sending two hundred to different places more or less near to London.[117] The Trinity Mission reported in 1891 that,

The Chief work of our Settlement in the summer is undoubtedly that connected with the Children's Holiday Fund. The Camberwell centre has moved its quarters hither and its operations have been extended so as to include almost all the poor schools in our giant parish of 280,000 people. We expect to send this summer about 1,000 children away for a fortnight.[118]

Individual residents where time permitted played their part in local politics. Trinity Mission for example, reported that Mr Dalton, topped the poll in the Vestry Election.[119]

Links with the Colleges

As in the case of all missions, the link with their Colleges was a vital lifeline if they were to flourish. In the last two decades of the nineteenth century there was considerable support from College heads, fellows, tutors and undergraduates alike, a support that was to decline during the war years and partly also as a result of the development of the Welfare State. Among the college heads, the Revd Dr H. Montagu Butler, the Master of Trinity from 1886–1918, was an example of whole-hearted commitment to the cause. On 7 November 1886 he was on holiday gathering his thoughts together and contemplating all that would be required of him in his new post. He wrote a number of resolutions in his diary, the eighth being 'to throw himself into all good moral and spiritual causes. (i) Trinity Mission. Make much of this.'[120] Butler was true to his resolve. Not only did he make much of it in his position as its President and Chairman of its business committee, he also played an important role as social host. Each year he welcomed the men and women from Camberwell who came down to spend a day in the College and to enjoy its facilities and the atmosphere of Cambridge. On one occasion, dressed in his black silk gown and velvet skull cap, he spoke informally in his clear musical voice and expressed the hope that 'all present would enjoy the day as much as Queen Victoria did when she stayed at the Lodge in 1847, to see her husband installed as Chancellor of the University'.[121] It is clear from the Trinity College Mission papers that Butler involved himself in matters such as the appointment of mission staff, work with the Ladies Committee in Cambridge, the level of ritual in the mission services, the appeals for funding for the new mission buildings and their dedication in June 1891.

Other college masters and wardens played similar roles also welcoming the Bishop of Rochester to preach in their chapels and arranging meetings with him and the college community. The Clare annual report for 1892 noted that on Bank Holiday the missioners and a large party of workers, 'including a goodly number of ladies', visited Cambridge and were entertained by the undergraduates of the College.[122] The Revd Dr Edward H. Perowne (1826–1906), the Master of Corpus, was President of their College Mission and was an active encourager from the inaugural meeting onwards.[123] William Hough, who was missioner of the Corpus Christi Settlement during the first 13 years of its existence, later recalled how during that period people from the Corpus Mission, sometimes more than a hundred in number, would descend upon the College. Here they were entertained and shown round the beautiful college rooms, enjoyed the cricket match, the easy chairs and the lovely 'Backs'.[124] Charles Andrews also vividly remembered that on one day each year groups from the Mission went up to Pembroke College and enjoyed the hospitality of the undergraduates in the college hall. An 'amusing cricket match took place during the afternoon and a concert was organised in the evening. Members often did not reach Walworth again until after midnight.[125] The Yelverton Club paid similar visits to Cambridge. *The Caian* for example, reported that 'On Bank Holiday 1899 a party of about fifty, including the Yelverton Cricket Club, paid a visit to Cambridge. The morning was spent viewing the town and the afternoon was devoted to watching the cricket match or playing bowls or croquet in the Fellows' Garden'. Tea was provided al fresco in the front garden of Tree Court with the undergraduates acting as hosts.[126]

To a large extent the head of college's support was also important if the supply of undergraduates and former college men was to be maintained. The missioners of these college missions all appear to have been warmly welcomed by their respective colleges on several occasions each year, given the opportunity to preach in the college chapel and to visit undergraduates informally in their rooms. William Phillips, for example, stated at the 1884 annual meeting that a number of undergraduates had resided at the St John's College Mission during the long vacation and had helped in the work.[127] Two years later he wrote, 'That interest in the Mission is felt in the College is shewn by the fact that there has been little difficulty in finding men willing to act as collectors for it during the present Term'.[128] Additionally, the Warden or Master's enthusiastic presence at an annual mission meeting went a long way towards encouraging staff and undergraduates to take an interest in its activities. The Trinity College Mission held its Annual General Meeting in November 1886 on the Saturday previous to the Bishop of Rochester's sermon in chapel.[129] The following year the meeting was held in college hall at 9.00 p.m. on 29 January and attracted almost a whole page of coverage in *The Cambridge Review* entitled, 'Trinity College Mission in St George's, Camberwell, S.E.'. The Master opened the proceedings with prayer and went on to speak of 'the growing conviction in minds and consciences of thoughtful men in their youth that there is work to be done for those less favoured than themselves'.[130]

External Influences

There seems little doubt that the Cambridge college mission settlements were motivated by a combination of later Christian Social thinking that had its origins in the theology of Frederick Denison Maurice and the practical and muscular Christianity of men such as Charles Kingsley. Among those who were active promoters and supporters of the Cambridge missions were Bishop Selwyn and Bishop Westcott of Durham and Edward Talbot, the former Warden of Keble College who became Bishop of Rochester in 1895. That said, undoubtedly the major player in all of this was Talbot's predecessor, the Evangelical, Bishop Anthony Thorold, who held the See from 1877–91. He clearly saw the promotion of settlements and mission settlements as an important part of his diocesan strategy. It was a good and cost-effective way of reducing the size of his more unwieldy parishes and injecting them with vigour and creativity. The extent and impact made by the settlers and undergraduate visitors together with the public school missions is a contribution to urban mission which appears to have been overlooked and is deserving of more attention than it has received in recent days. It says much for Thorold's vision and Catholicity that, notwithstanding his Evangelical convictions, he was able to embrace the mood of the time and become an active promoter and supporter of the Settlement Movement. Thorold clearly developed a growing social concern and social theology during his time at Rochester. Speaking at the Church Congress in 1886 he declared:

> We recognise, welcome, and proclaim a salvation for both worlds, and for the body as well as the spirit, and for time as well as for eternity, and for week-day as well as for Sunday; – a salvation which shall diminish social burdens, make food cheap, literature clean, house-room decent, schooling complete; a salvation which shall open up to the artisan in the town, and to the labourer in the village, that door of hope for material progress which give such a spring of action to us all, and which might vastly help to heal that brooding discontent against God and our neighbour which breeds atheists and nurses revolution.
>
> The more we can introduce the social element into the religious and devotional, and missionary life of the Church, the more they will recognise a real need of the same. If ever the masses are to be really converted to God, it must be by an organised lay body.[131]

Thorold was tireless in visiting the Cambridge colleges both to envision them and to enlist their support as well as spending time with the missioners and familiarising himself with the work of their districts. When Thorold first heard of Trinity College's decision to found a mission, he wrote that 'the news about Trinity comes like a bottle of port wine to a weak man'.[132] The following year Thorold was present at their annual general meeting and expressed his thanks for all that the College was doing in St George's. 'It made his heart leap', he said, 'to think of the way in which our colleges and schools were coming forward to help solve the difficult problem of the poor and neglected masses in London'. Two years later in 1888 he wrote encouragingly to Dr Butler endorsing the College's £7,000 appeal for new buildings and offering the support from the Rochester Diocesan Society.[133] When Corpus Christi College contemplated establishing a mission, they consulted with Thorold who helped them decide on a district in Camberwell and then worked with them to find the right man as their missioner.[134] Clare College reported that the Bishop of Rochester had 'shown the greatest interest in this movement from its inception, both in advocating its claims at Cambridge, and preaching in the Mission Room'.[135] Their Annual Report of 1889 noted that 'the Bishop of Rochester has continued to manifest all his former interest in the Mission'.[136]

When St John's held a meeting in their college hall to consider the possibility of establishing a mission, Thorold sent his diocesan representative, the Revd Charles Grundy, and as a result of his encouragement, a district in his Rochester diocese was chosen.[137] The Bishop was present in person at the Mission's AGM in College Hall in November 1885 and stated in his talk that 'the work being done in Walworth was 'solid and satisfactory' and although the results would not appear at once, 'they would be well worth waiting for'.[138] Four years later, when it was decided to raise funds for the building of a new Mission Church, Thorold attended the meeting and expressed his hope that the building operations would not be put off till the following year but begin in October coming.[139]

Thorold also devoted a good deal of time to encouraging Pembroke's mission plans and activities. He preached in the college chapel in November 1885,[140] was present at their Mission AGM in November 1888, and spoke on behalf of the mission at a meeting of 'Old Pembroke Men' in the Jerusalem Chamber, Westminster expressing 'his sincere growing thanks to Pembroke for the aid it was giving to South London'.[141] On 4 November 1890, 'A General Meeting of College Missions' as held in Pembroke College Hall at which Thorold gave the main address in which he touched briefly on the work of the different missions. The Vice-Chancellor in response said that, the Bishop of Rochester took a deep interest in the College Missions of his diocese. In most cases he has witnessed their earliest commencement and growth, and apart from his actual support, they owe to him an inestimable debt of gratitude for his warm and ready sympathy. For this before everything else, all Mission enterprise has looked to him, and by this has always been inspired with what it most requires, courage, confidence and hope.[142]

There is no doubt that Thorold regarded College missions as a very important supplement to what was clearly an inadequate parochial system. In his opinion, a handful of parsons, however self-sacrificing, could not counteract the stolid indifference of people who were content to live without God. Thorold spoke on occasion of missions as 'reviving the Apostolic method'. College missions were not what he termed 'drum and trumpet work' (a reference to the Salvation Army) they were 'a work of faith and labour of love'.[143]

When Thorold moved on to the See of Winchester it is clear that Cambridge college missions were conscious of a great loss. In the event both of his successors at Rochester doubtless did what they could to continue the support and encouragement that Thorold had so fully given but they were never quite able to sustain his momentum. Andrew Amos of the Clare Mission spoke of his thankfulness for Bishop Talbot's visit in 1893 and his remarks, which were 'distinctly encouraging'. After having learnt from some of the residents and helpers the particular methods of the work, 'he expressed himself as extremely pleased with what he had seen'.[144] Edward Talbot continued Thorold's practice of calling the college missioners together at stated times in the year to share experiences and to pray together. The Revd James Pridie who took up office as the Clare missioner in 1898 wrote of the strength and encouragement that he derived from these gatherings. 'This Meeting together', he wrote, 'has unified and knit closely the work of College Missioners, and made all the Missioners feel what a really great and important work the College Missions are doing; and thus fresh energy and hopefulness are kindled'.[145] Two years later Pridie noted that at the November meeting of the Missioners' Conference, the subject chosen by the Bishop was, 'The Permanent Value of the Schools and College Missions as Instruments of the Church'.[146] Talbot, who had earlier been a great source of inspiration behind the founding of Oxford House in Bethnal Green, noted that our forefathers 'thought they had done all that was necessary for the work of the Church by building and endowing churches'. But he went on to assert that missions with their spiritual life and teaching, together with their varied social and philanthropic agencies are protests against such a 'laissez faire' policy.

There is no doubt that the Cambridge presence in parts of South London, together with public school and other mission agencies, had a significant impact on the life and work of their districts. Their programmes and activities were perhaps not on such a grand scale as those of Toynbee Hall and Oxford House in the East End but there is little doubt that they improved the quality of the lives of many of South London's poor. As was the case with the Oxford settlements and missions in the East End, so the cultural level of some of the lectures and classes organised by the Cambridge missions must have been well over the heads of many who darkened the doors of their men's clubs for a smoke or a game of billiards. That said, however, the settlers and temporary residents did at least demonstrate their care and concern by their presence and their practical action.

5

PUBLIC SCHOOL MISSIONS

At the same time as the universities were setting up their missions in East and South London more than twenty public schools were active in forming similar institutions. Indeed some public schools founded their missions well before Toynbee Hall was established at Whitechapel and their movement was well under way by 1883. Along with the universities, many public schools were also stirred by the detailed investigations and surveys of London's poor and were alarmed at the physical squalor in which the workforce who formed the backbone of the Empire were living. In total some twenty-four schools either supported existing mission work or set up their own missions in London before 1900. Most of these came to embrace Toynbee Hall's settlement principle in some form and at the very least encouraged both their old and present pupils to come and share in the work.

Motivational Factors
A range of different factors helped to inspire or provoke public schools to establish their missions. One of these was the 'Muscular Christianity' movement, which seems to have emanated from influential Victorians such as the Christian Socialists, Charles Kingsley and Thomas Hughes and the reforming Headmaster of Rugby School, Thomas Arnold. Hughes in particular advocated muscular Christianity in his *Tom Brown's School Days* (1857) and *The Manliness of Christ* (1879).[1] In his former book, Hughes extolled this central theme through the exploits of Tom and his friends who venture out of school to go fishing, climb trees and view birds' nests. It reaches a high point in Tom's fight with 'slogger Williams', his protection of young timid Arthur from the bullies such as 'Flashman' and his prowess on the cricket field. At one point in the book, Hughes interjects a comment of his own that 'the object of all schools is not to ram Latin and Greek into boys, but to make them good English boys, good future citizens; and by far the most important part of that work must be done, or

not done, out of school hours'.[2] In his preface to the sixth edition, Hughes reflected that Arnold 'taught us that life is a whole, made up of actions and thoughts and longings, great and small, noble and ignoble; therefore the only true wisdom for boy or man is to bring the whole of life into obedience to Him whose world we live in'.[3] Edward C. Mack in his biography of Edmond Warre, Eton's headmaster from 1884–1905, showed how he made games the central and dominant focus of the school's life and how boys were given high status on account of their prowess on the games fields rather than for their academic ability.[4] Bishop F.R. Barry who was a pupil at Bradfield recalled the chapel preachers of a slightly later period who 'exhorted us to take God onto the football field' or 'they gave us healthy advice about Christian manliness'.[5] This was an emphasis which spread quickly in the last decades of the nineteenth century among those schools in membership of the Headmasters' Conference. Ability in sports became a deciding factor in the appointment of some headmasters and chaplains to major public schools. It also accounted for the rapid growth of football in the lives of working-class youths in London, which was so strongly promoted in the boys' clubs set up as part of the school missions.[6] When the Revd Arthur Allcock was appointed Headmaster of Highgate School in 1893 it was noted that among his other accomplishments, he was a first-rate fives player, and was anxious to place the game once more on a sound footing.[7]

Some public schools' missioners were socialist in their sympathies but the schools with which they were associated had little truck with Socialism either as a philosophy or a political system. That said, there seems no doubt that Socialism was at the very least an underlying influence in all of this. Many of those who were attracted by the settlement ideal drew on the thought of Maurice and Kingsley and shared their very practical concerns regarding sanitation, slum dwellings and public health.[8] In fact the Dean of Westminster, at a meeting that was held to launch the Westminster Mission in 1888, spoke of the influence of Frederick Denison Maurice, Thomas Hughes and Charles Kingsley in making the middle classes aware of what they owed to those of inferior social position.

The image of the school was also another key factor that helped to stir teachers, pupils and governors to get involved in work among the poor. They wanted it to be seen that their school was making pupils aware of their responsibilities towards the needy and providing them with opportunities for serving others. This was the age of empire when people were conscious of their responsibilities to others. There was a concern to lift up the downtrodden by example and by organising clubs, penny banks and educational activities. In a sermon preached on Founder's Day, 10 October 1867, Dr Montagu Butler, the Headmaster of Harrow, said:

> ... they enjoyed very peculiar advantages for working out with wisdom and vigour the remedies which our times demand, and as if in them the grand language of the Prophet might be conspicuously fulfilled, 'They shall build the old wastes, they shall raise up the former desolations, and they shall repair the waste cities, the desolations of many generations. No more glorious future for any Public School could be desired than that its scholars might become distinguished, singly and in co-operation, for works of this exalted type-men 'leaders of the people ... rich men furnished with abilities, living peaceably', but not idly, 'in their habitations', men who were honoured in their generation', and were the glory of their times.[9]

In a letter to Old Marlburians, W.M. Furneaux, the Secretary and Treasurer of the Marlborough College Mission Fund, felt sure that former pupils would be glad to hear that their old school is 'recognising the duty of helping, in its degree, the great Missionary work which lies before the Church of England amid the teeming population of our large towns'.[10] The following year, the Revd Noel Smith, the school missioner, addressed a business meeting of London Marlburians and told them 'they must build a Church – not a makeshift, but one worthy of the school'.[11] Two years later *The Marlburian* urged all its readers to be generous in subscribing money for the new mission buildings 'for the honour of the school'.[12] In March 1886 when Smith visited the school, he was proud to be able to tell his hearers that the new mission church in Tottenham 'would cost a £1,000 less than the Clifton church and would contain 100 more seats'.[13] Tonbridge School also became involved in the work of the parish of Holy Cross King's Cross out of a sense of duty. The entire district in which the parish was situated had been left to the school by Sir Andrew Judd and yielded a very substantial income to the governors. When therefore the incumbent, the Revd Albert Moore, came to the school and described 'the poverty and ignorance of the parishioners' it was felt that the parish 'has a distinct claim upon us'.[14] Everywhere in public school circles there was a strong sense of concern. As C.L.C Fletcher observed, 'In 1880 the air of England was thick with similar schemes, "hostels", "settlements", "halls", "missions", to enable the rich to understand and sympathise with the poor'.[15]

For quite a number of schools the founding of a home mission or settlement was an extension of the support that they were already giving to

*Edward Thring, distinguished Headmaster of Uppingham School
and pioneer of public school missions.*

some foreign missionary enterprise. They had been inspired by the exploits
of Empire pioneer missionary explorers such as David Livingstone
(1859–75)[16] but now suddenly the demands of the home front seemed
more urgent and furthermore offered the chance to boys to actually become
practically involved. When an old Uppingham boy was consecrated as the
first Bishop of Honolulu and another went to Japan as a missionary,
Edward Thring, the headmaster, was filled with happiness to see the
Christian life of the school spreading out to distant lands. It caused him to
make collections in the school for foreign missions. In 1865 £60 was sent
to India and about the same time another year the sum of £24 7s. 6d. was
sent to a clergyman in New Brunswick.[17] Then in 1859 Dr Edward
Tufnell,[18] the newly appointed Bishop of Brisbane, gave a lecture to the
school shortly before his departure for Australia and this led to the first
official school mission to the Diocese of Brisbane.[19] Thring's biographer
noted that he 'was always quick to adopt methods likely to develop the
Christian as well as the intellectual activities of the boys'.[20] It was not long
after this that Thring recognised that what his pupils really needed was
something more 'hands on' and it was this that led to the founding of the
school's home mission in London's East End in 1869.[21] *The Elizabethan,*

the Westminster School magazine, reflected this need in an article in 1885 in which it noted the growing feeling that something must be done, not only to preach 'the gospel to the heathens at home or abroad', but also to do 'something to attack the vast mass of poverty, squalor and spiritual deadness which has been revealed of late to hundreds who never thought of it before, in the dark places of this great city'.[22]

The Bradfield School Mission began collecting money in 1889 to support the work of the Universities' Mission to Central Africa and in particular for the support of the crew of the 'Charles Janson', the society's largest vessel which carried members of the mission along the shores of Lake Nyassa.[23] However, by the autumn of 1893, the school Sub-Committee for Missions recommended 'a scheme for supporting a curate in one of the most destitute districts in South London', the parish of St Chrysostom Peckham, where the Revd Herbert Bicknell, one of their former pupils, was vicar and 'hard at work grappling with unusually heavy difficulties with practically no funds at command'.[24]

For a number of years Highgate School had supported missionary work in Delhi where the Revd Edward Bickersteth, the eldest of five brothers who had been at the school in the 1860s and 1870s, was working. When Bickersteth became Bishop of Japan the masters and boys started to send out contributions towards his work. However the boys never showed much serious interest in converting the Japanese and in March 1894 the masters and sixth formers got together to discuss the formation of a home mission. In fact the school was clear that 'the English working classes were in as much need of Christian support as foreign natives'.[25] Following the principle adopted by other public schools, Highgate chose the parish of Whitechapel as its first parish mission because one of their Old Boys, the Revd Ernest Saunders, was an incumbent there.[26] Wellington College's Christian concern for others began in the later 1870s when Mr Carr, an assistant master, formed a school missionary society. It undertook each year to give a small sum of money to a mission in St Agatha's London Docks run by Mr Linklater and £30 a year to the Peshawur Mission.[27] With the passing of time the work at St Agatha's had been given up and the Master having met with Old Wellingtonians in Oxford was prompted to take fresh action. In consequence a meeting was held at Lambeth Palace in London at the invitation of Archbishop Benson who had been the first Master of the College. There it was suggested that a district of some five thousand people in south London, previously offered to Clare College, should be adopted.[28] This proposal was formally agreed at a meeting at Lambeth in March 1885 when Mr S. Ball proposed that the district chosen be that in St Peter's Walworth. The Archbishop accepted the office of chairman and before the meeting adjourned, prayed for God's blessing as they had the future task of selecting the mission clergyman.[29]

Old students were a significant factor in many public school missions both in the initial stages of encouraging the school to get started but perhaps more importantly in sustaining the work by their visits and residence in the mission district. It was a letter from an Old Carthusian which stirred his former school to take the plunge and set up a mission in South London. He wrote as follows:

TO THE EDITOR OF THE CARTHUSIAN
Sir – I have heard a great deal lately of missions being started in different parts of London, under the auspices of a few of our Public Schools – such as Eton, Westminster and Winchester; and am informed that these schools contribute solely to the expenses of their several Missions. Why should not one be got up in connection with Charterhouse? I feel certain that if you would kindly take the matter up, many Old Carthusians, as well as present ones, would be only too glad to follow the good example set them. I personally should be very pleased to do all in my power to forward any plan that may be suggested. Hoping this proposal may meet with approval – I am yours. AN OLD CARTHUSIAN.[30]

A very similar letter came from the pen of Herbert Sutton to the Revd Dr J. Merriman,[31] the Headmaster of Cranleigh. Sutton, who knew of the school's interest in the St John's College Mission, suggested they support the work of Peter Green,[32] a former pupil of the school, who had recently begun work as their 'third missioner': 'Would it not be a grand opportunity for Old Cranleighans in conjunction with Present Boys', he wrote, 'to take as a body, an actual share in the Church's battle against the sin, suffering and indifference abounding in South London by providing the necessary funds for Mr Green's stipend?'.[33] Sutton went on to organise a gathering of Old Cranleighians at Walworth in October 1894 and urged as many former past students as possible to involve themselves in the work of the St John's Mission.[34] The Seventh Earl of Shaftesbury who was one of Harrow's most distinguished old pupils, attended the meeting in June 1883 which was organised in support of the school's proposed mission. On being asked to say a few words, he stated that the objects before them would 'tend to the real interests of the country, by advancing its moral and spiritual condition, and by doing everything to make it great and good among the nations'.[35]

The Revd H. Walsham How, the son of the Bishop of Bedford, had a singular impact on the mission of his former school, Marlborough College. In a letter to *The Marlburian* in October 1880 he referred to the mission work done by the masters, boys and Old Wykehamists in the East End of London and then went on to issue a challenge.

> What Winchester and Eton can do, we can also do. May I suggest that some of the VIth take counsel with the Master and Assistant Masters, and see if Marlborough cannot help in doing some good of this kind. With a school of over 500 boys and 30 masters, with hundreds of O.M.'s in the country, it would surely be very easy to raise £150 a year to support a curate.[36]

How went on to make the point that if Marlborough would provide the funds for the payment of a curate, 'it will be but too easy to find him a sphere of work'.[37] As a result of How's letter a meeting was arranged and it was unanimously resolved to form a mission and the Master was authorised to make contact with the Bishop of Bedford to discuss the matter in more detail.[38] Support from former pupils proved to be very strong and at a subsequent meeting of 'some seventy' Old Marlburians at Westminster Canon F.W. Farrar moved the first resolution 'that this meeting of Old Marlburians hails with pleasure and sympathy the resolve of their old School to take part in the Home-mission work of the Church; and rejoices that the actual conduct of the Mission has been entrusted to an Old Marlburian'.[39] The meeting went on to hear their new missioner, Edward Noel-Smith, say 'they must build a church – not a makeshift, but one worthy of the School'.[40] Two years later however Smith challenged some of those who had shown so much enthusiasm to put it into practice by 'taking up their quarters in Tottenham instead of the West End'.[41]

Encouragement from Bishops and Clergy

Not only were the schools, their headmasters, teachers, pupils and former students active in seeking to form missions and settlements, the church was also active in promoting them. Among its clergy none were more energetic in the cause than William Walsham How, the Bishop of Bedford and Anthony Thorold, the Bishop of Rochester. Both men, as has already been noted, were simultaneously involved with the University missions and settlements. Thorold believed missions were a vital supplement to the large parishes in his diocese. His strategy was to break off a fragment of 4,000 or 5,000 working people and plant a young energetic clergyman in their midst. With the passing of time the mission would expand and become a parish in its own right. Such indeed was later the case with many of the public school missions that were founded during his episcopate.[42] C.H. Simpkinson, who was Thorold's Examining Chaplain and biographer, was also fulsome in his praise for How and recorded the fact that it was his 'stirring summons that had aroused colleges and public schools to organise mission work in the East End'.[43]

Both Thorold and Walsham How were involved in the early stages of Eton's mission at Hackney Wick. In May 1880 the Bishop of Rochester went down to the school and addressed a meeting of masters and boys in the drill hall. During his address he pointed out 'how much good might be done, and ought to be done, for charitable work by such a large and rich School as Eton'. In consequence a resolution was passed 'That it is desirable to connect the School with some charitable work in London'.[44] However, at the meeting of the School Mission Committee on 23 June, it was decided that the district to be taken should be in the East of London and it was unanimously agreed to accept the district offered to the College by Bishop Walsham How.[45] The bishop continued to take an active interest in the work and in February 1882 he returned to address another meeting in the drill hall and was encouraged that 'so much progress had already been made since his former visit to Eton'.[46] At the end of the meeting the Provost proposed a vote of thanks to the Bishop of Bedford, which was 'carried with the utmost enthusiasm'.[47] How also gave early encouragement to the Malvern School Mission and was instrumental in directing them to the parish of All Saints Haggerston.[48]

Walsham How offered strong support to the Marlborough Mission. As the father of three former pupils of the school, the mission was of particular interest to him. It was he who arranged for the School to have a district in Tottenham of 3,000 souls 'almost all poor and belonging to the labouring classes'.[49] The school magazine noted with confidence that 'the Bishop will watch over it with all the more interest, from his old connection with Marlborough'.[50] Three years later *The Marlburian* commented that 'the Bishop of Bedford has been from the first a warm friend and wise adviser. We have not forgotten the bright stirring address that he gave in the Upper School when we were beginning our enterprise'.[51] The Bishop for his part responded with a letter of encouragement in which he wrote:

As the Marlborough Mission is now taking a forward step in the acquisition of a site for a church, I will ask you to allow me to express in your columns my great interest in the work your school is generously aiding. I need not tell you that you have an admirable representative in the curate-in-charge, Mr Noel-Smith. He is doing a thoroughly good work, and I hope the School will heartily support him. I am especially anxious that Old Marlburians should come to the rescue, and do what they can towards providing a much-needed church ... I can pledge myself to do all in my power to help forward the work so full of present usefulness and future promise.[52]

A.F.B.Williams wrote in response 'to thank you most heartily in the name of Old Marlburians, past and present, for the kindly interest you have always taken in our undertaking'.[53]

What How did for the East London public school missions, Anthony Thorold did for those south of the Thames. He had a major hand in encouraging the Charterhouse Mission in Southwark. It was he who arranged to assign an ecclesiastical district consisting of parts of four parishes, among them St George the Martyr.[54] Shortly before he left the Rochester diocese on his translation to Winchester early in 1891, Thorold was able to open the Cheltenham College Mission at Peckham Grove where there was 'a good attendance and many men'. During his last weeks, according to his biographer, he paid visits to all the college and school missions, 'the introduction of which he felt to have been one of the chief distinctions of his episcopate'.[55] Bishop Alfred Barry, Suffragan to the Bishop of Rochester who was a former Headmaster of Cheltenham College, gave much support to the establishment of the school mission in Nunhead.[56] Other bishops with pastoral responsibilities in East and South London also gave encouragement to public school missions as and when the opportunity arose albeit on a lesser scale. The Bishop of Colchester dedicated the new Malvern Mission Iron Church at Canning Town to St Alban and the English Martyrs on St Andrew's Day 1894 and the missioner subsequently spoke of the 'greatest interest' that had been taken in the Mission by the late Bishop of Colchester.[57]

Aims of the Public School Missions
Almost all the public school missions that were founded in the last quarter of the nineteenth century had a specifically religious objective as a part or the central aspect of their agenda. Whilst they felt the Liberal ideas set out by Toynbee Hall were altogether too broad, a number of them did embrace

Toynbee's emphasis on settlement and residence and felt it vital that former pupils of the school should be encouraged to take up residence either at their mission or in the mission district. In very general terms public school missions had three overarching concerns: to Christianise the locality, to provide recreational and social activities that would keep people from gambling, drink and anti-social behaviour and to enhance the quality of life of the residents by offering opportunities for educational and self-improvement. At the inaugural meeting of the Hailebury Mission the Revd E. Hoskyns, Rector of Stepney, drew attention to the efforts that were being made to reduce the gulf between rich and poor. What was needed, he urged, were men who had enthusiasm for lifting people out of the mire, first towards civilisation and next towards Christianity.[58] When the Malvern College Mission was re-established in Canning town in 1894 the first missioner, the Revd G.F. Gillet,[59] described the ambition of the mission as being 'to carry on the church's work amongst her people from both a religious and social point of view and to be the centre of religious influence and social good'.[60] Part of thinking behind the Highgate School Mission was that of 'introducing the boys to a class of fellow countrymen they rarely met'.[61]

Harrow School Mission.

The Harrow Mission which was established in 1883 had as its overriding objective 'uniting and directing the work of Old Harrovians amongst the poorer classes in London or elsewhere'.[62] When the missioner, the Revd W. Law, spoke to the school on 6 February 1883 he stated that his motto in working the district was going to be 'Help them to help themselves', for if they valued 1s., if they saved it themselves, more than a pound would be given to them. He hoped to start on this principle, coal, clothing and blanket clubs'.[63] There was also a Christian aspect to Harrow's endeavours and it was noted in the first official history of the Harrow Mission that on New Year's Day 1883 'William Law planted the standard of Harrow "for Christ's sake and the Gospel's" not in East London, as had first been suggested, but amid the laundries and piggeries and brick-kilns of the extreme West'.[64] The aim of the Marlborough Mission was 'that a fund be raised for the support of Mission work in London' and 'that its aim should be to provide the stipend (say £150 a year) of a Mission Clergyman'.[65]

Wellington College Mission began with a very similar set of objectives, two resolutions being passed at the initial meeting of masters and prefects in November 1884. The first was 'that the school should provide £150 for five years for mission work', and second 'that a committee should be nominated to carry out this purpose and to seek the co-operation and advice of O.W.'s'.[66] At a subsequent meeting in the spring of the following year a scheme was established which stated 'that this Mission be called "The Wellington College Mission", and have for its object the social, moral and religious amelioration of some destitute district in South London'.[67] The college missioner, the Revd J.T. Steele, speaking at the Annual General Meeting of the mission on 2 July 1887 made the point 'that secular work was perhaps the runner that started with the lead at the very beginning and so made the pace, as the expression went, but religion was the runner that was to win in the end'.[68] At the first meeting to discuss the founding of Cheltenham College's mission it was stated that their objective was 'to send a man into one of the populous districts ... If possible, they wanted to get an Old Cheltonian – (applause) – someone who would be united to the school by ties of memory and of loyalty and to his work by love for Jesus Christ'.[69] At a subsequent meeting, the school Principal, the Revd H.A. James, stated that another object of the school was 'that they might teach the boys something outside their ordinary school life – that outside them lay a world of great misery and poverty, which they could, by some slight sacrifice, do something to alleviate'.[70]

Some schools rather than setting up their own missions put their energies into supporting a particular club or activity of an existing settlement or parochial mission organisation. Repton School for example

Edward White Benson, Headmaster of Wellington College, 1867.
Later he became Archbishop of Canterbury.

supported the Repton Club at Oxford House[71] and Berkhamsted School was commended by the Head of the House for 'the steady support given by the boys there to our boys' work'.[72]

School Mission Districts

In almost all instances the school mission districts were selected in conjunction with one of the bishops with pastoral oversight of East and South London. In most cases this was either William Walsham How of Bedford or Anthony Thorold of Rochester although some of the later foundations were helped by their successors. The majority of the missions were districts of about 5,000–7,000 people, which were carved out of one or more adjoining parishes in the poorest and most disadvantaged areas. Their vicars and rectors who were overburdened with the enormity of the task of trying to care for the souls of so many poor and down-trodden people were invariably only too willing to give away a slice of their territory. In general the larger and more prosperous schools were drawn to the idea of setting up their own missions although in some instances they joined in with the work and ministry of an existing parish.

One of the very first missions to be founded was the Winchester College Mission in the East of London. The first missioner described it as follows:

> The place of my labours consists of an area of about one thousand by six hundred yards, containing upwards of 10,000 people, not six of whom keep servants; they are all very independent and hardworking, and are very much left to themselves; about 800 or 1,000 are absolutely destitute. Very many of the people are Irish and from the north country; and the accommodation provided for large numbers of them consists of three or four courts, such as you probably have never seen; a hole in a wall, not large enough for any beast of burden to enter by, leads to a sort of rabbit warren containing in reality sometimes thirty or forty houses.[73]

The Charterhouse Mission District was described as 'a very poor one' formed out of five Southwark parishes with its northern boundary just south of the church of St George the Martyr, Tabard Street. The population that centred on this corner South of the Thames was described as one of the 'most degraded and vicious and poor in the whole of London'.[74] The 1884 Annual Report of the Charterhouse Mission noted that the courts in Tabard Street 'are considered the lowest in the Borough'. The houses were let in what were called 'furnished apartments' and 'unless the rent is paid on Saturday night the people are turned out, and consequently there is a very frequent change of tenants'.[75] The main occupations and trades of the residents included fur-pulling, cigar-making, brush-drawing, onion-peeling, jam-making, wire-weaving and leather bag-making.[76] The heart of the Dulwich College Mission area was described by Charles Booth in his *Life and Labour of the London Poor* as 'a cesspool towards which poverty and vice flow side by side. Bad buildings, bad owners, mismanagement on the part of the Church – all have contributed to these things which now demand the best united efforts to put right'.[77]

The Harrow Mission was established in an equally downtrodden area of Notting Hill, which at the time was known for its brick making and pig-rearing.[78] The main occupation among the men was bricklaying and most women were employed in laundries earning 2s. 6d. or 3s. a day.[79] The area, which was affiliated to the parish of St Mary Abbots, Kensington, had a population of 6,000 and was described as 'an extremely poor one'.[80] There were nine public houses and it was said that the poorest one was still able to realise takings of £50 week.[81] Harrow School and its old students gave generously to the needs of the mission such that by the summer of 1895 the missioner was able to report that 'the Mission had become a well-equipped parish; and the main task was to maintain and strengthen what had been done rather than to undertake new work'.[82] Highgate School began their mission in Whitechapel but later transferred their allegiance to the parish of St Mark's Dalston, an area in which 'overcrowding is very common' and 'many a house can be pointed out where three and four and even five or six families have their homes'.[83] The Malvern Mission District, which was a section taken from the parish of All Saints Haggerston, contained some six thousand people 'for the most part, very poor' being 'mostly gas-workers, dockers and casual dockers'. The school missioner described the usual dress of children in the area as 'no boots, trousers ending half-way up to the knees, torn shirt, and ragged coat'.[84] The Bishop of Colchester in a letter to the masters and scholars of the college wrote: 'The district, crowded with the tenements of artisans and dock-labourers, seems to call aloud for some mission work carried on by men of Christian principle and devotion, which may elevate, cheer, and brighten the laborious and often dreary lives of these toilers'.[85]

The Marlborough Mission at Tottenham was located in a district of 3,000 souls 'almost all poor, and belonging to the labouring classes' taken out of an area that was 'miles of houses'. There was one particularly bleak spot where a number of houses that were little better than wooden sheds were grouped around a large indiarubber factory.[86] The missioner, the Revd E. Bailey-Churchill, reported that, 'Up to the present time these toiling thousands have no civilising or religious influence brought to bear on them. A single moment's reflection will show how grievous is the need of a great evangelising effort to save them from practical heathenism; how wide and fresh and ample is the field of our Mission Work'.[87] The Wellington College Mission was established in St Peter's Walworth, an area where 'the people's needs were very great, numbers of them being unemployed and not able get work of any kind'. The missioner, the Revd Herbert Lucas (1854–1940),[88] felt that 'the hardest work of all was no work, and this was all numbers of them had'.[89] Tonbridge School Mission was located at King's Cross, an area noted for extremes of poverty and ignorance.[90] Cheltenham College was assigned a district in Nunhead for its mission. It was described as 'about the size of the College playground, containing 5,800 people, mostly very poor, living in houses which had been built for better class population, but which had gone down in the world'. A mission committee report added the further comment that 'the dreariness of the district is increased by the constant stream of hearses that make their way to Nunhead Cemetery'.[91]

The choice of these very poor districts was regarded as meeting two important objectives. First, they were an important way of supplementing and bringing new life to a parochial system that was inadequate and stretched to the limits. Many incumbents were not only glad to share their field of labour with a school or college mission, they were also encouraged by the presence of fresh enthusiastic young men in their locality. Second, these very poor urban areas ensured that pupils would have the opportunity of witnessing poverty at first hand, the experience of which would inspire in them a desire to engage in practical action and care. In all cases it was felt that the promotion of this kind of involvement would help to civilise and enhance the quality of the lives of the inhabitants and in some instances would assist in quelling social unrest and civil disorder.

Role of Headmasters

The success of school missions was inevitably very largely dependent on the influence of head teachers. If they were enthusiastic they would share the vision with staff and pupils and take a leading role in linking with Old Boys to raise funds for missioners' salaries and new mission buildings. In addition, missioners would be welcomed to the school and be invited to address the masters and pupils and speak in the school chapel. The school chaplains for their part would raise termly collections and from time to time take pupils to visit the mission. Where the headmaster was wholehearted in support of the school mission one particular benefit was an annual summer visit by people from the mission to the school.

Significantly the great majority of public school heads in the middle and later years of the nineteenth century were themselves clergymen who were deeply concerned at the plight of London's poor and acutely aware of the Church's failure to minister to their needs. Many heads were undoubtedly inspired by the life and teaching of Thomas Arnold (1795–1842), the reforming head of Rugby. He had instilled into his pupils at Rugby their duty to Christianise the English nation. In his *Englishman's Register* he urged that the situation of the times demanded that the rich should be made aware of social conditions of the poor. He was of the opinion that if men of privilege who possessed social, economic and political power could be persuaded to accept the ethos of service and help the poor as their duty, then the whole nation could be Christianised. An article in *Harrow Notes*, written following the announcement that Dr Montagu Butler was leaving the school after twenty-five years as headmaster, stated that Dr Arnold 'had begun that great reform which was destined to renew and rehabilitate, while preserving its essential characteristics intact, the whole public school system throughout England'.[92] The article went on to state that Arnold's influence could not fail 'enormously to increase the responsibility and influence of Headmasters'.[93]

The first school to respond to the kind of ideal that Arnold was advocating was probably Uppingham under its progressive Head, the Revd Edward Thring (1821–87).[94] The school's concern was first awakened by an address by the Revd J. Foy, a priest from the Additional Curates Society, in the schoolroom in April 1869 on East End London life. The school magazine reported that 'his admirable lecture on Home Missions could hardly have failed to rouse the energy and compassion of his whole audience and incite them to do something in this great work'.[95] His words evidently challenged a group of pupils who then asked Thring if the school could start a mission. Two entries in Thring's diary capture his evident enthusiasm.

April 17th – An excellent lecture last night from Mr Foy for the Additional Curates' Society; one of the best I have ever heard.
April 25th – The School has determined to start an East London mission in consequence of Mr Foye's lecture. We think we shall get £100 a year, and it will interest the boys. I am very pleased with the idea. We had £17:18: 3. 3/4d for our special offertory to-day.[96]

Thring was totally committed to the scheme and the following year the first public school missioner, the Revd Wynford Alington, began his work in North Woolwich. What Uppingham did was to pay the stipend of one of the assistant curates, which was not a mission in the fullest sense. That said, other public schools saw in Thring's action the beginning of what became the Public School Mission Movement.[97] Thring's major concern was to keep his boys in regular touch with the mission so that they would be constantly aware of its poverty and its day to day needs. Each year the missioner or someone from the mission came to inform the school about the needs and the progress that had been made. These visits were returned and Thring in particular was an enthusiastic participant. When a new church was consecrated in 1872 he recorded the following entry in his diary:

September 24th – Back from North Woolwich after one of the most remarkable days in my life, and one that I verily believe will mark an epoch in England. We took up forty boys on Wednesday, housed them in London, and brought them to North Woolwich next morning. In all, reckoning masters, ladies, and old boys, Uppingham mustered seventy-four strong on that day.[98]

Thring's account of the day was a lengthy one and he went on to comment on the Bishop of Rochester, 'a real man', whose 'excellent manly sermon'

and brief words at the lunch 'the boys will not easily forget'. The service, he
noted, was 'very good' and then in a few words which revealed his sensitive
nature, he commented that 'the singing sounded full and sweet, for we
brought up a strongish choir, but I was anxious about the effect of their
singing with the local singers and I told them to be careful to follow their
lead, as we came to help not to show off'.[99] Thring ended his reflections,
writing, 'I am sure that day will not pass out of our school life easily ... I
less and less set my heart on this Uppingham here and its buildings and the
local work'. 'England', he continued, 'has never before had this fastening of
a school on to real life work in the world outside. May it increase and
spread'.[100] Thring later reflected that 'the School Mission is the best
possible supplement to the purely intellectual atmosphere of the university,
the best corrective to its unpractical tendencies, and the best preparation for
the high and true thinking on life subjects'.[101]

Although Thring's involvement at North Woolwich and Poplar marked
the start of public school involvement in London parish work, Winchester,
'the mother of us all', was seen by many as the creator of the first wholly
independent school mission. This followed a meeting at the school that was
held in December 1875 and addressed by Robert Linklater[102] on the
miseries of London's East End. Following his challenging presentation, it was
resolved that the school should be responsible for a mission of its own.[103]
The district that was chosen was a section of the parish of St Michael's
Bromley in East London and the Revd E. Donne was chosen as the agent of
the school mission. In the autumn of 1880 a new mission church was
opened near the East India Dock. The Consecration service took place on
Michaelmas Day with the Bishop of Bedford presiding and Dr George
Ridding,[104] the Headmaster of Winchester, preaching the sermon.[105]

The Headmaster of Cranleigh School, the Revd Dr Joseph Merriman, a
Fellow of St John's College, Cambridge, was the founder and driving force
behind the school's mission which he subscribed to generously and visited
regularly. The Headmaster of Dulwich College under whose direction the
school mission was started in 1886 was Arthur H. Gilkes (d. 1922) who
came from Shrewsbury School where he had combined social work with his
other commitments. Gilkes took up his appointment in 1885. He was
something of a disciplinarian and, according to one obituarist, had a firm
conviction 'that small boys should be kept in their place, and that a low
place'.[106] Together with the Revd George Allen,[107] Gilkes founded The
Dulwich College Mission Home for Working Orphan Boys in Walworth
Road. As he saw it, the Mission mirrored the faith and aspirations of the
school's founder, and in the early days he visited it on Sundays whenever

time permitted. The extant Dulwich College Mission Visitors' Book shows that Gilkes was a frequent visitor even in later years. In 1891, for example, he made 31 visits.[108] In the early days the school made itself responsible for half the cost of the upkeep of the mission, the funds being raised by voluntary subscriptions. In theory contributions were voluntary but at the end of term Gilkes read out the contributions made by each class and it was felt to be a disgrace to be at the bottom of the list. The school mission remained close to Gilkes' heart until the end of his days. The preacher at his Memorial service recorded that 'every Sunday for many years, indeed, almost to the end of his time at Dulwich, he walked over to Walworth, or rode very slowly on his bicycle, to maintain his intimacy with the work and the boys'. After his retirement in 1914 Gilkes lived for a short time in Dulwich but then took holy orders in 1915 and became curate of St James, Bermondsey.[109]

Edmond Warre, the Headmaster of Eton, was the first treasurer of the Eton Mission at Hackney Wick from 1880–4 and, according to his biographer,

> he retained his interest in it to the end of his life'. It was apparently his delight to trace its growth from Mr William Carter's first meetings of twenty or thirty poor people in a back kitchen, and a Sunday School of forty scholars, to the full-blown splendour of Bodley's church ... which holds eight hundred people and is always full on Sundays at Evensong.[110]

Warre was made deacon by Samuel Wilberforce in March 1867 and ordained priest on 22 December the same year.[111] The Headmaster of Harrow from 1860–85 was Dr Montagu Butler. He had long wanted to establish a permanent link and mutual bond between the school and the poorer classes of society. The school's closeness to London seemed to suggest that this was the obvious place. When therefore Dr Billing, the Bishop of Bedford and Suffragan for the East End London, addressed the boys and pleaded for a mission or settlement in his part of the diocese, Butler pledged the help of the school. A committee of masters and boys was set up and an Old Harrovian appointed as first missioner.[112] H.S.S. Trotter related that Butler 'threw himself with characteristic vigour' into this new departure which was to crown his own work and extend the beneficent influence of the school'[113] Butler spent his fiftieth birthday at the Harrow Mission 'by going to hear some of our leading boys sing to William Law's poor people in London'. He remarked to a Mrs Galton in a letter that,

It was a touching sight to see the intense delight of the poor women, many of them with babies in their arms. To-morrow Law brings 65 of them, babies and all, to spend a long afternoon in our garden, and we shall do our best to make them happy with tea, cake, fire balloons, etc. Before they start for home, some of the boys will sing to them again in the speech room.[114]

The Harrow Mission flourished and by 1885 it became necessary to secure the legal right to control its patronage and to convert the district into a separate parish and to erect a new church. In all of this Butler proved both adept in administration and skilled when it came to inspiring support. As he left the school in 1885 he took the opportunity to address a 'Farewell Appeal to Old Harrovians and Friends of Harrow'. The sum for which he asked was £7,000 but within three years the money was raised and the church consecrated on Trinity Sunday by Dr Temple, the Bishop of London. In his address, the Bishop said he must as a former headmaster of another great public school, be profoundly impressed with such work as this, which testifies to the determination of the great public schools of England to use that brotherly spirit which binds men together, and their vast resources – moral, material, and social – for doing their duty by those classes unable to help themselves'.[115] The Revd J.E.C. Welldon (1854–1937), who succeeded Butler as headmaster, was also strong in his support for the school mission. Speaking at the laying of the foundation stone of the new mission church in Latimer Road, he said that if Harrow was not as foremost as she ought to have been in starting a work to fulfil their duty to their poorer neighbours, it would not be too much to say that it has been foremost in the energy with which the work has been carried on'.[116]

Arthur Allcock, the Headmaster of Highgate, was the leading influence in the founding of the school mission, which was first mooted in 1894. Under his direction a strong committee was appointed to set out the lines on which the mission would work. On a number of occasions the lads of the Mission Brigade in Dalston visited Highgate and enjoyed what became 'the great event of the season', the hospitality of the Headmaster.[117] *The Cholmeleian* reported that the Headmaster kindly invited the Whitechapel boys to visit the school on Saturday 24 July 1897 noting that many would remember his 'generous hospitality' from last year.[118] Malvern's head played a prominent role in the College Mission helping it to locate first in Haggerston and then being instrumental in its subsequent move to the parish of Holy Trinity, Canning Town in 1894 pledging the school to double its former subscription.[119]

The Revd C.G. Bell, the 'Master' of Marlborough, met with Walsham How, the Bishop of Bedford, to discuss with him the possibilities of a mission district. Once this had been established he continued to give much support to the work in Tottenham. On a number of occasions he both visited and preached at the mission and during the 1883 Christmas vacation he attended a congregational social gathering.[120] Speaking at a meeting after the consecration of the new Tottenham mission church on 8 April 1887, the missioner stated that the success of the mission was due in large measure to those who had originated it and 'he must express his thankfulness to what he called the two fathers of the Mission, the Bishop of Bedford, and the Master of Marlborough College (cheers)'.[121] It was the Warden of Radley who first invited the Revd Robert Linklater to the school on 6 March 1881, to give an account of the district of St Peter's London Docks.[122] It was this that led to the school supporting the work of the parish as its Mission.[123] In a similar way the Revd Theophilus Rowe was instrumental in the founding of the Tonbridge School Mission in King's Cross in 1883.[124]

The headmasters themselves came from a variety of backgrounds. Gray of Bradfield for example, was a moderate and liberal churchman. Described as a broad-minded Evangelical he had no use for sacerdotalism or ritual, took a receptionist view of the eucharist and had a thorough distrust of High Church ways.[125] In contrast it seems probable, judging by the fitments and furnishings of the College mission church, that the Revd C.G. Bell, the Master of Marlborough, was High Church in his convictions.[126] George Ridding of Winchester was Broad Church in his sympathies as was Edward Thring of Uppingham while James Welldon of Dulwich and Harrow began life as an Evangelical but eventually shook free of party labels.

Commitments by the Schools

Most schools began their commitment to mission by undertaking to raise the salary of their appointed missioner or mission curate for a term of three to five years. The missionary concern of the Victorian era certainly did not pass by Winchester. 'A rousing and humorous address in 1875 by Robert Linklater on the miseries of London's East End led to the inauguration of the College's Mission there the following year. It was situated in an area close to the East India Dock.[127] Later, when it was decided that a church was needed, the money was very quickly collected.[128] A meeting of masters and boys in the school drill-hall, Eton College in the early spring of 1880 guaranteed a sum of not less than £200 per annum for two years in support of its mission in Hackney Wick.[129] Later in December of the same year a meeting at Marlborough College agreed to provide a missioner's stipend of

£150 per annum for five years.[130] At another later meeting in March 1882 it was unanimously resolved on the recommendation of the Bishop of Bedford that a committee should be appointed to collect funds for the building of a church, and for providing the mission clergyman with a colleague.[131] The masters and boys of Harrow gave a somewhat more demanding commitment in the spring of 1883 when they 'made themselves responsible for the salary of the Missioner for at least seven Years'.[132] In addition the ladies of Harrow agreed to pay the mission woman's salary. The Harrow community was particularly generous in its giving. There was a rapid response to the Master's request for funds to build the new mission church and all the required £7,000 was raised and the building completed in three years.[133] It was small wonder that the *Harrow Notes* reported: 'The Harrow Mission began on the first day of 1883, and has been nobly supported by Harrow men and boys, and by other friends of the school'.[134]

In November 1884 Wellington College undertook to raise £150 for five years for missionary work in London.[135] At a subsequent meeting it was agreed that this should be located in a district of the parish of St Peter's, Walworth.[136] Bradfield held a meeting on St Andrew's Day 1893 at which they agreed to raise the sum of £100 to support a curate in the parish of St Chrysostom, Peckham. The school magazine commented that 'following the example of other and larger public schools' Bradfield is likely at no distant date to support a definite Home Mission'.[137] Cranleigh agreed to provide the stipend of the Revd Peter Green, the third missioner at St John's College Mission, in Walworth.[138] The headmaster, Dr Merriman, agreed to make a personal contribution of £5 per annum.[139] For their mission Dulwich College decided to take on the responsibility of running a boys home. The details of its location in Walworth Road were worked out between the Master and the Bishop of Rochester. Each form in the school was required to make a termly collection and the sums collected were published in the school magazine. This brought about a competitive spirit with the result that not inconsiderable sums were collected. *The Alleynian* reported that the 1891 spring term collection had amounted to £41 11s. 0 3/4d.[140] In March 1894 Highgate School made a regular financial commitment to support the Boys' Brigade and underwrite the salary of a curate in the parish of St James Whitechapel where an Old Cholmeleian, the Revd E.A.B. Sanders, was its rector.[141] At a general meeting of the Malvern College Mission on 4 February 1893 it was resolved to act on the proposal of the Archdeacon of London, the Ven William Macdonald Sinclair, and guarantee the sum of £200 per annum for the salary of the missioner in the parish of All Saints Haggerston.[142] In the autumn of 1900 it was announced that Radley's terminal subscriptions were to be given to the Radley College Club in the parish of St Peter's London Docks.[143]

The Missioners

Ultimately the key to the success of a school mission lay with the missioner. If he was a lively communicator and at ease with people in general, he would both be able to draw people into the mission activities and inspire the staff and students with the vision. It was vital that the missioners were able to gain the support of headmasters who in turn would organise opportunities for them to address the school, preach in the chapel and link up with former staff and students. The enthusiasm of the missioners and their reports back to the school were also a major factor when it came to raising funds for mission churches, halls and other buildings.

The first missioner of Winchester College's Mission, which began in 1876, was the Revd E. Donne. He stayed in post until 1882 when on his removal to the parish of Limehouse, the college decided to move its mission nearer home to Portsmouth. Donne was evidently a good speaker since the school magazine recorded that the account that he gave of his work in January 1879 'to a large number of both Boys and Masters' was 'listened to with evident appreciation'. Later the same evening Donne preached in the chapel at the evening service and pointed out 'the great social differences that exist between class and class, and the duties which those in the higher grades of life owe to their poorer brethren'.[144] With the approval of the Bishop of Rochester, Charterhouse chose as their first missioner, the Revd J.G. Curry, who had been Curate of St Mark's Kennington. The 1884 Annual Report described Curry who had been educated at Wellington, as 'a clergyman singularly adapted by character and experience for the work he has undertaken'.[145] Cranleigh decided in the autumn of 1894 to support the St John's College Mission, and did so by providing the stipend of the third missioner, the Revd Peter Green who was an Old Cranleighan.[146]

It was often the case that the school either chose an Old Boy as their missioner or decided to support an existing parish where one of their former students was the incumbent. This obviously gave the school a closer link with their mission since the missioner was able to reminisce about his time as a pupil. Such was the case at Uppingham. In 1870 the Revd Wynford Alington, a former pupil of the school, was appointed to the post of missionary curate and sent to work under the incumbent of North Woolwich, the Revd Dr Henry Boyd who was later to be Principal of Hertford College Oxford.[147] When he moved on from there to take up missionary work in South Africa, the school transferred its mission to another poverty-stricken parish in Poplar which was under the direction of another Uppingham Old Boy, the Revd Vivian Skrine.[148] The first missioner of the Eton College Mission was William Carter. Like Green an Old Boy of the school, Carter was described as 'a straightforward and courageous character'. He was a keen footballer and one of the founders of West Bromwich Albion.[149] The first missioner appointed to the Harrow Mission was the Revd William Law described by the Master as 'a devoted Old Harrovian'.[150] Along with Carter, he was a distinguished cricketer having been four years in the Harrow Eleven and four years in the Oxford University Eleven. He was subsequently curate to the Hon. and Revd Edward Carr Glynn, first at Beverley, then at Doncaster and lastly at Kensington.[151] He enjoyed a particularly close and warm relationship with the Master, Dr Montagu Butler, who seemed always ready to entertain people from his mission district and welcome them to the school to address the masters and boys.[152] Law, who had always said that his work would be done in seven years, eventually left the school mission at the end of 1889 to become Vicar of Rotherham. His replacement was Arthur Gordon (1858–1924),[153] another Old Boy and captain of the School Football Eleven in 1877. He went up to Trinity, Cambridge, and was ordained in 1881. Unhappily Gordon's sensitive nature proved unsuited to the work of the mission and he was compelled to resign in 1892 after a long illness.[154] Gordon was followed by W.H. Heale, who had represented the school against Eton in 1878, and after studying at Balliol was ordained in 1884. His health also failed and he too was forced to resign in 1895.[155] D.J. Learoyd who followed him proved to be strong in health and remained in the post for the next thirteen years. During his time the ministry developed into a strong parish and the nature of the work was to maintain and strengthen what had already been established rather than engage in new initiatives.[156]

The Headmaster of Highgate School called a meeting in March 1894 to discuss the formation of a school mission and it was decided to support the work of an Old Cholmeleian, the Revd Ernest Saunders, in the parish of St Mary's Whitechapel. When in 1897 Saunders moved on to St Mark's Dalston, the school decided to transfer their missionary concern to his new parish.[157] In February 1881 Marlborough College felt the time had come for them to found a school mission. The Master, the Revd G.C.Bell, inserted a letter into the school magazine in which he begged 'any into whose hands this paper may come to aid us in finding a fit man, perhaps a Marlburian or other public school man, to take charge of this good work'.[158] It was Bell's chief concern that the one chosen 'should have power to attract the sympathy and stir the hearts of the masters and boys here –

and thus not only deepen their interest in his own people, but may be plant the seed of harvests richer than his own'.[159] The first missioner, the Revd E. Bailey-Churchill, began work in the parish of Tottenham in June 1881 and remained in post only until the following year when he was succeeded by Edward Smith.[160] It was noted in the school magazine that he was 'the younger brother of two distinguished Marlburians' and it was stated that he came to Marlborough in August 1863 and remained until Christmas 1868 before going on to take his degree at Oxford.[161] At a meeting of Old Marlburians held shortly after his appointment had been announced, Canon Farrar said that 'his experience as a London clergyman had taught him that public school men were exceptionally valuable'. He then went on to state that 'of Public School clergymen Edward Smith was a good specimen. He came of good stock; he had a large and varied experience; he had the greatest of all gifts for the work – that spirit of enthusiasm which won converts now as it had done in the early days of Christianity'.[162] When Wellington College decided to establish a mission they took a long time to decide on their missioner but eventually the Revd H. Lucas was selected. On his first visit to the school he was 'most warmly greeted by a very largely attended meeting'. Lucas said that their welcome reminded him of his own school days at Uppingham when they used to greet their missioner in a similar way. He now felt 'more than half a Wellingtonian' but he was proud of his old school for two reasons, 'first for its prowess in the cricket field, secondly, and especially because it was the first public school to take up such a work'.[163] Lucas was succeeded by an Old Wellingtonian, the Revd J.T. Steele, who served as missioner for almost ten years. On his retirement from the post, *The Wellingtonian* commented: 'It would be hard to find anyone who could have been more suitable for the work, a thorough public-school man, and an excellent athlete, he threw a freshness and manliness into the work he undertook'.[164]

Role of the Missioners

The public school missioners had two major roles; to maintain close links with their schools who in most cases paid their salaries and to sustain the work of their mission churches, clubs, societies and educational ventures. The principal means for most missioners was by visits to preach in the school chapel and by regular mission updates and progress reports in the school magazine. For example, Highgate had a terminal service on behalf of their mission in the school chapel with the offertory going to Mission expenses.[165] When the Uppingham mission moved to St Saviour's Poplar they changed their method of keeping in regular touch with the mission.

The chapel choir, together with musical masters and ladies of the school, visited the parish and gave a concert.[166] Winchester organised regular visits to the school for their missioner, Mr Donne. He would address the boys on a Saturday evening and then preach in the school chapel on the Sunday following with the collections being given to their East London Mission.[167] Some schools gave detailed reports of these occasions. The following reports in *The Marlburian* that recounted the school visits of their missioner, Edward Smith, were typical of most school magazines. On Saturday 25 February 1882 it was noted that 'he addressed the meeting for nearly an hour' and that on the following Sunday evening he preached in the chapel from Luke chapter 14 verse 23: 'Compel them to come in'.[168] The next year there was another lengthy report of 'a numerously attended meeting' at which Smith delivered an interesting address richly stored with humorous anecdotes of his past year's work'. Once again Smith preached in chapel on the Sunday following.[169] Two years later, the school magazine again noted that the Revd Edward Smith paid his annual visit to the school and gave a detailed account to the 'well-attended meeting' presided over by the Master.[170] He urged all present when they prayed for the progress of God's kingdom, 'to devote some special thought to that little corner of it which had been committed to his charge at Tottenham'. The meeting closed with some words from the Bursar in which he described his recent visit to the Mission when he preached for Mr Smith. He was struck by the hearty services, admirable singing and the effective temperance work'.[171] Smith, who died in 1908 at the comparatively young age of 58 was described as 'one of the most loyal Marlburians, never failing in gratitude to his School for founding and steadily supporting the Mission, and to the many Old Marlburians, with the Bishop of London at their head, who responded to his appeals for money or personal service'.[172]

School missioners also fostered the relationship between their missions and their schools by encouraging present pupils and Old Boys in the school to visit and where possible stay and become involved in the work. A number of schools arranged for groups of boys to go down to their missions and entertain people from the mission district by giving concerts and other forms of entertainment that included, musical items, drama and sketches. Magazines of schools such as Berkhamsted, Eton, Harrow, Wellington and Winchester give detailed accounts of some of these occasions. In the early 1890s Highgate boys and masters were going regularly to Whitechapel in the evenings where they taught 80 members of the Mission Club to play chess, draughts and bagatelle. They also provided them with a vaulting horse and 'a liberal supply of boxing gloves'.[173] In October 1895 the school gave its first concert at their mission with Miss Crich, the matron of school house, accompanying soloists on the piano.[174] Members of the Common Room, boys and Old Alleynians were regularly encouraged to visit the Dulwich College Mission and Hollington Club.[175] The Revd St Clair Donaldson (1863–1935)[176] appealed to all Old Etonians who found themselves able to stay at Hackney Wick for any length of time to do so. He reminded them that there was room at the new house for five laymen and that they would always be most gladly welcomed.[177] *The Malvernian* of December 1894 stated that the key to their mission becoming a centre of Christian influence 'is for everyone to go down there'. It went on to point out that 'it is an easy journey from Liverpool Street or Fenchurch Street, and there are buses and trams from the City'.[178] *The Radleian* for June 1899 gave a lengthy account of 'a pilgrimage to St Peter's London Docks' when members of the school went up to Wapping and entertained the people of their mission district with two short plays and some musical items'. All was reported to have 'gone exceedingly well' with the audience 'enjoying the humour and the jokes'.[179]

For many missions the annual visit to their sponsoring school was the event of the year. The outing began with a large party of children and helpers, often more than seventy in number, setting off by train. On their arrival at the local station they were greeted by representatives of the staff and pupils and escorted back to the school. There they were given a generous lunch in the school hall or gymnasium. The afternoons were usually taken up with a cricket match and various other activities such as croquet, river trips and seeing round the school buildings. Later in the afternoon there would be a tea on the headmaster's lawn and sometimes an entertainment. The day usually concluded with a service in the school chapel before the homeward journey began. School magazines made frequent mention of these occasions. Children from the St John's Mission for example, were taken to Cranleigh School in the summer of 1885.[180] In the summer of 1888 the Wellington missioner, the Revd J.T. Steele, took a party of 87 from the Working Men's Club to the College. After dinner the visitors enjoyed the swimming pool while others enjoyed the gymnasium or watched the rain-interrupted cricket match. The visit ended with tea and some brief speeches.[181] *The Carthusian* of October 1886 reported on the summer visit of 300 youngsters to Charterhouse School. They arrived at Godalming Railway station and were transported up the hill to the school in specially provided closely-packed wagons. The treat, as was the case in the previous year, was organised by Mr and Mrs Davies. After dinner, a variety of activities were laid on including games, swings, see-saw, and

A visit to Charterhouse School at Godalming by children from the school mission, c. 1885.

skipping ropes. Later in the afternoon there was tea and a chapel service with a few words from Mr Curry, the missioner. The children, according to *The Carthusian*, 'sang their hymns very nicely – heartily, but without shouting or screeching'.[182] The Annual Report for 1894 noted that 'Charterhouse generosity' was displayed for the ninth time on 8 August when a party of more than 350 visited the school and found 'the hosts attentive to the smallest details'.[183]

Sustaining the Mission

Public school missioners needed to be men possessed of a strong constitution and enormous energy since their week was one continuous round of clubs, activities, night schools and involvement in local affairs. It was small wonder that numbers of them suffered ill health and were forced to resign the work after relatively short periods in office. It would be impossible within the scope of this one chapter to do justice to the wide range of activities that were promoted and fostered by the missions. That said, various passing references in the school magazines enable us to catch a glimpse of the dedicated labours of the missioners, their staff and helpers. Christ's Hospital ran the St John's Working Men's Club, a men's Bible class and sunday school classes, social and musical evenings, a cricket club, debating society and a library.[184] The Harrow Mission ran a mothers' meeting, a Church of England men's society, a boys' club with cricket and football sections, a girls' club 'with about two hundred members of the rougher class', a musical society and gymnastic and drill classes.[185] Highgate School Mission could boast a Sunday School with 250 children, a lads' brigade, a penny bank, a gymnastic club, a reading and games room, a Brigade Band of Hope and a weekly Bible class.[186] Among its activities, the Marlborough Mission in Tottenham included a Church lads' brigade, a women's guild, and a men's club. They also supported a mission nurse who was 'much beloved in the parish, especially among the children'.[187] Marlborough had a Provident Work that, among other things, sold 70 tons of coal to its members during 1884. The Blanket Club was 'greatly used' and the two penny banks boasted 400 members. In addition there was a clothing club and a temperance society.[188] Wellington had a girls' club, a men's club and a farmhouse in Essex which had been lent to them as a holiday home for children.[189] When the situation demanded it school missioners did what they could to provide practical relief. Charterhouse for example, lent blankets and gave out coal and tickets for meat and grocery during the severe winter of 1894 but the missioner was careful 'to give to people who seem most deserving'.[190] His policy was only to give from mission funds to 'those who are personally known to us or have been visited in their homes'.[191] In its first year the Cheltenham College Mission set up a soup kitchen and over 600 gallons of soup were distributed[192] and later in 1897 a coffee tavern was opened just opposite the mission with a view to increasing temperance among the people of the neighbourhood.[193]

A concern for temperance seems to have occupied quite a number of the public school missions for the reason that drunkenness reduced family incomes and that in turn led to poverty and crime of various kinds. Temperance societies and Bands of Hope thus became part of the work of a number of the missioners and their helpers. Uppingham Mission in Woolwich had a total abstinence society. Eton held a temperance mission in Hackney Wick in November 1899[194] and Harrow had a flourishing temperance society, managed by a committee chosen from the working classes as well as two juvenile temperance societies.[195]

Impact of the Missions

It is not difficult to be critical of public school missions and to put them down as primarily designed to enhance the image of their schools and to impress parents with the notion that their boys were being trained in responsible citizenship. It is also easy to portray their endeavours as condescending attempts on the part of the upper and middle classes to play their part on behalf of the poor. They can also be criticised for not being more involved in local politics or grappling with the roots of poverty but the reality of life was that there were limits to what could be achieved with small resources. The fact is however that the missions and mission settlements made significant contributions to the life and worship of their districts.

One aspect of this impact, which has recently been revisited, was the impact of the missions on sport and Association Football in particular.[196] Historians of the game have acknowledged the significant contribution of the public schools in the development of the game during the late Victorian years. Public school Old Boy teams dominated the FA Cup in the first years after its introduction in 1871. 'Wanderers', a team consisting of 'Old Boys' from a number of public schools, won five of the first seven FA cup finals.[197] As schools such as Eton, Winchester and Repton began to establish youth clubs as an integral part of their missions, it was inevitable that football would have a central place. A number of missioners, as has been noted, had been prominent footballers and therefore put considerable energies into training their mission teams. The formation of The London Federation of Boys' Clubs in 1888 with which many mission clubs were affiliated provided a further stimulus by creating a competitive element. There is no doubt that the public school mission movement was an important influential factor in the spread and growing popularity of the game among working-class lads of London.

It is apparent that the missions had a measure of success in bringing the working poor of all ages, and indeed numbers of men, into the church. Most mission churches were able to report good congregations at their Sunday and weekday services. Their missioners, nurses, helpers and other staff did much to lessen the burden of pain and poverty of London's poor. There may have been an element of condescending charity in their activities but their educational and social work widened people's horizons and implanted in them a desire for self-improvement. The remarks of the Revd Edward Smith of Marlborough College on 'the civilising effects of the Mission' were typical of many annual reports. He noted with satisfaction 'the reformation in manners and mode of dress he had succeeded in introducing among the factory girls'.[198]

Perhaps the one area of disappointment was the relatively small numbers of boys and old students who personally involved themselves in the work of their school missions. This was due in part to the fact that most had very little accommodation for residents or for short stay visitors. Perhaps the last word should go the Bishop of Bedford who had no doubt from what he had witnessed of the work of missions that 'the lower classes of working men and women were most appreciative of kindness, and most respectful of the church'.

6

NONCONFORMIST SETTLEMENTS

Several of the Nonconformist denominations were attracted to the settlement principle as being a positive step towards doing something constructive to reach London's poor with the Christian message in ways that were more than just words. Among the most significant were the Wesleyan Methodist Settlement in Bermondsey and the Congregational settlements in Canning Town and Walworth. All three institutions were inspired by the social conscience of their leaders who had all in varying degrees been inspired by *The Bitter Cry* and the work of the Barnetts at Toynbee Hall. Before 1901 the Roman Catholics, who were also challenged by Mearns' pamphlet,[1] founded one settlement for men in Southwark and three others in London that were staffed by women. They were small in comparison with the other Nonconformist settlements and were all connected with Catholic parishes.

The Bermondsey Settlement
The first warden of the Bermondsey Settlement was John Scott Lidgett (1854–1953). He had had a solid Methodist upbringing and was said to have been a product of the 'Wesleyan Methodist Aristocracy'. The influence of his maternal grandfather, John Scott, remained with him throughout his whole life. His father, John Jacob Lidgett, was a wealthy ship-owner who divided his leisure time between church activities and philanthropic work. He had already served in the ministry for 15 years before he went to live in Bermondsey. Young John was studious by nature and a voracious reader. He was particularly influenced by *The Life of Kingsley* published in 1877 which 'fed the flames of my social enthusiasms and stimulated me to various forms of social activity'.[2] Of no less importance was the publication in 1881 of *The Life of Frederick Denison Maurice*, which extended his theological

thinking.[3] Lidgett was also impacted by discussions on the fatherhood of God which he had with William Burt Pope whom he later described as 'the greatest systematic theologian that Methodism has ever possessed'.[4] As a small boy he heard a sermon which prompted him to offer himself for the ministry. Then in later years after his arrival in Cambridge he recalled that as he walked back from a preaching engagement he had resolved to plant a colony in one of the poorer districts of London that would be evangelical 'but with the broadest possible educational and social aims'.[5]

The start of his more specific interest in the settlement ideal began when as a young man he met with John Richard Green and Brooke Lambert and discussed with them the possibility of 'doing something for the poor'.[6] Another crucial moment occurred one night in November 1887 when 'under a moonlit, but stormy sky, I vowed to God that I would renounce all other interests and endeavour to plant a colony, somewhat on the lines of Toynbee Hall in one of the poorest districts of London'.[7] Bermondsey, the selected area, was chosen for several reasons. It was a poor neighbourhood but it was also relatively healthy which was important if young undergraduates and professionals were going to take up residence there.[8] An additional factor was the close proximity of Guy's Hospital from which several staff and medical students had already expressed a willingness to be involved in the work.[9] The next step was to gain approval from the Methodist Conference, this at a time when the Wesleyans had 'a strong fear of any preaching that could not be called evangelical'.[10] In the event the required permission was granted in 1889[11] and the necessary funds were raised. Together with William Moulton and Morgan Harvey, the scheme treasurer, Scott-Lidgett placed a letter in *The Methodist Times* asking for financial support for the project in this 'much-neglected part of London'.[12] The letter strongly emphasised that all the objectives of the settlement were inseparable from evangelism, religious teaching and Christian fellowship. They stated the integral relationship of these two vital elements as follows:

> The extent to which Christ is realised as present and set forth in His saving mercy will be the measure of our success. But no setting forth of Christ will be complete which does not seek to provide counteractions to the terrible temptations to which multitudes are exposed, and the healthy expression of all the powers, mental and social, which Christ has redeemed.[13]

The dream finally began to be realised in December 1891 when the *Pall Mall Gazette* announced that 'A freehold site has been secured in

Farncombe Street, Bermondsey, for the Methodist Universities Settlement in London'. The article went on to inform readers that the building 'is to be erected by the architect of Toynbee Hall, and in some respects – notably in the provision of a larger lecture hall and gymnasium – Toynbee Hall will be considerably improved upon'.[14] The aim was to provide a permanent residence for twenty young professional men and a number of additional helpers.[15] Lidgett later wrote in his autobiography, 'The work which I started in January 1892 was, to begin with, chiefly educational' and 'while basing my arguments on spiritual, and indeed evangelical grounds, I set social rather than ecclesiastical duties to the foreground'.[16] The main building, which was opened on 6 January 1892 by the Right Hon. Sir John Lubbock MP,[17] was to be the warden's home for the next 59 years.

Aims of the Settlement

Lidgett was Methodist to the core and spoke of his denomination as 'the greatest movement of compassion towards the multitudes in England since the Reformation'. In consequence, he said, they had 'the highest qualification for social work'.[18] Lidgett was particularly taken with the endeavours of William Booth's scheme for the social salvation of the submerged tenth and was vehement that Christians must do all in their powers to remove the causes which brought about the widespread ruin that existed in many areas of London. As he saw it, they were primarily bad housing, drink and the lack of education and healthful recreation.[19] Lidgett believed that the formation of trade unions for the unskilled and vigorous evangelism were both vital necessities and he urged support to make Booth's plan 'as perfect in conception and as efficient in execution as can possibly be'.[20] Lidgett was influenced by the Toynbee concept in that he felt that a settlement should be a community of social workers[21] who had come to take up residence in order to assist in promoting the well-being of the neighbourhood by means of friendship and co-operation. He differed in his conviction that the settlers must also be overt in their proclamation of the Christian faith.[22] Lidgett was firm in his conviction that a settlement, as opposed to a mission, was based on Christian principles, not ecclesiastical organisation. He also seemed unperturbed that other Methodists appeared to be unwilling to take up the settlement ideal.[23]

The aims that Lidgett set out for the new settlement were the same combination of evangelism and social action which he had earlier stated in his appeal letter to *The Methodist Times*. In his first annual report, he wrote: 'Our recognised principle in these matters must always be the production of Christ-like character by the power of the Holy Spirit, yet there is a duty resting upon us to make the general conditions of life as favourable to the formation of such characters as possible'.[24] Lidgett defined the aims for the Bermondsey settlement under six heads.

(1) To bring additional force and attractiveness to Christian work;
(2) To become a centre of social life, where all classes may meet together on equal terms for healthful intercourse and recreation;
(3) To give facilities for the study of literature, history and art;
(4) To bring men together, to discuss general and special social evils and to seek their remedy;
(5) To take such part in local administration and philanthropy as may be possible.
(6) And so to do all this that it shall be perfectly clear that no mere sectarian advantage is sought, but that it shall be possible for all good men to associate themselves with our work.[25]

In all of this Lidgett aimed to build a bridge that would span the gulf between the 'two nations', the rich and the poor. He saw this objective as the 'constructive philanthropy' of the Forward Movement as opposed to the 'remedial philanthropy' which was offered by so many of London's churches.[26] Such philanthropy, he wrote in his report of 1892, must nevertheless always be in concert with 'directly evangelistic work' to which 'we attach the highest importance'.[27] In his report for 1897 he wrote that the role of settlements was 'to show to the religious people with whom they are in contact, how broad and humane the Christian ideal is, and how closely bound up with the highest spiritual interests are the general educational and social activities which settlements create'.[28] Much of their evangelistic efforts were made in conjunction with the services at Southwark Park and Silver Street Chapels where among other commitments, they provided Sunday school teachers and gave help with the temperance work.

A number of the earliest residents who came from a variety of religious backgrounds[29] were not from the universities. Most of them worked in London offices during the day. In his report for 1891 Lidgett stated that all men and women who sought the kingdom of God in Bermondsey would be equally welcome to share in the work of the settlement. That said, he deliberately aimed to attract university graduates. He went on to record his gratitude that members of the Wesley Societies at Oxford, Cambridge, Edinburgh and Aberystwyth 'are earnestly entering into our work'.[30] In the year from September 1891 to September 1892 six Oxbridge men were reported to have been in residence.[31] Following the strategy adopted by the

Barnetts, Lidgett sought to awaken young people to a sense of their great responsibility of serving both God and the people.

Activities

The core activities centred around the gymnasium, games room and class room activities[32] and the main hall where lectures on all kinds of subjects were provided and classes held in mathematics, languages, public health and even theology.[33] The theology classes for Christian workers were a source of deep pleasure to Lidgett who was himself a scholar of distinction who gave public lectures on biblical topics.[34] Almost all the students who attended these classes were found to be between the ages of 16 and 25 and residents of either Bermondsey or Rotherhithe. Most were artisans, clerks and shop assistants. These classes were later organised as the settlement's Working Men and Women's College.[35] It continued to grow in popularity and in the year ending in September 1895 there were 1,054 attendees at the classes.[36] By 1899 the number who enrolled had further increased to 1,364.[37] A significant aspect of the work of both the men and women's settlements were their temperance activities. This had been one of Scott Lidgett's concerns even before the doors of the settlement were opened.[38] He noted in his annual report for 1900 that temperance work has continued with a hundred names on the roll.[39]

Lidgett's concern was that residents should be fully involved in the life and work of the local community and he certainly exemplified this in his own life by becoming one of the most prominent members of the London County Council.[40] He was also active on the London School Board[41] and was one of eight Bermondsey settlers appointed as local school managers.[42] Lidgett was particularly concerned for the welfare of pupil teachers and in 1893 the settlement undertook to house and support a number of pupil teachers who were working in the local area.[43] A significant aspect of Bermondsey's work with children was the Guild of Play set up by Grace Kimmins (1871–1954). Her initiative which established links with similar initiatives on the part of Mary Ward's Settlement and Hugh Price Hughes' West London Mission, argued that education should not be confined to school timetables and designated hours. In her view, it needed to take place in streets, parks and other public areas. In 1894 Kimmins also helped to set up 'The Guild of Poor Brave Things' which aimed to establish alternative learning strategies for children with disabilities. The guild was initially located at the settlement premises. In addition to promoting educational work Lidgett was also active as a Poor Law Guardian being first elected to the St Olave's Union in April 1892. To this work he wrote, 'I have devoted much time and thought'.[44] At a later point Lidgett referred to the Infirm Wards as 'above all, the great human problem'. He wrote:

> There men and women spending together the closing years of their life, for whom it is necessary to secure, not only healthful, religious, and moral influences, but rational interests; some degree of freedom, above all, from the wearisome monotony of routine, and some sense that they are not beyond all concern of the community, but are still objects of sympathetic thought and care.[45]

Lidgett went on to urge that Settlements should make Poor Law Work a major concern because they are the most likely to have among their number men and women of compassion who can 'redeem administrations from self-seeking and harshness, or weakness and stupidity'. Lidgett further maintained that 'Poor Law problems admit to the very heart of those social evils which settlements are seeking.[46]

In his second annual report Lidgett stated that the settlement would 'seek to acquire and promote a better understanding of pressing social problems and shall endeavour to bring about common action for their solution'.[47] In order to facilitate this objective a continuing series of lectures on social and economic topics were organised and supplemented with conferences which included the religious and moral aspects of these issues. Although Lidgett never considered himself to be an active member of the Labour Party he was a strong supporter of Trade Unions believing them to be vital in the case of unskilled workers. Arising from his concern for the casual labourers a Private Labour Agency was established during the course of 1893 and employment was found for a number of 'deserving men'.[48] A free legal advice centre patterned on Mansfield House was also started with one of the residents who was a barrister giving free legal advice on Saturday evenings.[49] Lidgett stood behind the London dock-workers in their dispute of 1889.[50] Lidgett's action together with the dedicated care and visiting by the resident nurses helped to create a strong bond of trust between the settlement and local unions. This was particularly apparent in 1899 when a large number of local Labour Unions and Benefit Societies formed a committee, which had as its object 'to help the Bermondsey Settlement whenever called upon, and for whatever purpose'.[51] Lidgett commented that they had subsequently had the pleasure of entertaining about sixty of those men to supper in the autumn.[52] Always concerned for the poor, Lidgett ensured that the Settlement gave what support it could to the Co-operative movement in Bermondsey[53] and actively supported Sunday closing in an effort to ensure a day of rest and relaxation for the working classes.[54]

Alongside the many social and political involvements of the Bermondsey Settlement, Lidgett was ever concerned to proclaim the Christian message in word. As he saw it, the 'ordinary street preaching' of 'the certainty of death, the awfulness of hell and of Christ offering a happy eternity' gave an incomplete idea of the Christianity of Christ. 'We must', he wrote in his report for 1892, 'set forth the whole Gospel in all its spiritual and ethical splendour'.[55] As far as he was concerned, it was only the practical care offered by the residents of the settlement that could achieve this. Writing in 1895 he stated that 'the great evangelistic advance for which earnest men are looking' was unrealisable unless those who were 'highly placed' would come and live among the poor and by their actions 'be interpreters of Christ'.[56] Five years later he reversed the order and spoke of the vital need for all the settlement's activities to have 'a spiritual temper'.[57] In addition to his many commitments Lidgett was also a Wesleyan Circuit minister with the oversight of a number of churches and clergy. There are several references in the settlement reports to the residents devoting their time and energy to specifically evangelistic work. For example, many of them took an active part in the great united mission that was held under the auspices of the Bermondsey and Rotherhithe District Council of the Evangelical Free Churches at Bermondsey Town Hall in the first week of November 1897. Lidgett stated in his report that this council had its headquarters at the settlement and that is was his honour to be its President.[58] Four years later Lidgett gave a full report of another similar evangelistic mission held in January 1901 at Bermondsey Town Hall and sponsored as before by the Bermondsey Evangelical Free Churches. Lidgett once again served as chairman and most of the organisation including house to house visiting was done from the Settlement.[59] A number of the residents carried out a house-to-house visitation of the district, delivering leaflets and giving personal invitations to the mission services and other activities. The settlement also trained the mission choir. Lidgett commented that, 'It is one of the privileges of an institution situated like the Settlement that it can serve in various ways the cause of Christian union'.[60] Although Lidgett was always engaged in reading, academic and journalistic writing[61] and involved in many social and philanthropic enterprises, he never lost his concern for the evangelistic work. In 1893 for example, he wrote with some satisfaction that, 'Our congregations here have shown a steady increase during the year, and almost the whole increase of church members has been in connexion with this society'.[62]

Mansfield House and Browning Hall

The Congregational churches had been made aware of the plight of London's poor from a very early point. *The Bitter Cry* had been produced by one of their own ministers, Andrew Mearns, and his report had been keenly debated in many of their churches and on their public platforms. This being so, it was perhaps surprising that they were somewhat later than the established churches in opening their settlements. Their two London Settlements, Mansfield in Canning Town and Browning South of the river at Walworth, which were formed in 1890 and 1891 were very similar in ethos and theological outlook. The *Mansfield House Magazine* for January 1896 stated that 'there are the closest bonds of sympathy uniting the two Settlements, and we hope for great development of mutual aid in the future'.[63]

During the later 1880s a number of Mansfield students had been spending some or part of their vacations working in Canning Town with the Revd F.W. Newland and this gradually led to a desire that there something of a more permanent nature should be established.[64] Thus it was that a scheme to set up Mansfield House was first mooted at a meeting held in the College Hall on 21 May 1890.[65] Twenty people were present including students and members of Council. Percy Alden who was on the point of completing the second year of his college course volunteered to act as warden and his offer was accepted.[66] The College Report for 1890 noted that the movement had not originated with the Council and was not under their control. They nevertheless 'heartily commend it to the sympathy and support of their constituents'.[67] Alden himself later emphasised that the motivation for the settlement had come from the students themselves. 'I ought to say, to the credit of the Mansfield students, that the movement originated entirely among the men themselves without, in the first place, any official interference on the part of the college'.[68]

Alden had been influenced in his thinking on social issues by both T.H. Green and Arnold Toynbee. He later wrote, 'What a friend Green was to every young man who showed that he had a craving for something higher and better than the satisfaction of a few selfish desires'.[69] It was largely through Green's influence that Alden went up to Balliol in 1884 to read 'Greats'. It was from there that Alden entered Mansfield and became a Congregational minister and warden of the College Settlement.[70] Alden was also influenced by F.D. Maurice whose theological writings had inspired an earlier generation of Christian Socialists that included Charles Kingsley and Thomas Hughes.[71]

Mansfield chose Canning Town as the district for their settlement partly because of their already established links with the area but also because it was rapidly becoming one of the most congested parts of the Borough of

Some of the 'squires' of Mansfield House with the warden Percy Alden (centre) in 1897. By kind permission of Mansfield College, Oxford.

West Ham, which had a population that had grown from 129,000 in 1881 to nearly 205,000 in 1891. It was also a purely working-class constituency into which casual labourers 'swarm up from the country continually but from which the well-to-do have fled'.[72] Canning Town lay to the south of West Ham and was described as a desolate dockland area where much of the labour was casual. A report in the *Mansfield House Magazine* described it as 'a flat, marshy expanse' with Shooters Hill in the distance and the masts of shipping and the gas works decorating the mist-barred flats.[73] Many of the men in the area were employed in the iron and gas works of the area.[74]

Browning Hall was formally inaugurated on 21 November 1895 by Herbert Stead (1857–1928), the son of a manse who followed his brother William into journalism. In 1876 however he felt a call to enter the ordained ministry and trained at Glasgow University where he graduated with honours and went on to further studies at four German universities.[75] Before taking up settlement work, Herbert Stead, unlike Alden, gained experience in the pastoral ministry serving Gallowtree Gate Church in Leicester from 1884–90. He then came to London as editor of *The Independent and Nonconformist*. Four years later he laid aside any hopes of a ministerial or theological career in order to serve the poor of South London. Browning Hall was however connected with the local York Street Congregational Chapel in Walworth. In earlier times it had been a flourishing centre of Christian life and worship but had then been a mission before finally being renovated and re-christened as Browning Hall after the poet who was baptised there in 1812.[76] In his boyhood and youth Robert Browning attended Sunday worship at the chapel and listened to the preaching the Revd George Clayton.[77]

Like Alden, Stead was influenced by the kingdom theology of F.D. Maurice and the earlier Christian Socialists. He later wrote that 'men are finding out the truth about the Christian religion. They are going back past priest and Church – back to Jesus Himself'. When working men do this they find him to be 'the Nazarene carpenter, the homeless wanderer, the despised agitator, the friend and champion of the poor and exploited and disinherited, the supreme social reformer'.[78] Stead went on to relate that these men were learning to put the stress on the doctrine of the Kingdom that Jesus taught was intertwined with the Fatherhood of God and the Brotherhood of Man. They were learning that the kingdom is 'no fire-escape' but a place where there is justice and abolition of physical want.[79] In an article he wrote in the *Mansfield House Magazine* Stead stated his conviction 'that to leave common brotherhood is to court certain failure, and so University Settlements, whatever they may be in actual practice, have always held this in theory to be their ideal'.[80] Stead, one of whose residents was Keir Hardie, became increasingly convinced that the Labour Movement could become thoroughly Christianised. As he put it:

Labour can think and write and rule. And once Labour has seen the real Jesus and drunk in His social ideal of the Kingdom of God, then we shall behold the most glorious revolution this land has ever witnessed. Then we shall see clearly that the Labour Movement in Religion is but the answer to the workers to the command of Christ.[81]

The Aims of Mansfield and Browning

Both Mansfield and Browning had very similar objectives that were in essence a combination of settlement, social and philanthropic programmes combined with evangelical preaching. Mansfield was clearly influenced by the work and example of Toynbee Hall. The settlement's appeal of 1925 spoke of their 'specially close relationship with Toynbee Hall, with which it has carried out several co-operative schemes'.[82] K.S. Inglis observed that of the Nonconformist settlements, Mansfield House was certainly nearest to Toynbee Hall in religious atmosphere'.[83] Perhaps this link was nowhere more obvious than at the laying of the foundation stone of the new

Mansfield House residence on 17 December 1896 when Canon Barnett was invited to give one of the addresses. Among other points that he made, Barnett stressed that 'a settlement is not a mission. A mission exists for a definite purpose, for the promotion of a fixed set of principles, such as Christian doctrine, teetotalism, socialism, or may be individualism'.[84] Barnett went to state that he had himself been involved in missions for many years and 'I don't deprecate their work at all'.[85] The key in all settlement work, he said, was to bring about unity by facilitating 'contact' so that church and people can both come together and get to know one another. Settlements must be places where people not only come together but become workers together. In all of this, as he saw it, it was vital to avoid 'vulgar party spirit'.[86] This thinking clearly resonated with the views of the Mansfield College Principal, Dr A.M. Fairbairn, who more than a decade earlier had made a similar point in a lecture to the Congregational Union. He urged that it was not enough to organise evangelistic missions and that religion should make industrial questions peculiarly its own.[87]

The aims of Mansfield House were clearly set out in a document that was published in 1893 and which included the following paragraph:

1. The name of the Association is 'THE INCORORATED MANSFIELD HOUSE UNIVERSITY SETTLEMENT'.
3. The objects for which the Association is established are as follows:-
   (a) The promotion of the religion of Jesus Christ in its most comprehensive meaning, but so that special attention shall be given to its social action and aims.
   (b) To provide religious educational and other charitable purposes for the people of the Southern Division of the Borough of West Ham and the poorer districts of London and elsewhere, to enquire into the condition of the working classes and the destitute, and consider, advance, and carry out plans and schemes to promote their welfare.[88]

Stead and the residents of the house constantly reiterated these parallel twin objectives. Will Reason (1864–1926),[89] one of the early residents and later sub-warden,[90] stated in 1893 that 'To carry out Christ's teaching we felt that a vigorous attack must be made on the evil conditions of life in the district'.[91] An anonymous publication put out by the house in 1892 stated that the 'deeply religious' aim of Mansfield was 'to bring the teaching of Christ to bear upon all the problems of a poor man's life'.[92] Another document published by some of the residents stated that they felt strongly that all the social work at Mansfield was as a result of their religious beliefs in consequence of which they had been able to overcome many prejudices against Christianity.[93] The Settlement Directory for 1894 stated:

> Mansfield House is a University Settlement, founded for practical helpfulness, in the spirit of Jesus Christ, in all that affects human life. We war, in the Masters' name, against all evil – selfishness, injustice, vice, ignorance, ugliness and squalor, and seek to build up God's kingdom in brotherhood, righteousness, purity, health, truth and beauty.[94]

The aims of Browning Hall were similar in many ways to those of Mansfield House, though with slightly more emphasis on proclamation of an evangelical nature. When the settlement was first opened *The British Weekly* expressed itself reassured that it was to be connected with a local Congregational chapel and would offer religious teaching that was non-sectarian but evangelical.[95] Like Mansfield there was strong emphasis on settlement. In Stead's own words, 'the general idea is that those who possess education, wealth, leisure, or other social advantages, should take up their abode among those who are less fortunate, in the hope of alleviating and enriching the life of the neighbourhood'.[96] The declared aims of the Browning Settlement were 'the furtherance of the Kingdom of God ... the amelioration of the life and lot of the people dwelling in the Borough of Southwark ... to promote the full and happy development of body, mind and soul'.[97] In the *Directory of Settlements* Browning Hall expressed a specific commitment to Labour:

> We stand for the Labour Movement in religion. We stand for the endeavour to obtain for Labour not merely more of the good things of life, but most of the best things in life. Come and join us in the service of Him who is the Lord of Labour and the soul of all social reform.[98]

Residents

For both Mansfield and Browning the concept of settlement was a vital aspect of their strategies. Shortly after the opening of the premises in York Street, Browning rented a house in the Camberwell Road about a quarter of an hour's walk from the Hall. Next to it was a common lodging-house, behind it was the railway and beyond some of the worst slums in Walworth.[99] In terms of their staff and helpers both provided residential accommodation for university students and both were non-denominational in their outlook. Mansfield stated in one of their early publications: 'We are not at all sectarian; our sole condition is a spirit of Brotherhood and desire to help. If anyone will come and help us to do the work of Christ in any way, we gladly welcome him, whatever his creed'.[100] While Mansfield drew most of its residents from its Oxford base Browning established links with Nonconformist students in Cambridge. The Cambridge University Nonconformist Union noted that a connection had been established with the Browning Settlement, 'by means of which members are enabled to come into actual contact with practical social work'.[101] Browning residents tended to be a little less dominated by university men. Besides professors, undergraduates and academics who represented the majority, there were others whose only training was in elementary or secondary schools.[102] Stead noted that the settlement's concern was always its neighbours, not its residents. It was also the case that Browning had not been a temporary resting-place for social nomads and he was pleased in later years to recall that they had not given support to the jibe that 'a Settlement man is a man who cannot settle'. Indeed he reflected that a good number had remained in the work for two years and some had spent ten or eleven years as residents.[103]

Both Alden and Stead set great store on the concept of brotherhood both among the settlers and in all dealings with the people of their respective districts. Writing in 1913 Stead was clear that throughout the course of the settlement, men and women stood on a footing of 'absolute equality'.[104] A Mansfield pamphlet published in 1892 stated that the aim of Mansfield House was 'to foster a practical spirit of Brotherhood and for this there is no better soil than the heart of the working man, when he is frankly and reasonably approached'.[105] Stead constantly warned his residents of the dangers of patronising attitudes and urged that Browning was to be the very negation of caste. 'The true resident', he wrote, 'has been found to be only a neighbour raised to a higher power of neighbourliness'.[106]

Activities

Both Mansfield and Browning fostered a wide range of educational and philanthropic activities, which focused on clubs, recreation and a variety of classes and university extension lectures. One of the first of Mansfield's ventures was Fairbairn House which was opened in January 1892 in Swanscombe Street but later in 1895 put down permanent roots in a former Boxing Saloon. Its one aim was 'to create and satisfy the widest possible range of interests among its boys'.[107] The Mansfield Men's Club similarly aimed to reach the men of West Ham irrespective of their political or religious views by offering as wide a range of activities as possible. The club commenced on a modest scale with one small billiard table, bagatelle, a few sets of chess, draughts, dominoes and cards but membership quickly swelled to 600. The occupation of the members varied, many being dockyard labourers and transport workers. Others were glass-blowers, boilermakers, lightermen, stevedores and clerks.[108]

A host of other activities were offered in conjunction with the club including cycling, rambling, cricket, football, gymnastics and concerts and entertainments. In addition there was a penny bank, loan society, sick benefit society, orchestral society and temperance bar. The latter institution proved 'a most distinct success' with a number of men reportedly becoming sober and temperate and some even becoming total abstainers.[109] The Sick Benefit Society was established in 1891 and gave benefit to any members who were prevented from working either through sickness or accident. In the early days a contribution of 6d. a week brought a benefit of 12s. per week for 13 weeks and 6s. for a further 13 weeks. Doctors' fees were also paid.[110] Percy Alden held many discussions with the men both from the district as well as from Fairbairn House from which it emerged there was a desire for educational improvement. In consequence, efforts were made to start university extension lectures during the winter of 1890–1. On Sunday evenings there were lectures on scientific, historical, literary and social subjects with an estimated 500 persons taking part. In the second year of is existence Browning organised the Walworth Centre of the London University Extension Society and a popular professor who knew the area gave a course of free lectures with an average of 430 attending. Other lectures followed in the succeeding years including 'Glimpses of English Literature' in 1898 and 'Electric Power and Lighting' in 1899 but the problem for Browning was that Walworth was not able to pay the lecturers. Besides these presentations there were many vocational and practical courses that included topics such as hygiene and cookery. Percy Alden followed the example of Canon Barnett at Toynbee Hall and organised a picture exhibition in 1895. Some two hundred pictures were loaned and mounted in the Boys' Club Hall and attracted large numbers of visitors. The event was repeated for a number of years.

Browning also developed a wide range of clubs and activities. These included the Goose Club which provided the family Christmas dinner for many homes, the Coal Club which secured coal at affordable prices, the Clothing and Boot Clubs and a Maternity Society which gave clothing for mothers and children at the time of the birth of a new child. There was also a well-stocked Blanket Club, which loaned out blankets during the winter months to people known to the settlement. The settlement had its own Clothes Store, which proved popular with many in the local neighbourhood.

The Slate Club, which was begun with 30 members in the second year of the Settlement, ensured members against sickness and burial. The Goose Club turned out to be by far and away 'the largest branch of the Settlement'. Beginning in 1897 with 253 members who each paid 7s. 6d. in weekly instalments, the club enabled them to obtain a large goose or turkey and a quantity of groceries. It rose by leaps and bounds every year until in 1908 there were 10,383 members who each received their Christmas meat and a five-pound parcel of groceries.[111] Stead commented that if the settlement had been so minded, 'it might have blossomed out into a huge centre of co-operative purchase and distribution of poultry and other Christmas goods'.[112]

Unemployment in Canning Town and West Ham was a constant problem with Alden reporting 5,500 men out of work during 1894.[113] For this reason the Wave Lodging House at 234–5 Victoria Dock Road was taken over and run as part of the settlement's work. 120 beds were available each night at a cost of 4d. a bed in the main building and 6d. a night in the quieter cottages at the rear. The 1897 annual report noted that there had been a wide variety of lodgers during the course of the year the great majority of whom were casual labourers who are 'very desirous of obtaining work'. The number of permanent occupants was a growing one and to encourage them a free bed was offered on Sundays to any who had spent the previous six nights at the 'Wave'. During the past year, 4,000 beds had been given in this way. Those men who were permanent took a great pride in the place and often put out a helping hand to strangers.[114]

In order to help these men and their families in the local community, Mansfield began an institution that became widely-copied by other settlements, that of 'The Poor Man's Lawyer'.[115] A college friend of Alden's, Frank Tillyard, who was a barrister, expressed a wish to help in the work of the settlement and thought his knowledge as a lawyer might be helpful to some poor people who were unable to pay for legal aid. Will Reason, who was for a time deputy warden of Mansfield, reported that in the first seven years of the service 'the total number of cases per annum has to be figured in thousands, the number that reach courts may easily be counted on the fingers'.[116] Reason went on to state that one of the settlement's lawyers had his practice in West Ham[117] and that there had been over 2,000 clients in 1898.[118] The most frequent cases dealt with by the Mansfield lawyers were quarrels between husbands and wives and disputes arising between employers and employees.[119] *The Mansfield House Report* for 1897 stated that, 'Increasing numbers of poor persons flock to the consulting-rooms every Tuesday night, amounting in the year to some one thousand clients. The lawyers seldom rise until after two-hours sitting during which their sympathy has been deeply aroused, and their minds fully occupied'.[120] Browning Hall also developed a Poor Man's Lawyer scheme. Stead later wrote that every Tuesday evening since the settlement began the little rooms at the back of the hall were used for this purpose. Over the years the number of lawyers who gave their services increased from three to six, one of whom continued in the work for 20 years. The major cases were 'those of matrimonial difficulty' but there were also frequent cases of breach of contract particularly in the sale of small businesses. Stead reflected that, 'Possibly nowhere in the Settlement is the Sermon on the Mount more pointedly enforced than in the consulting rooms of the Poor Man's Lawyer: "Agree with thine adversary quickly whilst thou art with him in the way", is the constant advice'. The Browning lawyers found that only a very few of those who came to them for advice actually went on to the law courts.[121]

While Mansfield House can be credited with initiating the Poor Man's Lawyer Scheme, Browning Hall can claim the distinction of being the inspiration that led to the start of old age pensions. Stead and his resident helpers became increasingly aware of the heart-rending struggles of the elderly working-classes to keep themselves out of the work house. Lord Rothchild's Committee met in the summer of 1898 and concluded that there were a million aged poor who were on the verge of the bread line and unable to make adequate provision for their most basic needs. Somewhat unexpectedly later in the same year the New Zealand government passed the first Old Age Pension Act in the British Empire which gave seven shillings a week to every needy and deserving person over 65. The Agent-General of the colony was invited to recount the provisions of the Act at the Browning Hall Brotherhood meeting on Sunday afternoon 20 November 1898. His explanation of the New Zealand scheme made a great impression on the Browning community and it resulted in another conference being called to consider how the action might be replicated in England. Charles Booth was invited to come and address what was intended to be a local affair with trade union and Friendly Society leaders from the neighbourhood. Some of the surplus conference invitations that were sent to Labour leaders in other parts of the country for information purposes unexpectedly resulted in a number of leaders of major trade unions attending what turned out to be a major national conference on the subject. Charles Booth called for pensions for all in old age and his proposals were adopted with total agreement. Delegates from Leicester and Newcastle-on-Tyne suggested that similar conferences should be organised by the halls in their areas. Booth consented and a series of conferences were arranged in the provinces in Newcastle, Leeds, Manchester, Bristol, Birmingham and Glasgow. At the suggestion of the Birmingham meeting the convening groups of the seven conferences formed themselves into the National Committee of Organized Labour and the agitation for a free state pension for everyone reaching old age was taken up across the country by Labour. The newly emerging Labour Party was totally committed to the cause and won public support from Archbishop Randal Davidson and Dr Horton, President of the Free Church Council. The protracted struggle finally came to a successful conclusion in 1908 when the Old Age Pension Act received Royal assent. A few months after the vote a member of the Cabinet went to Browning's Annual General Meeting to extend the government's thanks to the Settlement for its 'splendid educational work in the cause of Old Age Pensions'. A memorial commemorating the campaign was later placed in the Hall. It read as follows:

This tablet is erected
in grateful commemoration of
The justice and grace of
GOD
when all parties in the State had left
unhelped and unhonoured
the Aged of this realm,
graciously chose to raise up in this Hall,
After exposition here on November 20th 1898,
of the first Old Age Pensions Act
in the British Empire, Passed by New Zealand:
by means of the Conference held here
December 13th 1898, with
CHARLES BOOTH
in advocacy of Pensions for All in Old Age:
and by means of the
NATIONAL COMMITTEE OF ORGANISED LABOUR
Which resulted from ensuing Conferences
with Mr Booth in Newcastle, Leeds, Manchester,
Glasgow, Bristol and Birmingham.
A NATIONAL MOVEMENT
which, directed from this Hall, the chief officers being
Frederick Rogers, George N. Barnes,
Edward Cadbury, Francis Herbert Stead,
eventually secured as a first instalment the
Old AGE PENSIONS ACT 1908,
thereby answering the prayers of His people
offered here and elsewhere 1898–1908.[122]

Following in the steps of most Settlements both Mansfield and Browning had the needs of children close to their hearts. Mansfield put on cheap dinners for poor Board School children reporting in 1892 that in the winter just ended they had provided 26,000 such meals.[123] They also organised 'A Happy Sunday Evening' each week for children and attracted about 300 boys and girls who were not touched by the Sunday School effort'.[124] In the summer there were excursions and summer camps, with the first Fairbairn Camp being organised in 1897.[125]

Country holidays became an important feature of Browning's ministry particularly so on account of the unhealthy crowded streets and low mudflats of Walworth. On Saturday afternoons residents took children out by tramcar to the parks or arranged rambles for a handful of adults. Over Easter and Whitsun there were outings to places further afield. Then in 1895 a joint August bank holiday camp for men and women was held at Court Farm in the Surrey village of Whyteleafe with the men sleeping in the great tithe barn and the women bedded in an out-house of the farm and all except very young children helping with the cooking. The event became the first in a long succession of happy camps, which continued for many years.[126]

Other Social and Political Action

In addition to being Congregational ministers with an evangelical conviction both Alden and Stead were fully committed to the cause of Labour. Both were strong supporters of trade unionism and enjoyed the company of men such as Keir Hardie, Ben Tillett and other leaders of the Labour Church Movement. Leonard Smith observed that the Browning Settlement rapidly became known as a trade union and labour headquarters.[127] Residents of Mansfield reported that 'sturdy trade unionists have stood up to say that they will gladly come to a church which has a gospel to proclaim'.[128] Alden was elected to West Ham Borough Council in 1892 and this marked the start of the Settlement's involvement in local social and political questions. In 1898, although he was strongly committed to the Liberal Party, Alden became a member of the coalition which formed the first socialist administration in English local government history. In 1901 he became editor of *The Liberal Echo* and resigned his position as warden. In 1905 he published a book entitled *The Unemployed: A National Question* which considerably stimulated debate and the following year he was elected Liberal MP for Tottenham. Despite Alden's personal commitment to the Liberal Party, Mansfield House had no political or party bias and residents were encouraged to take up positions in local government in the sphere of 'pure politics'. In the words of one resident, 'When we became settlers we became citizens, and recognise our responsibility as such'.[129] Several others from Mansfield House were active in local politics. *The Quintinian* noted in November 1892 that not only had Alden been returned as a member of the Borough Council but that another of Mansfield's 'most prominent workers' – Mr Will Reason – had been elected to the district School Board.[130] In December 1897 congratulations were offered tom A.J. Shepheard on his re-election to the School Board for London.[131]

In addition to its campaigning for Old Age Pensions, the Browning Settlement also had other strong involvements in local politics. Stead was conscious how they and many other churches often sang the hymn 'Crown Him Lord of all!' but the key question was how to crown Him Lord of our public life? No part of Browning's activities caused more hostility than their endeavour to assert the Lordship of Christ in municipal and local politics. Their first step to try and make this goal a reality came following the Parish Councils Act, which required for the first time that Vestries were to be elected on a democratic basis. The long list of local candidates was carefully scrutinised by the settlement's Public Life Committee and then a selection was made regardless of party on the primary basis of good character. The names of those selected on this basis were then pinned up on the hall notice boards. Local party activists were incensed.

In the Vestry Election of 1897 the Public Questions Committee issued a circular to all ratepayers reminding them of their duty to vote and to vote only for those of sound character whose first concerns were those of the ratepayers and would work for better sanitation and better lighting. Prior to the County Council elections of the following year Stead put out a pamphlet entitled 'What would Jesus do if he were in My Place?', in which he set out the key issues as he saw them. It was rare in any of the subsequent elections for the Public Questions Committee to fail to put out a leaflet of some kind. At the time of the 1906 General Election a full manifesto was prepared which set out Ten Plain Duties involved in obedience to the Son of Man. They were: put law for war; find work for the unemployed; honour the aged by pensions for all in old age; provide food for underfed school children; let the people more completely control all State-supported schools; reform the poor law, abolish the pauper class recognising only fellow citizens to be helped or criminals to be punished; facilitate the housing of the people by publicly organised locomotion and by garden suburbs to accommodate the out-flowing population; provide counter-attractions to the public house; penalise the publication of betting odds; pass land laws to carry out the purpose for which God made the land.[132]

Browning Hall was very concerned over the slum conditions of the area of south London in which they were situated and they publicised the fact that the ground landlord of the worst slums in London was the Church of England. Residents from the Settlement became personally involved in two slum areas of Walworth, which were built on land owned by the Ecclesiastical Commissioners. Many of them were flooded during the high tides causing the sewers to back up. The matter was brought to the Bishop of the diocese and the Secretary of the Commission visited the area in question and 'after a few years' 22 acres of the worst dwellings were cleared away. The settlement also played its part in the clearing of the Tabard Street area where the Charterhouse School Mission was also working. Described as 'the Southwark Inferno', the Tabard area was 13½ acres of tumbledown dens of infamy, disease and death'. There was a widespread feeling that no action would be taken since the project was estimated to cost 'nearly half a million pounds'. However, following strong representations, the London County Council, to the surprise of many, agreed to embark on this, the largest clearance that it had ever undertaken.[133] In the face of such activity it was not surprising that even the *Mansfield House Magazine* reported that 'Browning Hall is fast becoming a centre of social reconstruction on the principles of Jesus Christ which we are also trying to follow at Mansfield'.[134] In 1900 Stead organised a special conference on 'Poverty and Overcrowding' at the Borough Polytechnic with Charles Booth, Lord Hugh Cecil and the Bishop of Rochester among the main speakers.[135]

In order to further extend the role of the Christian faith in the world of labour both Mansfield and Browning established organisations that had this specific end in view. Mansfield set up a Brotherhood in the spring of 1895 with Brotherhood Pledge Cards. These spelt out the Brotherhood's decidedly social aims. The following principles were adopted as the basis of the new Society.

1. To propagate the principles of Universal Brotherhood and Industrial Co-operation.
2. To cultivate a more general appreciation of the franchise.
3. To seek to bring about, both by example and precept, all those reforms necessary for the welfare of humanity.
4. To observe and report all unsanitary and unhealthy conditions of the Borough.
5. Advocacy of temperance and total abstinence policies.[136]

Browning formed a group from those who attended their main 'Pleasant Sunday Afternoon' service. Founded on New Year's Eve in 1895 it was known as the 'P.S.A. Brotherhood'. Its aim was quite simply 'The Labour Movement in Religion' and to lay stress on the Kingdom of God as a present reality.[137] A few years later Stead also established 'Labour Evangelists'. They were men and women who continued in their ordinary daily work in industry or the factory floor but at the same time devoted themselves to 'the promotion of the Labour Movement in Religion,– bringing of the working classes of to-day the good news of the Kingdom of God'. The Labour Evangelists agreed to spend time in Scriptural study of the Kingdom of God and also to speak in the open air on these matters.[138]

Religion at Mansfield and Browning

As has already been noted both Mansfield and Browning were up-front about their Christian commitment and this was readily apparent in their specifically religious activities. One Mansfield publication stated that the Settlement had since its foundation endeavoured, by means of a Sunday meeting that is open to everyone 'to apply the Christian faith to the practical issues of every day living'.[139] In 1892 attendance at the Sunday afternoon service in the Congregational Chapel was averaging 500 and similar numbers were attending the Sunday evening discussions on social issues at the Institute.[140] A Bible class was established at Fairbairn House to engage in the systematic study of the teaching of Jesus Christ. It was open to all regardless of their views and aimed to promote free and open discussion.[141]

The focal point of Browning's worship was 'The People's Hour' Sunday evening service, which included hymns, prayers and frequent evangelistic appeals. Other activities followed which included musical items and lantern presentations. These later occasions produced a variety of contributions such as poetry, biography, recitations, marching music, Jesus in art and sculpture, and Christian views on issues of the moment. The Lord's Supper was celebrated monthly and was highly valued as bringing 'a deep infusion' of spiritual life. A correspondent of *The British Weekly* attended The People's Hour on the last Sunday of January 1898 and recounted the experience in a whole page coverage. There were some sixty adults and about thirty young boys and girls when the service commenced but the hall began to fill up as the service progressed. During the final hymn men, women and children started to stream in through every door in order to secure seats for the lantern lecture which followed. The worship was much like that of an ordinary chapel with several hymns, prayer and readings from Scripture. The correspondent found Herbert Stead's sermon 'woefully disappointing' probably because of its social content. 'Can it be', he stated, 'that the old Gospel has lost its power, and Christ's ministers have nothing but these dry husks to offer their people'.[142] Every Sunday morning a Bible class was held for adult men with the teaching done either by Herbert Stead or Tom Bryan. Because the residents of the settlement came from so many different backgrounds and churches it was felt right that these denominational links should be retained but members were given the opportunity to commit themselves to one another by joining 'The Fellowship of Followers'. This group was started in January 1897 and quickly achieved a membership of two hundred. Its members met once a month and their aim was to promote deep and lasting friendships and mutual support in the work.[143]

Newman House

One Roman Catholic Settlement that was established for men in the Victorian era was Newman House in Southwark with a hostel at 108 Kennington Road and clubrooms in the adjoining street at 21 Westminster Bridge Road. The main reason why the Catholic contribution to the Settlement Movement was small was that strictly speaking their young men were forbidden to attend the universities of Oxford and Cambridge and Trinity College, Dublin. In practice however, one or two leading upper class families acted against the proscribed line and a few others managed to obtain a dispensation from their bishop that enabled their children to read for a degree. An official pamphlet published in the early 1890s stated, 'there are at present at Oxford between thirty and forty Catholic undergraduates and at Cambridge between fifteen and twenty'.[144] It wasn't in fact until 26 March 1895 that Papal approval was finally granted to the petition by the English bishops that Catholics be officially allowed to attend Oxford and Cambridge.[145] The result of this was that in the 1880s and 1890s there was only a very small pool of Oxbridge graduates from which the Catholic Church could draw potential residents for settlements and missions.

The original idea for the settlement resulted from a talk given to the 'newly-formed Newman Society'[146] in Oxford by James Britten, a convert to Catholicism, who worked on the staff of the British Museum and ran a South London Catholic Students' union and boys club in his spare time. Britten, an impassioned pioneer of many Catholic causes, related what was being done outside the Church and spoke amusingly of his experiences with the Catholic Lads' Club in South London and about his Catholic Students' Union which he and John Gilbert were leading. Britten so stirred people's enthusiasm that James Hope, Francis Urquhart and Sidney Parry were appointed to examine the matter. The upshot was that the premises were taken in Kennington Road. A governing Committee was formed of representatives of various Catholic public schools from which it was hoped workers would be forthcoming. The Committee found a sympathetic Patron and President in Bishop Butt of Southwark. The work of Newman House was formally inaugurated by the Bishop of Southwark on the evening of Tuesday 6 August 1891 in the presence of more than a hundred invited guests. The settlement provided accommodation for the St George's Students' Union and the St George's Catholic Club. The first speech was given by Mr B.F.C. Costelloe, a Roman Catholic who had worked in St Jude's parish in the mid-1870s and then been active in the affairs of Toynbee Hall.[147] Costello, who was an open exhibitioner of Balliol and a double first of Oxford and held a Glasgow degree, had close connections with the Barnetts and lectured on various subjects at Toynbee. He was also active in Poor Law Work and was a member of Mrs Barnett's State Children's Association Committee.[148] In his address Costelloe spoke of 'the advantages of both settlements alike to the people of Southwark and to the settlers. The former would be raised out of the dull dead level in which the majority of our fellow brethren live, whilst the latter would learn much of practical use in after life'.[149] The objective of the house was clearly that of promoting the Catholic faith, a point made by the secretary, Mr Sidney Parry, who stated that 'without the help of the clergy no such social work can either succeed, or indeed would merit success'.[150] The bishop who was a very warm supporter of the venture, urged those present to come and give their personal help, if possible for one week night each week to start with. In this way he believed that people's interest and commitment would grow. Besides the various clubs and other social activities, Newman House provided a range of educational and cultural activities. These included a choral class with the Revd F. Widerspin, a science class with Mr McGann and Shakespeare with Mr Kegan Paul. Other classes including mathematics, French and Italian also formed part of the curriculum. There were also classes on a number of practical subjects on Wednesday evenings. A settlement publication, *The Newman House Chronicle*, was also issued quarterly and the reference library was open to members every evening, including Sundays.[151] Newman House followed in the steps of most other settlements in that they soon formed cricket and football clubs and rented fields from the London Playing Fields Committee. Even the back garden of the settlement was pressed into service as a bowling pitch with 'Gerry Weigall' a famous MCC and Kent cricketer giving coaching sessions. A highly successful Catholic Lads' Brigade was formed and drilling and boxing matches also became a popular feature as the movement expanded.

Newman House proved to be a relatively short-lived venture but it made an impact on the wider Catholic Church. Its educational activities led to the development of Catholic Educational Summer Schools for Catholic teachers. Newman House's activities also helped to influence Cardinal Vaughan's decision to lift the ban on Roman Catholics studying at Oxford and Cambridge.

The Nonconformist settlements may have been few in number but they certainly didn't lack for energy or support. Between them they developed a very wide range of activities and clubs which enabled them to build many bridges into their respective local communities. Not only did they raise the quality of life for those who shared in their organisations, they made significant contributions in local government and local politics. Like their Church of England counterparts they depended on the help of recent university graduates and undergraduates. Mansfield House being linked to a university college was fortunate in being able to make regular Whit Monday visits to Oxford[152] but both Bermondsey and Browning drew support from Nonconformist students at Cambridge, London and elsewhere. The distinctive contribution of these three settlements taken together was seen in their links with labour and the trade unions and their involvement in local politics. All three settlements helped to secure an improved representation for Labour in their respective districts. All three gave shelter and encouragement to trade unions in their localities and played a part in providing educational development for the workers and their leaders. Newman House in contrast was much closer in ethos to Oxford House and other Oxbridge Mission Settlements, which had strong religious agendas and were less committed to supporting labour and trade union activities.

7

WOMEN'S SETTLEMENTS

Alongside the work and the contributions that were made by the men's colleges of Oxford and Cambridge, a number of women's settlements were established in London's East End and south of the river. In fact several of them began in association with one or other of the men's settlements. Such was the case at Oxford House in Bethnal Green and at Mansfield House in Canning Town. There were a number of factors that prompted the setting up of women's settlements, the most obvious being that there were many women and children whose needs demanded the specific skills that women settlers were able to offer. London and East London in particular was, as Walter Besant observed in 1901, noted for its many needy and exploited factory girls. 'They are girls', he wrote, 'who make things, girls who sew things, girls who sell things'. He described them as 'poor, driven, sweated creatures, for sweating once begun is handed on from one to the other as carefully and as religiously as any holy lamp of learning'. They work 'like bees' from early morning till evening.[1] Most of the women's settlements made this very needy section of London's poor a major focus of their attention and endeavours. The later years of the nineteenth century were a time when middle-class women were beginning to venture out from the domestic sphere and seeking fulfilment in education, medicine and social work. Octavia Hill (1838–1912) who had worked for many years to improve the quality of London's housing overcame her initial reticence when she saw the potential for harnessing the enthusiasm of the young women who were offering their time and talents to London's poor. In time she was able to set up a training course suitable to all social workers whether voluntary or professional.[2]

In 1887, just a short time after the founding of Oxford House and Toynbee Hall, some of the women students from both Cambridge and Oxford helped to form the Women's University Settlement in Southwark and this paved the way for a number of similar ventures which were established in the years that followed. The Southwark scheme was also supported by women from London University and the Royal Holloway College. At a quarterly meeting of Women's Federated Settlements in 1897 seven settlements were represented and the attendance was very large.[3]

Women's University Settlement at Southwark

The Women's University Settlement had its origins in a meeting of the Cambridge Ladies Discussion Society in February 1887. They invited Mrs Barnett, Samuel's wife, to address them on the Settlement idea. At this meeting Miss Alice Gruner, a former student at Newnham College, spoke of her experience of working from 44 Nelson Square in Southwark which, according to Charles Booth's survey, was the second poorest area of London after Bethnal Green. Very shortly after this gathering representatives of Newnham, Girton, Lady Margaret and Somerville Halls combined together and established the Women's University Settlement. It was located in Miss Gruner's house, which was large enough to provide accommodation for several others. It opened its doors on 12 September 1887 with the aim of promoting 'the welfare of the poorer districts of London, more especially of the women and children, by devising and advancing schemes which tend to elevate them, and giving them additional opportunities for education and recreation'.[4] At the first Annual Meeting which was held at the Temperance Hall, Blackfriars on 19 June 1889, Mrs Alfred Marshall took the chair and gave the opening speech in which she reiterated the point: 'Our Settlement is to work more especially with children, and I believe we can do nothing which is more important than to try and raise the character of women'.[5] In the same address she referred to their small group of residents at the settlement as 'our new sisterhood' and went on to say that unlike earlier sisterhoods it 'lives in the world'. She also confessed to being somewhat alarmed at the amount and variety of work that they had attempted in their first year.[6] These activities included excursions to the Zoo, Botanical Gardens, the Natural History Museum, helping with swimming lessons, tennis instruction for pupil teachers, mothers' meetings, musical drill-classes for factory girls, and magic lantern lectures.[7]

The WUS committee appointed Miss Alice Gruner to take the post of head-worker. She was described by one writer as the 'maid of all work' since she was housekeeper and general secretary, and was responsible for the health and general supervision of all the settlement.[8] Alice Gruner proved immensely hardworking but she left the settlement in March 1889. A number of others including Edith Argles, a former Vice-Principal of Lady Margaret Hall, held the wardenship for relatively short periods of time until

Miss Margaret Sewell of Newnham College took up the reins in 1891. She remained at the helm for the next decade and during her time as warden the number of residents grew steadily so that in 1894 the freehold of numbers 44, 45 and 46 Nelson Square was acquired for £4,800 and the problem of accommodating 31 resident workers was solved.[9] In addition to their number there were 61 non-resident helpers.[10] The Lady Margaret Hall Old Students Association Reports list the names of a number of former pupils who gave varying periods of time to assisting in the settlement activities.[11]

Although the WUS engaged in wide diversity of club and social activities several projects came to occupy the bulk of their energies. One of these was education. Both Alice Gruner and Constance Elder were elected as School Board managers in Southwark, and the settlement as a whole became particularly concerned over the training needs of pupil-teachers. Contributing to the Childrens' Holiday Fund was another regular annual concern. In 1898 for example, £173 13s. 1d. was contributed.[12] Efforts were also made to meet the educational needs of manual workers in the locality by holding evening classes and in 1893 the settlement, in conjunction with the London School Board, organised a variety of classes each evening of the week.[13] There was also a particular concern for medical provision. In 1892 the settlement took over responsibility for all the Southwark cases from The Invalid Children's Aid Association (ICAA) with the result that numbers increased from 45 in 1892 to 185 in 1905.[14] Special attention was paid to the needs of the handicapped and a registry was set up in 1894 to help them to find employment. Two years later a workshop was opened with facilities for 12 crippled boys to receive apprenticeships in shoe-repairing.[15] The subject of nursing was raised at the 1892 Annual General Meeting. Among others who addressed the assembled company was the Revd Canon Henry Scott Holland who spoke of 'the benefits to be derived from a good nurse, and the blessing of her presence in cases of severe sickness, especially among the poor'.[16] During the year a fund had been raised by the friends of the late Miss Eleanor Benson, a daughter of the Archbishop of Canterbury, with the intention that it be used to provide nursing care for the poor of Southwark. It was agreed to place £30 a year at the disposal of the settlement for this purpose. Subsequently a branch of Metropolitan and National Nursing Association was established.

The WUS also took an active part in promoting The Co-operative Women's Guild and organised a Women's Benefit Society to protect its subscribers in times of sickness and incapacity. The numbers who joined the scheme rarely exceeded forty and in 1899 it was decided to transfer members' separate accounts to The National Deposit Society.[17] One of the WUS resident workers gave time to assisting Octavia Hill with rent collecting and work arising from that, as well as assisting her with the concerts and entertainments at Red Cross Hall which was at the centre of Miss Hill's work.[18] It was reported in June 1896 that the settlement was 'glad to remain intimately connected with Miss Octavia Hill's work in Southwark'. It recorded that she had under her care some dozen courts and buildings worked by ladies, three of whom were residents of the settlement.[19]

Following the lead given by the Barnetts at Toynbee Hall, the residents of the WUS were also of the view that helping the people of their district to appreciate high culture and art in particular was an important aspect of their work. It was a means of instilling in the poor a desire for what was just, lovely and of good report. For this reason Eleanor Benson, a former student of Lady Margaret Hall, Oxford, and the Hon. Miss Hugessen, a former student of Newnham, organised a loan exhibition of pictures in connection with the settlement that was opened in May by Princess Christian. It was managed in the same way as the Toynbee Exhibitions with present and former students of the women's colleges acting as interpreters to the visitors.[20] The exhibition was well-received and became a continuing feature of the work. The Annual Report of June 1893 noted that the loan exhibition of pictures had been held again at the polytechnic, under the auspices of a joint Committee formed of representatives of the Women's University Settlement, Morley College and the Polytechnic. The number of visitors had increased from between 17,000 and 18,000 last year to 24,812 the current year.[21]

Despite the fact that Alice Gruner had resigned as warden feeling that too much emphasis on training was a distraction from the main aims of the settlement, the WUS came to regard it as being of increasing importance. Octavia Hill felt much more drawn into the WUS when Margaret Sewell took over as head worker and began to initiate formal training for the workers as a specific part of the settlement's agenda. In 1891 a course of lectures was begun by Bernard Bosanquet and Octavia who had persuaded the settlement to expose the women residents to a wide variety of relief work.[22] As the theoretical side developed the WUS joined forces with The Charity Organisation Society (COS) and The National Union of Women Workers. The latter body was a conservative, philanthropic and religious organisation of Middle-class women that later became The National Council of Women Workers during the Great War.[23] Notwithstanding her emphasis on training, Sewell was quick to stress to Octavia[24] that 'important though we believe education and method to be, we do not hold them of FIRST importance. We do not suppose that by training and teaching we can dispense with, or render superfluous, that loving zeal which yearns for the souls of men, that instinct to come at all costs to the help of the helpless'.[25]

Mayfield House

Two years after the establishment of the WUS, Cheltenham Ladies College opened Mayfield House in Victoria Park Square, Bethnal Green. It seems that the various individuals connected with the school had been inspired by reports of the work at Toynbee Hall.[26] In 1888 Elizabeth Raikes read a paper to the Guild suggesting that past members of the College should engage in some collective charitable work. She went on to say that more Guild members lived in London than anywhere else and 'it would be hard to find any place that cries out more strongly for help'.[27] It was decided as a result of this gathering to appoint a Committee of Management to consider the matter further.[28] Miss May Wolseley-Lewis who was one of the prime-movers of the scheme, stated that their idea was that there should be

i   An experienced worker in charge.
ii Other workers, coming for a longer or shorter time … that these
    should be occupied (under the head worker) in such work as the
    parish most needs and they can best do – such as district visiting,
    teaching boy's and girl's night schools, the organisation of work
    rooms, and sales of work at low prices to the poor, superintending
    soup kitchens, providing entertainments and society of all kinds
    for all classes.[29]

It was proposed that a house should be taken in the parish of St John, Bethnal Green, where the Revd Henry Bromby (1840–1911) was the vicar. He had connections with Cheltenham since he was the son of Bishop Charles Henry Bromby, the first Principal of the Training College and Vicar of St Paul's church, who had been instrumental in the development of the Ladies' College. In a letter to the Guild, Bromby described St John's as 'a typical East End parish of the better sort' with a population of nearly 13,000 of which 'there are but few of the depraved and dangerous classes'. The people are chiefly shoemakers, cabinet-makers, labourers and match-box makers.[30]

Mayfield House was formally opened on Saturday 26 October 1889 for joint occupation with the ladies of Oxford House with a short service arranged by Mr Bromby. The Cheltenham ladies were however entirely responsible for the settlement, the house being taken in its name and the committee of management consisting only of Guild members.[31] Miss Kate Newman who was a trained nurse generously volunteered to undertake the management of the work at her own expense.[32] She had a number of close connections with the college having been for some time a member of the Council. She was well-known by most of the committee and her offer was accepted. The ideals of the Ladies College Organising Committee breathed a strong air of condescension. As one of their number put it:

> Something we hope can be done by regular and occasional visits, but it is only by going down to live among the poor that the more cultured are able to fully share the advantages of their education, their knowledge, their refinement, that increased power of sympathy, which is the true part of culture, with less privileged classes. It is the daily personal contact with the more cultured, the living side by side with them, which is what is wanted, and this can surely be brought about most satisfactorily by settlements in their midst.[33]

Catherine Newman, who was inspired by the example of Father Lowder, worked with great commitment as a number of her letters in the Ladies College Mission archives so clearly show. In a letter dated 22 May 1889 she wrote of having been engaged in trying 'to get workers down from the West End'.[34] In another she wrote of the difficulty of having helpers who stayed for less than three months since the girls at the club, do not readily take to strangers'.[35] Later she had to cope with the tensions of whether to continue sharing the premises with the ladies of Oxford House or to embark on a separate course. In the midst of all this activity events took an unexpected turn in December 1894 when Catherine died after only a few days illness, of diphtheria, following upon influenza.[36] Her funeral took place on 12 December at All Saints, Cheltenham, where the choir of the Ladies College chanted the Psalms and sang, 'Now the labourer's task is done'.[37] A memorial service was held at the same time at St John's Bethnal Green with an address given by the Head of Oxford House.[38] One of her obituarists stated that 'she has worked in Bethnal Green for nearly five years, and has won the hearts of all those with whom she has come into contact by her unselfishness and devotion'.[39] She was replaced by another salaried head, a Miss Corbett.

As was the case with almost all the Boys' School Missions, the role of the head teacher also played a vital part in the birth of the Ladies College settlement at Mayfield House. Miss Dorothea Beale (1831–1906), the Principal, was a person with a deep social concern and a number of her close friends who were engaged in full-time social work had encouraged her in that direction. Her time as a student at Queen's College, London and her close association with Frederick Denison Maurice had made her acutely aware of the city's growing social problems. Indeed it seems likely that it was Maurice's influence that confirmed in her the decision to teach as being one of the most effective forms of social transformation.[40] She became Principal in 1858 and remained in post until 1906. In July 1884 a meeting of one hundred and fifty friends of the college including nearly eighty former students was held. They resolved that an association of Old Girls should be founded to be known as *The Guild* and that it should meet biennially. It was this group that felt there was a need to establish some form of social work in which both the College and the Guild could be actively involved. It was largely their initiative which led to the link being made with St John's Bethnal Green. Dorothea Beale who was an ardent supporter of women's suffrage and concerned to widen the career opportunities for women feared at the time the decision was taken that the inexperience of the Guild in social work might result in the failure of the venture. Nevertheless she gave the scheme her wholehearted support as if it had been the result of her own devising. Her concerns about the wardenship were allayed when Catherine Newman offered to take on the responsibility for the work. She was further encouraged by the fact that the ladies of Oxford were preparing to open a settlement in the same district and that they could share the same house with them under Catherine's direction.

On his return from Tasmania, Henry Bromby departed from his father's low church evangelicalism and identified with the ritualism of the later Tractarians. That said he was always insistent on conversion and in his early days 'a muscular Christian – fond of riding, cricket, tennis, shooting and rowing'.[41] Dorothea Beale did not share his gradual change of views stating on one occasion her dislike of 'the excessive attention paid to ceremonies in some churches'. She was 'highly disapproving of Confession' and expressed herself in 'great dread' of Romish opinions.[42] Despite their differing views, Miss Beale seems not to have run into any conflict with Bromby over the links between Mayfield House and the work that was undertaken by the college in his parish. It was a work which included district visiting, mothers' meetings, Bible classes for men and women, and Sunday schools.[43] In addition, there was work with The Invalid Childrens' Aid Association, which involved holding a small school for invalids once a week. There were also some more specialised activities such as leather and brass work and iron work for the boys.[44] Miss Thornton became one of the managers of St John's School and the administrator of the School's Penny Bank.[45] A Miss Bucknell also became a Mayfield School Board worker and devoted much time to The Children's Holiday Fund, which brought her further contact

with local teachers.[46] Residents of the House also engaged in local politics
and worked hard canvassing in local elections for Poor Law Guardians.[47]
Miss Corbett who became Head of House after Catherine Newman became
a member of The Women's Trade Union Association and served for a time
as a member of the organising committee.[48]

In many of these endeavours there was a clear underlying missionary
agenda which doubtless emanated from Bromby and his staff. It was
epitomised in a comment that Miss Williams, the District Nurse, 'uses the
influence that her intimate knowledge of the people gives her to draw them
to the Church as much as she can, and she has brought many babies to
Baptism and older folk to confirmation during this year'.[49]

From the very early days, the Ladies College shared Mayfield House with
the ladies who worked in conjunction with Oxford House. The
arrangement seemed a very happy one and was felt to make good economic
sense. However despite the good relationships there was a desire on the part
of some of the Oxford supporters to establish a separate house for their
residents. Catherine Newman also reported that there were two of her
Cheltenham residents who were apprehensive about continuing to work
with the Oxford ladies although she herself was decidedly in favour of
maintaining the relationship. She wrote in a letter dated 30 August 1889 to
Miss Anson that 'Miss Beale and myself feel so desirous on every account
to combine forces'.[50] However by the spring of 1890 it was reported that
for the first time there had been a feeling of two sides in the house, which
she had been anxious to avoid. 'No one', she reflected, 'has ever thought of
comparing the two parishes or two churches until now, and it would be
fatal to the House if this tone should spread'. She expressed her
thankfulness that the Cheltenham workers had behaved very well but still
felt apprehensive about the future since one or two are quite young'.[51]

The Guild report for the spring of 1893 reported that the Oxford
residents had now departed and that there was ample room at Mayfield for
regular as well as temporary residents.[52] Although there were fears that the
Cheltenham subscriptions alone might not be sufficient to meet the
running costs of Mayfield House the committee elected to stay in Bethnal
Green for the time being. The life enjoyed by the residents seems to have
been one of convivial graciousness that must have contrasted starkly with
the surrounding environment. Josephine Evans, who was a temporary
Oxford resident, penned the following impressions of her brief stay.

Lest the idea of residing in a settlement among other women workers
should appear unattractive, let me inform all those who are already

aware of the fact that they are not shoppy or parishy at Mayfield House, and that the atmosphere is that of a refined and pleasant home. There is time found by all the residents for journeys to the West to see friends or to do sightseeing – there is time found for reading, not only works on social problems but also poetry, novels, – works on every subject, – the daily and weekly papers.[53]

Despite the pleasant atmosphere and the agreeable intercourse that took place on the premises, it became apparent to all concerned that the Guild Settlement would have to move elsewhere. It was noted that 'apart from the drains, the high rent and rates, and the landlord – "a most unsatisfactory person to deal with" – the ladies' branch of Oxford House, doing the same work, had established themselves on the other corner of the square'.[54] There was also the additional factor that Charles Bromby who had many close links with the College had moved to Bristol to take up a new work as incumbent of All Saints, Clifton.

The decision was finally taken to re-locate in Shoreditch and on 26 April 1898 a new settlement to be known as St Hilda's East was opened with rooms for 14 residents in Old Nichol Street which ran along the back of Shoreditch High Street. The vicar of the parish was Septimus Buss, the brother of Mary Buss who had taught in the school in earlier days'. He reported that the new house was altogether healthier being built on gravel and that in consequence it was 'a healthy place' and quite safe since 'the very dangerous class of population had moved on.[55] The finances were put on a sound basis by issuing debenture shares to members of the Guild and this raised the sum of £3,800 in a relatively short time. Calculations suggested that an annual sum of £250 was going to be needed in order to meet the basic running costs of the new set-up. In 1899 Marion Bruce, an Old Girl of the college, became the warden and remained in office until 1932. Her obituarist wrote of 'her devotion to duty, her strict sense of justice, her insistence on accuracy of thought and thoroughness of work'.[56]

The new location proved to be very satisfactory with the house always being full and the work going ahead steadily in several different centres and in St Saviour's parish.[57] Two years later it was reported that fresh work had been taken up 'in connection with St Philip's, our parish church'.[58] In order to sustain the interest of the school in the work of St Hilda's it was necessary for the wardens to go down to Cheltenham whenever suitable opportunities arose and there were occasions when Miss Corbett visited the various boarding houses and urged the college girls to come and visit Mayfield House during their holidays.[59]

St Margaret's House, Bethnal Green, 1893

In August 1892 the ladies who worked in conjunction with Oxford House left the Mayfield residence[60] and the following year relocated across the square in new premises which they named St Margaret's House. In 1896 it enlarged its quarters by adding University House close by. The premises, which included an oratory, reflected the fact that the residents shared the Anglo-Catholic convictions of Oxford House.[61] Some of the residents were a little more inclined to socialist ideals than their former colleagues at Mayfield House. Miss Portal, one of their workers, represented the St Margaret's at the Christian Social Union Conference in Glasgow in October 1894.[62] In the January following, John Ludlow addressed the local Women's Bethnal Green CSU branch at St Margaret's House on the beginnings of the Christian Socialist Movement in 1848. He gave details of the experiences and projects that he had shared with Frederick Maurice and Charles Kingsley.[63]

The residents fairly quickly began to develop a variety of activities that included a girls' club for 8 to 13 year olds which was named St Margaret's Guild and a junior club for 13 to 15 year olds. The latter group engaged in singing classes and dress-making.[64] In 1894 a Tuesday night club was started 'for factory girls not quite suited to St Margarets' Senior Club'.[65] In September 1894 St Margaret's House, under the leadership of Miss B. Harrington, was reported to be making a marked influence in various ways but particularly through 'its self-denying efforts on behalf of young girls and women in the immediate neighbourhood, which is one of the poorest in East London'.[66] In November of the same year it was reported that there was 'a very fair house-full of residents to carry on autumn and winter work' which included classes in drawing, singing and drama.[67] The Oxford House Chronicle reported on two highly successful Christmas parties and entertainments with dancing, singing and magic lantern, all which gave the girls 'great satisfaction'.[68]

Women's Settlements in Canning Town and Bermondsey

The Women's Settlement that was set up at Canning Town in 1892 was intended to work closely with the men of Mansfield House[69] but with a particular focus on women and children. The settlement was both independent of Mansfield College and Mansfield House.[70] It had rooms for a small number of residents although it was reported that during 1894 no less than ten had been 'tightly packed into our close quarters'.[71] It was established as a medical mission and hospital with its own doctor and chief nurse. There was also a dispensary with three nurses for dressing wounds and dealing with minor injuries.[72] Margaret Sewell reported that there was a widespread need for gratuitous medical aid.[73] Two days each week, Monday and Friday, were devoted to giving free advice to those women and children who lacked sufficient funds to pay doctor's bills. The number attended to by this means in 1897 was 5,584.[74] In addition, 1,835 patients were given surgical dressings, 1,894 visits were made by the outpatient doctor and 1,723 visits were paid by the nurses.[75] Home-visiting continued to be a major aspect of the settlement's work and an old clothes store was set up on the premises run by the head worker, Miss Rebecca Cheetham, and opened between ten and eleven each morning.[76] There was also a workroom for needlewomen,[77] a Sick Benefit Society[78] and a scheme that provided dinners for the very poorest children each week day apart from Mondays. During the winter of 1894, 28,978 meals were provided.[79] The residents ran a lively Sunday afternoon worship service with 'the nucleus an orchestra, consisting of a cornet, two violins, and a viola'.[80] There were 540 names on the register for those attending during 1894.[81]

The Bermondsey Settlement was opened in Rotherhithe in 1892. The Annual Report of 1892 stating that 'from the first we felt it important to enable women to take part in our work. In concert with the heads of a number of Schools for Girls, we have taken a house for Women Workers, No. 149 Lower Road, Rotherhithe, S.E'.[82] The House, which was in the charge of Mrs J. Shirley Richardson, shared the same objectives as the men's settlement. It had rooms for a small number of residents who could work on a full or part-time basis.[83] Accommodation was also provided for a nurse in connection with Queen Victoria's Jubilee Institute for Nurses.[84] In addition, there were two district nurses associated with the work. There was a wide range of educational and philanthropic objectives that were designed to 'bring force and attractiveness to Christian work'.[85] The 1892 annual report stated that all these classes were mixed, 'though no men have yet aspired to learn either dress-making or cookery'.[86] Following the example of Toynbee Hall, the Bermondsey Womens' Settlement were committed to sharing the best in culture with the people of their locality. Acting on the suggestion of Octavia Hill, artists' proofs were presented to the residents and hung in the public drawing room.[87] Alice Barlow House, as it was known, organised support for the Country Holiday Fund[88] and set up a remarkably successful Working Girls' Club which, in 1893,[89] achieved an average membership of more than 80 each week. The programme included gymnastics, dressmaking, drawing and painting, arithmetic, algebra and singing.[90] Temperance work was also an important aspect of the Settlement, which became the home of the Bermondsey and Rotherhithe branch of The

British Women's Temperance Association with a hundred members on their books in 1895.[91] There were further reports of the branch's good work in the following months.[92]

Lady Margaret Hall Settlement, 1897

Mother Edith Langridge, the first warden, looked back in later years to the founding of the Lady Margaret Hall Settlement.[93] She recalled a talk in the parks with Maggie Benson about Oxford House and Toynbee Hall in which they discussed whether Oxford women could follow the men and have such a settlement somewhere in London. Their conversation ended with the hope that if they kept the matter firmly in view they might eventually have their own LMH house in the not too distant future. Sometime later she found herself debating with Nelly Benson and Mary Talbot the possibility of becoming part of The Women's University Settlement in Southwark. They concluded that joining it need not eliminate the possibility of realising their cherished hope of having a LMH and definitely Church settlement.[94] In 1897 their dream was finally realised when the college launched out on its own to establish the Lady Margaret Hall in Lambeth. Many of the people in the chosen district were engaged in making pottery at Doulton's but the greater number were observed to be on the lower rungs of industry and engaged in bottle-washing, street-selling and rag-picking.[95]

The house, garden and small chapel at 129 Kennington Road were ready for opening at Easter. According to the tenth Annual Report of the WUS, there was no spirit of rivalry when this decision to form the new institution was taken. Indeed the WUS felt sure that the two settlements 'with their common aims will remain firm allies, and that the Association will join the Executive in heartily wishing the new Lady Margaret Settlement in Lambeth all success'.[96] It aimed to operate on church lines and the Bishop of Rochester promised to guarantee the rent of the house for one year.[97] Notwithstanding this expression of goodwill, some were opposed to the new establishment. At a meeting held in Lady Margaret Hall in October 1896 a letter was read from a Miss Mary Wood who 'expressed her disapproval of the formation of a separate settlement, as likely to be prejudicial to the interests of the Women's University Settlement'. In the discussion that followed, the Principal, Elizabeth Wordsworth, pointed out that a separate settlement for the hall on Church lines had been projected at the time when the WUS was first launched.[98] Eventually a resolution was passed: 'That in the opinion of this Meeting, a time has come when the Hall might endeavour to found a Settlement on Church lines for the promotion of charitable work in or near London'.[99] In reply to the question as to whether this might injure the existing Women's University Settlement in Nelson Square, the general opinion was that the time was favourable for the inauguration of a new settlement, as the debt to the former was paid off.[100] It was made clear that the need for settlements in the Rochester Diocese was great and there was widespread agreement that the proposed new work should be located south of London.[101] It was also felt that the settlement would be good for the hall in that it would further strengthen the link between the present members of the hall and Old Students' Association.[102] The motion to go ahead with the new settlement was approved unanimously and at an extra-ordinary meeting it was decided to take the house at No. 129 Kennington Road.[103] There is no doubt that the founding and ethos of the new settlement was strongly influenced by Tractarian worship and theology. The LMH Old Students' Association reported that the effect of Oxford House on the life of the hall had been 'bracing and stimulating'. The Principal, Elizabeth Wordsworth, was the eldest daughter of Christopher Wordsworth, the Bishop of Lincoln. Her biographer noted that she and all her siblings were reared in a Tractarian tradition that was 'reverent, reticent, and deeply imbued with the consciousness of the Church's historic past'.[104] Elizabeth was observed to be the closer to her father than any of her six brothers and sisters and shared his religious convictions with particular earnestness.[105] Bishop Talbot of Rochester who had formerly been Warden of Keble College and was chairman of the LMH council also gave much encouragement and 'advised that the work should be begun as soon as possible'.[106] The first Warden of the LMH Settlement, Edith Langridge, resigned in 1902 in order to become Head of the Oxford Mission to Calcutta that was based at the Community of the Epiphany.[107]

The projected aims of the settlement included work with parochial organisations such as district visiting, Sunday school teaching, girls' clubs, mothers' meetings, boys' evening classes and provident collecting.[108] All such work would be under the direction of the vicar in whose parish the work is done. The O.S.A. reported that in the first year there were four residents and a number of others who gave help on at least one night a week.[109] One immediate need in the locality was education for invalid children and a small school was quickly set up.[110] This venture, for which the settlement was entirely responsible, became the North Lambeth branch of the Invalid Children's Aid Association. By the close of 1898 there were about seventy children involved.[111] Eventually the branch covered ten parishes and gave instruction to over eight hundred children.[112] Their mothers received advice regarding hygiene and where necessary children were sent to private doctor or a hospital in an attempt to prevent serious illnesses setting in.[113] In 1897 it was resolved that the settlement should affiliate with The Federation of Women's Settlements and the following year Edith Langridge was appointed as Head of Settlement with a salary of £50 per year.[114] The settlement took a particular interest in the pupil teachers who were working in the area and organised a series of 'at homes' for them.[115] In the summer of 1899 the Head of the Settlement announced that a number of present Lady Margaret students would take up residence for a short period during the long vacation'.[116] During 1901 the next door house, No. 131 Kennington Road, was taken which meant that an extra income £120 a year was required. However old students rose to the occasion and it was reported that there were few who had not subscribed to the settlement.[117]

Other Women's Settlements

Other women's settlements were founded in the run up to the end of Queen Victoria' reign. They included St Mildred's House in Millwall, Isle of Dogs, that was founded in 1897 under the leadership of Miss A.M. Harrington and the Trinity Settlement that opened at Stratford in 1898 with Miss Yatman as 'Head Worker'.[118] Both of these were Church of England projects affiliated to St Margaret's House in Bethnal Green.[119] The United Girls' School Mission, which began about the same time, stated in 1897, 'We hope to set forth by deed and word a Christianity that is bright and social – that touches men's bodies and minds as well as their souls – that concerns weekdays as much as Sundays, home life as well as Church and Church-going, work and play as well as worship – that looks upon everything as 'religious' and nothing as merely 'secular'– and that aims at making 'the kingdom of Heaven' begin down here upon earth'.[120] In the spring of 1900 a group of six or seven ladies took a small house from which to organise the help given by women interested in the work of St Luke's church in Peckham. They called themselves 'St Luke's Women's Guild of Aid'. There was a deaconess, a servant and a guest-room. Among other activities there was a crèche on the first floor and on the ground floor clubs were organised for younger and older girls. One particular feature of the Peckham Settlement was The Depot where a variety of second-hand goods and clothing were sold. The idea was possibly derived from the success of William Booth's Household Salvage Brigade, which had been operating in a number of areas of London. The settlement workers sent out sacks to people who had surplus goods and clothes that they were willing to donate. All that they had to do was to secure the neck of the sack and pay 6d. to a local carrier who would take it to the settlement depot. The whole philosophy of the scheme was one of self-help so nothing was given away except in the cases of 'great distress or illness' and in those circumstances only through the Relief Committee.[121] In September 1901, the settlement moved into larger quarters at 2 Commercial Road and the work markedly increased in the decade that followed.[122]

In 1899 the Presbyterians founded a settlement at Esk House on the East India Dock Road in Poplar under the superintendence of Mrs Ellis Hewitt. It was established in response to the local Presbyterian call for more workers to assist in the practical work of its east London churches. Indeed the minister of their church in Plimsoll Street when asked if there were not sufficient workers in the East End, replied, 'You might send an army of them down here, we could do with them all'.[123] The settlement, which was set up by the denomination's Church Aid Committee, aimed to 'render further practical aid to our East End Churches who are faithfully struggling under great difficulties, to lift up the banner of the kingdom among the masses'.[124] The settlement house which was purchased by a Mr Robson and 'tastefully furnished by his wife, provided accommodation where women could come and reside for a month or longer. It was formally opened by the Presbytery of London North on 24 March 1899.

Esk House established many of the usual mission settlement activities including a goose club, a prayer meeting on the last Sunday of the month, a Bible class and two mothers' meetings that were linked with the Millwall and Bow Churches. In connection with these there was regular sick visiting with three hundred visits being made during the first nine months. One woman who received such a visit remarked, 'I likes to hear the minister read the Bible, and I likes to hear you read it, but when I opens it myself it's one of the most stupidest book I ever came across'.[125] The settlement's distinctive and dominating feature was its work among factory girls. This developed through the endeavours of the first resident worker, a Miss Locke who came from Kensington. According to the first Annual Report, 'she took special interest in the work among factory girls, sparing no trouble to secure for them the much needed holiday at the sea-side or in the country'.[126] As a result of Locke's initial inspiration the residents began regular lunch-time factory visits during the girls' dinner hour and a club for factory girls was set up at Esk House on Tuesdays and Thursdays at which members could sew, chat and play games. In all of this work there was a strong evangelistic objective. In 1900 it was decided to hold a quarter of an hour's service at one of the factories once a week during the girls' dinner hour because 'we simply long to win these young hearts for Christ'. The report went on to observe that the older women who were visited were 'hardened by their long continued evil habits' with the result that it is impossible to get them to be Christians. In contrast the younger girls were found to be 'easily impressed and very responsive to kindness'. This was demonstrated by the fact that 'about forty Bibles and marked Testaments had been bought by the girls'.[127] The Annual Report of 1901 stated that the work among factory girls had been 'another successful year'. It did however note that 'the greatest problem of our factory girls is drink' and that gambling was proving another temptation for some.[128]

Roman Catholic Women's Settlements

The man who succeeded Henry Manning (1808–92) as Archbishop of Westminster was Herbert Vaughan (1832–1903) who came from an old Catholic family. Although he was less skilled than his predecessor in identifying with the working classes he had a genius for enlisting the help of the aristocracy in the ventures which he planned. This was particularly so in the matter of the women's settlements which were established in conjunction with The Catholic Social Union, an organisation which he founded in November 1893. It had three main objectives:

1. To bridge over the chasm separating the east from the west, and to unite one part of the Catholic population with the other on a basis of friendly interest and mutual good.
2. To save a great multitude of Catholics from becoming lost to their religion and to Christianity.
3. To safeguard society in the future by strengthening the hold of the Church upon the rising generation.[129]

CSU focused its energies on the youth of both sexes between the ages of 14 and 21 years and 'on those who are most open to good influences', because they are 'not yet hardened and corrupted' and will therefore 'give the best results for care and kindness bestowed upon them'.[130] The principle means by which CSU set out to meet these aims was by starting clubs and classes 'for music, drill, gymnastics, drawing, and handicrafts, such as carving, modelling, basket making, shorthand and telegraphy, magic lantern lectures, sewing, dress-making, cookery and other subjects as may be attractive and useful in the locality'.[131]

Two sisters of the Duke of Norfolk, Lady Mary and Lady Margaret Howard, were among the first to be drawn into the work. Lady Margaret who was then 31 years old had for a long time wanted to work in London's

East End but had been put off by the ways in which other aristocrats 'made a craze out of it' and 'spoke of the East Enders as if they were animals in a zoo'. Although her private income meant that she was a wealthy woman, she had no desire to enjoy the pleasures of the high life and gave most of her money to charities. When Vaughan recognised how strongly she wanted to work amongst the poor, he invited her to go to Mile End, which he regarded as 'the most unpromising portion of his diocese'. In consequence she and her sister rented No. 24 Tredegar Square[132] where they were soon joined by two other volunteers, Miss Emma Lowe, a former Anglican nun, and Miss Clementine Annesley, another younger convert. The initial plan was that Lady Margaret Howard and her friend, Lady Clare Fielding, would live together in the house for a month in order to get the project established, after which time they would take it in turns to live in for a month at a time. The settlement, which was linked to Guardian Angels Church, was named St Philip's House after St Philip Neri and the ladies took up residence on 14 February 1894. An entry in the Catholic Directory gave the following information, which indicates the overt nature of the settlement's religious agenda.

ST PHIILIP'S HOUSE
24 Tredegar Square, Mile End, E.

This house has been established for ladies who wish to work among the Poor in the East of London, and who are willing to reside there for a few weeks at a time to carry on various works of Charity and instruction under the direction of the Rector of the Mission. The works undertaken are: Visiting the sick and poor, teaching in the Sunday School, and holding the meetings of the children of Mary and other Confraternities, Instruction for the sacraments, Superintendence of Mothers' Meetings, Clothing club, & c., & c. Ladies wishing to join the work, or willing to help it by gifts of money, clothes, & c., are invited to apply for further particulars to Miss Lowe, 24 Tredegar Street, Mile End, E.; Lady Margaret Howard, 1 Wilton Crescent, S.W.; Lady Clare Fielding, 5 John Street. May-Fair, W.

The ladies began the settlement work by visiting Catholic homes with Miss Lowe and Miss Annesley going their separate ways and the two aristocrats staying together for fear of going out alone. Jean Maynard observed that 'visiting was to take place every day, and was considered an essential element in the settlement work in order to befriend parishioners and get them interested in the settlement activities'.[133] Within a few days of their taking up residence a club for teenage boys was set up and this was soon followed by a similar venture for factory girls. Their first encounter with the girls was somewhat nerve-racking as they found them big and rough but the ice was broken when they started to play the piano and the girls got up to dance. Other activities including cookery, dress-making, drill and singing soon followed. A mothers' meeting was started with instruction classes on the sacraments and the sick were visited. There were grants of food, clothing and coal and in the winter free dinners were given to the poorest children. There was also a savings club and Emma Lowe started a men's club.[134] Following in the footsteps of other settlements St Philips started to organise excursions into the countryside. The first of these took place on Whit Monday 1894 with 120 girls going to Arundel for the day. The proceedings began with girls being taken in horse drawn vans to Victoria Station and then by train in specially-reserved compartments to the Sussex coast. There they were entertained to an excellent lunch and spent the afternoon exploring the castle and castle grounds. They arrived back in the vans late the same evening, tired and singing.

The work of the settlement had a significant impact on the life of the parish and during the first five years the number of baptisms doubled and large numbers of people were received into the church. The Roman Catholic School, which was linked to the church, also witnessed a considerable increase in the number of pupils, which meant that more teachers had to be recruited and extra classes built with loans from Lady Margaret.

By the close of the century there were two other Roman Catholic settlements, both of them in East London and both with women residents. St Anthony's House in Great Prescott Street had been established under the leadership of the Dowager Duchess of Newcastle in 1894[135] and St Cecilia's House in Albert Square, Commercial Road, had been the initiative of Lady Edmund Talbot in 1900. St Anthony's House devised a strategy for systematic local visiting and started a boys' club with drill-classes, football, cricket and religious instruction. St Cecilia's House was very similar in ethos and aims to St Philip's. In fact the opening lines of their introduction in the Catholic Directory were almost identical with an additional sentence which stated that residents paid 25s. a week.[136] All three institutions worked closely with the parishes in which they were situated and combined Catholic evangelistic work with a wide range of charitable and educational work that was very similar in character to most other settlements. Some of their residents and helpers also took an active part in local government. The only significant discouragement was the failure of the Mile End Boys' Club, which was forced to close through lack of numbers. Almost all the money

that was needed to sustain the three settlements came from the three titled
ladies. Life in the East End was always demanding and frequently unhealthy
and it was therefore no surprise that residents' days there were sometimes
short-lived. Lady Clare Fielding caught pneumonia and died in May 1895.
Lady Margaret suffered illness and died in November 1899 and just six
months later Emma Lowe, who had been warden at St Philip's, fell ill and
died at Bournemouth where she was convalescing.

Denouement

In April 1894 the Women's Settlements of East London came together to
form The Federation of Women's Settlements. It comprised of the following
institutions: The Women's University Settlement, Southwark; The
Settlement for Women Workers in connection with Mansfield College; The
Grey-Ladies, Blackheath; York House in North London; The Women's
House of Bermondsey Settlement; The Society of Friends, Bishopsgate;
Mayfield House; and St Margaret's House in Bethnal Green.[137] Strictly
speaking, according to William Reason, the College of Women Workers on
Blackheath Hill, commonly called The Grey Ladies, and the North London
Ladies' Settlement, Holloway Road, both founded in 1893, were hardly
settlements in the strictest sense of the word since their houses were not
located in their chosen district areas and the residents were sent out to
parishes that in some cases were a considerable distance away.[138]

Considering the women's settlements as whole, it is clear that they shared
a number of common objectives. Most obviously, they all drew their
support from educated women who with the exception the Cheltenham
Ladies College were for the most part university graduates. The majority
seem to have been inspired and motivated by some kind of religious
conviction or ideal. Most had clear links with one of the mainstream
denominational churches. In the case of St Margaret's House and to a lesser
extent Mayfield House and its successor the link was with the Anglo-
Catholic wing of the established church. Whilst St Margaret's was an
integral part of the work of Oxford House and shared its Keble College
convictions, the Cheltenham Ladies Settlement was also impacted by
Dorothea Beale's views which had been shaped partly through her
friendship with F.D. Maurice but also from her respect and friendship with
men such as Arthur Winnington-Ingram and Charles Bromby.

Both the St Mildred's Settlement and the Trinity Settlement in Stratford
were formed as outposts from St Margaret's House and shared their Tractarian
convictions. Whilst it was the case that The Women's University Settlement
in Southwark had no specifically religious agenda, it clearly had links with the

Church of England since Canon Henry Scott Holland was a member of its
Council and Eleanor Benson, who was the daughter of the Archbishop of
Canterbury, was one of the residents. The Lady Margaret Hall Settlement
that was formed in 1897 by some of the members of The Women's University
Settlement did however adopt a distinctly religious objective. The
Presbyterian Settlement in Poplar was specifically Evangelical in outlook and
the Women's Houses in Bermondsey and Canning Town were connected
with the Methodist and Congregational Churches respectively.

There seems no doubt that women's settlements offered real and varied
opportunities to educated middle-class women. Their humanitarian and
Christian values, together with a sense of duty, gave them a desire to
contribute to the welfare and betterment of the less fortunate. Women such
as Anne Gruner, Eleanor Benson, Octavia Hill and Dorothea Beale were role
models to a rising generation of women who were graduating from Oxford,
Cambridge and institutions such as Bedford and Queen's Colleges, London,
which were situated on the doorstep of the city's deprived boroughs and
slum areas. Both the Southwark and Canning Town settlements recognised
the very real value of providing a place where workers could be formally
trained in the various branches of social and philanthropic work. These
included nursing, district visiting, public health, housing, sanitation and
basic life skills. The Southwark Settlement obtained endowed scholarships
from the Pfeiffer trustees, which enabled them to train a limited number of
students for a year or longer.[139] The Women's Settlements made the needs of
the young women and the factory girls a particular focus of their activities.
Nearly all of them also took part in school management in girls' clubs and
in The Children's Country Holiday Fund.

8

UNIVERSITY HALL,
A NON-SECTARIAN SETTLEMENT

Whilst it was the case that almost all the settlements and missions were aligned with orthodox Christian belief, University Hall, established by Mrs Humphry Ward in 1890 was unique. It was founded on theological modernist ideas and its educational programmes were largely focused on spreading advanced liberal theological ideas among the working classes. *The Freeman*, a Baptist periodical, dubbed Mrs Ward 'the high priestess of the New Religion' and stated that 'this attempt at Christianity without Christ will be watched with interest' and 'may be well supported'.[1] The original University Hall was divided into two parts with the south wing and library being purchased for use by Dr Williams' Library, whilst Mrs Ward and her committee took the North Wing and Annex. It contained sufficient suitable rooms for a warden and a number of residents together with some space for educational and philanthropic purposes. Initial attempts to attract shop-workers from the Tottenham Court Road area were unsuccessful and the focus of the hall's activities moved much more towards the needs of children. But in a further effort to meet the needs of the poor, Marchmont Hall was taken for use as a base for a variety of evening clubs, lectures and concerts. Mrs Ward's underlying philosophy was stated clearly in a printed circular distributed in March 1890 asking for funds. It concluded with the words:

> We appeal for help in carrying out such a scheme to all those who have at heart the adaptation of the faith of the past to the needs of the present – who desire to live their lives in the faith of God, and in the memory of His noblest servants on earth, – while holding with a firm conviction that God is manifest, not in miracle or special revelation, but in the ever-widening experience of conscience ....[2]

Mrs Humphry Ward

Mary Augusta Ward (1851–1920) was born in Hobart, Tasmania, in 1851 and brought to England in 1856. She was the daughter of Thomas Arnold (1823–1900), who was for a time, Professor of English Literature at the Catholic University of Dublin, and the granddaughter of Dr Thomas Arnold of Rugby and the niece of Matthew Arnold. She spent her early days in Oxford where in 1872 she met and married Humphry 'Thomas' Ward, a fellow of Brasenose College. Mary helped in the founding of Somerville College and for a brief period from 1879–81 served as its secretary. Like many of her generation Mrs Ward had a crisis of faith brought about largely by Biblical criticism. It was said that while she was at Somerville she reached the conclusion that 'Christianity could be revitalised by discarding its miraculous element and emphasising its social mission'.[3] Mary's religious thinking was clearly influenced by the writings of the English philosopher, Thomas Hill Green (1836–82). She said on one occasion that the two most important influences on her life were Matthew Arnold and T.H. Green and that her mission in life was to popularise Green's thought.[4] In summary, she followed Green's rejection of Anglican creedal orthodoxy and was of the view that Christianity was best expressed in action rather than in a form of words. She wrote a number of novels several of which addressed these themes and none more so than *Robert Elsmere*, first published in 1888.

Robert Elsmere

It was this novel that was destined to have the most personal impact on Mary's own life in that it led to her founding the University Hall Settlement. The story centres around Elsmere, a young modern priest, who through conversations with his local squire, Wendover, eventually found he could no longer believe in miracles and was plagued by severe doubts over other aspects of the creedal faith. Eventually, much to the distress of his devout wife, Elsmere returns to his university to seek advice from his former Professor Henry Grey, a Fellow of St Anslem's College (Balliol) who is clearly modelled on Thomas Hill Green. Grey had been an inspiration to him in his undergraduate days although Elsmere had not at that time shared his tutor's abandonment of the creedal faith. In consequence of his interview with Grey, he resigned his country living and went to live in a poor part of London where he came into contact with Murray Edwardes, a Unitarian minister, who left the confines of his denomination and was teaching working men in the area a simple ethical and unsectarian creed. Elsmere though impressed was not drawn to Unitarianism, which he considered to be generally unattractive to the working classes. Edwardes directed him to an educational club for working men, which Elsmere soon attached himself to. There he quickly became a popular and leading figure giving lectures on a humanistic Jesus and what his life and teaching should mean in terms of everyday living. The social and philanthropic work that Elsmere there entered into, he came to regard as being the true Christian gospel.[5]

It seems highly likely that Ward's model for Elsmere was taken, at least in part, from another Green, in this case her husband's friend, John Richard Green, the incumbent of St Philip's Stepney. Mirroring Elsmere, Green had had a crisis of faith and came to the view that the way forward was to go and live among the poor and seek to bridge the gap between privilege and poverty. Well before the founding of either Oxford House or Toynbee Hall, Green, together with Edward Denison and the Revd Brooke Lambert, had conceived the idea of setting up a social settlement in London where 'colonies of urban gentry' could give something more valuable than money to those in need. The book received increased publicity on account of Gladstone's critical review and Mary's forthright defence of it. The book earned £3,200 in its first year and sales were said to have reached two hundred thousand copies in America. One grateful American publisher sent a gift of £100 that Mary duly passed on to the Barnetts for the work of Toynbee Hall. Robert Elsmere was eagerly read by the British public it being particularly popular among those who had been impacted by the growing climate of doubt in the wake of publications such David Strauss's *Life of Jesus* and Charles Darwin's *The Descent of Man*. The success of the novel, it is said, led Mrs Ward to found the settlement.

University Hall, Gordon Square
In 1881 the Wards moved to London where Mary's husband had commenced work as an art critic for *The Times* newspaper. It was then that Mary began to contemplate the setting up of a spiritual centre where the Bible and other sacred writings, including those of other faiths, could be studied. She envisaged a community where people who shared Elsmere's loss of faith in accepted Christian teaching could share their concerns and interpret them to others. For Mary, having lost faith in a God 'out there', the important thing was now to search for God within and she came increasingly to rely on her conscience and on feelings of compassion. She spoke of conscience as God's revelation within each person. Whereas settlers in other parts of London were motivated by their commitment to Tractarian principles or acting under compulsion to share the evangelical message, Mary Ward was clearly driven by social conscience combined with a strong sense of duty that was still informed by a residual liberal Christian

theology. Traditional moral values regarding marital faithfulness, family and
gender issues were very strong in her and she believed that her liberal brand
of Christianity could both impact society and make it secure. Among those
she drew into her circle were the Liberal Peer Lord Carlisle and Mr Stopford
Brooke who shared Mary' own crisis of faith. Carlisle was of the view that
the Unitarians would best run the new centre but Mary still had a slim
attachment to the Established Church, possibly cherishing a hope that she
might one day be able to broaden its outlook. The Unitarians nevertheless
sent a donation of £7,000 and this may possibly have carried some weight
in the appointment of Philip Wicksteed as the first warden. The plan was
that the settlement would be housed in University Hall in Gordon Square,
which had been built in 1848 as a hall of residence for University College
and had recently been purchased by the trustees of Dr Williams' Library. In
1890 a circular was put out explaining the ideals and the aims of the
proposed new settlement.

> It is proposed to establish a Hall for residents in London, somewhat
> on the lines of Toynbee Hall, with the following objects in view:-
> (1) To provide a fresh rallying point and enlarged means of common
>   religious action for all those to whom Christianity, whether by
>   inheritance or process of thought, has become a system of
>   practical conduct, based on faith in God, and on the inspiring
>   memory of a great teacher, rather than a system of dogma based
>   on a unique revelation. Such persons especially, who, while
>   holding this point of view, have not yet been gathered into any
>   existing religious organisation, are often greatly in want of those
>   helps towards religious life, whether in thought or action, which
>   are so readily afforded by the orthodox bodies to their own
>   members. The first aim of the new Hall will be a religious aim.
> (2) The Hall will endeavour to promote an improved teaching of the
>   Bible and the history of religion. To this end continuous teaching
>   will be attempted under its roof on such subjects as Old and New
>   Testament criticism, the history of Christianity, and that of non-
>   Christian religion.[6]

An early document stated that the hall would contain rooms for about 15
residents who would engage in religious and social work similar in character
to that done by the residents at Toynbee Hall, or the workers of Oxford
House.[7] It was also proposed that the hall would work in sympathy with the
Manchester New College, Oxford, and with the various social and religious

activities carried on at Essex Hall.[8] The link with these institutions was due to the fact that most of the first committee that Mary drew in were prominent Unitarians.

Mary Ward's Theological Views

There can be little doubt that many in late-Victorian England were dissatisfied with the life and religious teaching of the denominational churches, chiefly because it was either too dogmatic or had become dull, lifeless and perfunctory. Yet the number of residents and middle-class people living within the vicinity of the University Hall Settlement, who shared Mrs Ward's views on biblical criticism and a liberal humanitarian Jesus, proved to be small. In fact it was soon the case that the University Hall where the lectures took place was half-empty while the social work that was developed at the nearby Marchmont Hall was throbbing with life. Significantly, Philip Wicksteed (1844–1925), a Unitarian Minister, mathematical economist and Dante scholar, who was eventually persuaded by Mrs Ward to undertake the leadership of her new project, had expressed his concern at the vagueness and ethos of the proposed programme. The son of a Unitarian minister, Wicksteed was educated at University College, London, and served churches in Taunton, Dukinfield and Little Portland Street in London. As the newly appointed warden, Wicksteed soon found that the locals were not going to be drawn to the classes by means of advertisements. Eventually he was reduced to going out into the streets and cajoling a handful to come in.[9] Mary Ward later recalled in one of her addresses that 'His first lecture was given sitting on the edge of a table to three or four people, who must have wondered what it was all about'.[10]

The aim of Ward's settlement was twofold: 'to bring together those who viewed Christianity as "a system of practical conduct"' and 'to provide opportunities for social work and the study of social problems, developing and organising educational and social work in the district'. Mary Ward later re-iterated this objective in an address in November 1898 to The Universities Association for Promoting Social Settlements at the Guildhall, Cambridge. On that occasion, she stated that

> they wished to create in the poorer parts of St Pancras a new centre for the action of social forces; to test thereby within a small sphere, the action upon life and within certain forms of religious thought, and they pledged themselves to help forward an improved study of the Bible and of religious history and tradition in general.[11]

She reiterated that her particular hope was that she would be able to attract to the settlement those 'for whom Christianity, whether by inheritance or process of thought, has become a system of practical conduct, based on faith in God, and on the inspiring memory of a great teacher rather than a system of dogma based on a unique revelation'.[12] She wanted University Hall 'to do for the west central and north-western districts what Toynbee Hall was doing for East London'.[13] On occasion Mary's social theory appeared somewhat more radical than that of Toynbee Hall and many of the other settlements, as her aim was 'equalisation' in society. She also became increasingly strong in her advocacy of women's rights although, perhaps somewhat strangely, she later became the first president of Britain's Anti-Suffrage League. The hope was to create places 'where men and women desirous of the common good may, no matter how different their outward lots, come together for study, amusement, and social intercourse'.[14] 'Such a place', she said, 'we desire to make Marchmont Hall, and such men and women we desire for our associates'.

Marchmont Hall Social Activities
An early fundraising flier entitled 'University Hall Marchmont Hall Scheme' stated that 'the poor and thickly populated area in which Marchmont Hall is situated, lying within the angle between Gray's Inn Road and Euston Road, is at present quite untouched by work of the kind contemplated, and indeed is singularly wanting in institutions designed to elevate the social and intellectual life of the people'.[15] The document went on to outline plans to furnish two small rooms for a club to be open each week-night for reading, games and refreshment, together with a boys' club focused on recreational and gymnastic activities and a library for the use of members.[16] The Marchmont activities soon proved to be captivating and in 1892 some of those attending the activities began to take a share in the management. A small printed card entitled 'Workers' Curriculum' listed the activities for the autumn of 1891. It included boxing, gymnastics, drill as well as story telling and reading, music and drawing.[17] Additionally, the library was reported to be flourishing with a growing book stock and 354 borrowers in the previous six months. The Saturday evening concerts had been 'greatly appreciated' with sometimes every seat taken and people standing. The women's club had enjoyed doing needlework and the girls' club had found singing, gymnastics and games to be popular.[18] Among other very practical aspects of Marchmont's work was the 'Holiday Fund'. With a promise from Mary Ward and a few of her friends to double any money saved, some of the members were persuaded to put money aside each week towards a summer

holiday. About forty 'Associates' as they became known, enjoyed a week or more outside London.[19] Despite the fact that early Marchmont flier asserted that religion is 'the noblest element of life' and 'the binding force by which the best men have been driven', Mrs Ward must have been disappointed that most of the residents seemed opposed to integrating religious teaching with the social activities. Thus the work developed in two separate spheres, with the social work among the neighbourhood poor at Marchmont Hall and the educational work at University Hall. It was education that was to become the dominant focus of the Settlement and of its successor Passmore Edwards from 1898 onwards.

Difficulties in Conveying the Vision

Mrs Ward had high hopes that the poor might have been attracted to her religious outlook on life but the reality of the situation was that a greater percentage of the few who were drawn to the Christian faith preferred something that was more traditional and most probably for the simple reason that it was easier to grasp. A further problem was that the residents who organised the clubs at Marchmont Hall resisted pressure to promote her thinking. There are a number of extant letters on the matter between her and Philip Wicksteed. On 18 February 1891 for example Wicksteed wrote. 'I am, as you may well suppose, very far from being satisfied with the attitude indicated by Mr Williams as that of the Residents generally, with regard to the Religious work at Marchmont Hall'. He went on to say that he proposed to hold a conference with them in a week's time, giving them plenty of notice, in order 'to get a clearer idea of what they really are at'.[20] He concluded by saying that he would value a full discussion with Mary after his time with the residents.[21] In a further letter to Mrs Ward after his meeting with the residents, Wicksteed was of the view that the men must not be pushed into preaching any form or Christianity to the men and women at the clubs. 'We must', Wicksteed wrote, 'give the men their heads, and we must let whatever power we give anyone be genuine'. He was firmly of the view that if the question of religion was not forced there was 'every prospect of a growing sympathy on their part'.[22] Subsequently a number of Mary's friends and sympathisers wrote in support of her desire to have religious teaching at Marchmont Hall. Among them was one from one of her committee members, W. Blake Odgers. He wrote:

> I entirely agree with your view as to one common religious impulse going through all our work, and I think the Residents will see it in that light, if we leave them to cool down a bit and come round. But I feel as

though the Committee had rather lost touch with them. Your influence ought to be supreme in the Hall; and the only reason it is not is because the young men do not understand your views and appreciate your wishes as they will do when they know you better. We must try to see more of them apart from Committee meetings, and co.[23]

However the resident men and their helpers held their ground and Mrs Ward felt it best not to pursue her religious objective.

There was a subsequent hope that they might have been able to attract the poor of the locality to the religious lectures at University Hall but that was never realised, largely because topics such as Source Criticism and the Gospels and lectures on the Book of Enoch were well beyond the grasp of those who could barely read. Instead, the premises were filled on Thursdays and Sundays with middle-class doubters who came to hear men like R.H. Charles lecture on the Old Testament and the Gospels. In addition, there were popular free lectures and concerts on Saturday evenings, classical music on Sunday afternoons and Mary herself came across on three Sundays to tell rationalistic Bible stories to the younger children. Beatrice Potter, the children's writer who later married to Sidney Webb, had recently become a part of Mary's circle and gave some of her time to the work.

Early Wardens

Philip Wicksteed remained in post as warden until 1893 and the work of the settlement flourished. The hall became a thriving centre of the University Extension Movement in the district. Indeed when he tendered his resignation at the Council meeting on 21 March 1891 the committee resolved that he be invited to take 'the title of President of the Hall, to retain the general oversight of the lecturing work of the Hall and to undertake for them in the future the same proportion of lecturing on similar subjects as he has done in the past'.[24] They further resolved that he be offered an annual salary of £250 in connection with the post.[25] Wicksteed had evidently found his work fulfilling for in his letter of resignation he wrote: 'I shall look back upon my work with the knowledge that it has brought much enrichment to my own life; and with the hope that, under the circumstances and within the limits of my tenure of office, it has been some use to the Hall ...'[26] Wicksteed's work was varied and demanding in that he was involved in both the social and educational work. During his tenure of office, courses in Biblical criticism were given by Dr Estlin Carpenter, Charles Hargrove and Professor Knight, and the course on the Gospel of Luke by the white-haired Dr Martineau was long remembered.[27] On the non-biblical side Mrs J.R.Green gave a series of lectures on 'The Development of English Towns' while Beatrice Potter gave a course on the Co-operative Movement'.[28] Wicksteed was responsible for the residents and for recruiting new ones. The Committee minutes for 24 June 1891 noted that 'he had addressed a meeting at Cambridge the day before under the presence of Dr Sidgwick on the aims of University Hall'.[29]

In 1894 Wicksteed was succeeded as warden by Mr John Russell who was a part-time teacher at University College School. He was appointed initially for one year at a salary of £150 per annum on the supposition that he would continue to work mornings at the school.[30] Mrs Ward was evidently taken with his contribution and spoke in an address of 'his increasingly good work' and 'his extraordinary gift of popular sympathy, whose eager 'choosing of equality', were never, that I could see, 'marred by the least touch of insincerity or self-advertisement'.[31] She noted that when Marchmont was closed down Russell's work had resulted in almost two hundred paying 'Associates'.[32] Not surprisingly therefore, 'the Committee received with regret' Russell's resignation in July 1895. It was not until December the following year that his successor was finally appointed. R.G. Tatton, a former fellow and tutor of Balliol College, had been a member of the Hall Council for some time and it was while he was at the helm that the settlement moved to new premises and took the name 'The Passmore Edwards Settlement'. Although appointed in 1896 it was not until 30 June 1897 that Tatton finally took up the office of Warden.[33] He had made a special request to be given time in which to satisfy himself that he was happy with both the courses and the management structure of the organisation.

Plans for New Buildings

Encouraged at the success of the social and educational work at University Hall, Mary Ward soon began plans to raise money for more adequate, purpose-built accommodation. For this reason, she approached the philanthropist, John Passmore Edwards (1823–1911),[34] for funding. At first he offered little more than a few words of encouragement, declaring that 'he had his hands full at present and was thus unable to help'. However, on 30 May 1894 he wrote to Mrs Ward in the most positive terms:

51 Bedford Square
30 May 1894

My Dear Madam,
Since I received your letter from Italy I have considered your suggestion in reference to the extension in ampler premises of

University Hall Settlement and thereby planting as you say a Toynbee Hall in the Somers Town district. I have also visited the district around Clarendon Square and am convinced that such an institution is as much wanted in North London as it was wanted in East London. I therefore cheerfully respond to your appeal and undertake to provide the necessary building within the limits of the sum you indicate, if somebody will provide a suitable site .... As a matter of course provision must be made for the building to be permanently devoted to the purpose now intended. In my opinion we have two things most necessary in Somers Town district for a Toynbee Hall:- we have a numerous working population requiring educational assistance and advantages and we have in the neighbourhood many able and willing workers ready to assist in works of intellectual, moral and social culture.

I remain

     Yours faithfully

       J. Passmore Edwards

Mrs Humphry Ward[35]

In January 1895 he wrote again to Mary Ward that, '... when you have made quite sure of your site I will send you a cheque for £1,000' and 'another cheque for £1,000 when you have completed the purchase and another for £2,000 when you lay the foundation stone'.[36] In a subsequent letter in March 1895 he stated, 'You are quite at liberty to pledge me to the extent of £7,000 and if you insist in calling it "The Passmore Settlement" then I insist on increasing my donation to £10,000'. In the event, Passmore Edwards finally supported the project to the tune of £12,000 and gave advice on the chosen site and the contractual arrangements with the Duke of Bedford.[37]

The New Passmore Edwards Settlement

The work of Marchmont Hall continued on until the end of June 1897 and the settlement moved into the new Passmore buildings in October the same year. The accommodation for the residents was finally ready just before Christmas and the Warden and five others took possession of their new rooms at 9 Tavistock Place, St Pancras, WC1. The new district, which was situated on the southern border of St Pancras, was described as 'having a mixed population of rich and poor to the south and a closely-packed working-class neighbourhood to the north and east'.[38] *The Daily News* described the area in the following lines:

To most it may seem that of all places bourgeois Bloomsbury, notoriously the land of lodging houses with a shifting population, is the least hopeful spot for the planting of one of these comparatively new-fangled things called settlements. But not so. Adjacent to the square and long unlovely street, lie squalid slums innumerable – not much more than a stone's throw, indeed, where there is crying need of some social explorer. The Euston road is one of the disgraces of our civilisation. Somers Town is notorious for its slums and squalor. Grays-inn-road, Kings-cross road, are close by; and a thousand and one byways, twisting and curving, which abut those great thoroughfares. It is a dark enough continent for the most zealous, the most intrepid, to grope his way through.[39]

Mary Edwards was herself very struck by the poverty of the Somers Town area, observing that it had a population of over 35,000 with a percentage of poverty of 42.3 per cent, rising in the east-central block to 60.3. Taking the district as a whole there were 166 persons to the square acre and in the worst part of the district the infant mortality rate was 256.40 per thousand, as compared to 154.8 for London generally.[40]

The new buildings set in this challenging locality contained rooms for 18 residents who, it was hoped, would be able to support the expanding work of the settlement. An article in *The Times* commented that 'residents will probably be, as a general rule, men who are engaged in their own profession or business during the day, but are willing to give time in the evenings and on Sundays'. The writer went on to note that 'their life will be collegiate, and will possess many of the charms of such life in the Universities'.[41] The architect's plan for the new settlement complex shows a very ambitious set of buildings on three floors. The basement contains a sizeable workshop, laboratory, gymnasium, kitchens and scullery. The ground floor contains a library, a reading room, dining room and billiard room. The first floor has a public hall with seats for 445 people with servants' quarters and bedrooms for the residents.[42] The aim was that these facilities would enable all classes in the local neighbourhood to come together on the common ground of fellowship. The whole complex seems almost exactly to fulfil the community to which Elsmere attached himself in Mrs Ward's London in her novel.

Three floors of rooms brightly furnished, well-lit, and warmed; a large hall for Sunday lectures, concerts, entertainments, and story-telling; rooms for the boys' club; two rooms for women and girls, reached by a separate entrance; a library and reading room open to both sexes, well stored with books, and made beautiful by pictures; three or four smaller rooms to serve as committee rooms and for the purpose of the Naturalist Club, which had been started in May on the Murewell plan; and, if possible, a gymnasium.[43]

Aims and Activities

The overall ethos of the newly housed settlement remained the same with its constitution and its aims entirely 'unsectarian'. In particular, the Council expressed the hope that they would continue to pursue 'a thorough and scholarly study of the Bible and the history of religion'. With this end in view, distinguished scholars established 'The Jowett Lectureship'[44] with the first aim of securing an annual course of lectures on this topic. In an address to mark the opening of the Passmore lecture session Mrs Ward again referred to their founding ideals:

> We have come to stand for an attitude and a spirit, and not for any special religious agreement. That spirit is a spirit of liberty, a spirit, we hope, of equal justice. What we want to avoid here in the treatment of disputed questions, economical or social or religious, is a temper of partisanship, the temper of polemics.[45]

She went on to make the point that in the matter of economic and social affairs, as in religion, they were committed to no party or school. Here again their stance was to be one of attitude not opinion.[46] In all of this one can readily see both Mrs Ward's own reaction against the often fiercely dogmatic and doctrinal struggles in both church and society. Yet despite her rhetoric the Passmore Edwards Settlement emerged with a strong set of ideals particularly in the matter of children's education, the family and the role of women in society. The aims, which reflected those of University Hall, were set out in a document entitled *Memorandum and Articles of Association of the Passmore Edwards Settlement*. They were 'to carry on all descriptions of Religious, Educational and Social Work' including the following:

(1) To promote the study of the Bible and of the history of religion in the light of the best available results of criticism and research.

(2) To promote the study of philosophy, history, or literature, or any other study which the Council for the time being shall consider may be suitably promoted by the Association, and to undertake

or assist the teaching of music, art, and technical work and science of all descriptions.

(3) To provide lectures and classes, and undertake examinations and the collection of statistics and other information on any subject the study of which may be promoted by the Association …

(4) To provide, organise, or promote clubs, gymnasia, benefit and other societies, libraries, art galleries, exhibitions, concerts, entertainments, social gatherings, reading parties, holiday excursions, and other means which, in the opinion of Council, may tend to promote the religious, moral, intellectual, or physical well-being of the people of London.

(5) To organise and support any movements for the reform of municipal and other local institutions.[47]

There was a formal opening ceremony for the new institution performed by Mr John Morley on Saturday 12 February 1898 when the purpose-built complex was duly renamed 'The Passmore Edwards Settlement'.[48] A prospectus noted that it contained a large concert and lecture hall, library and entertaining rooms, club rooms and gymnasium with accommodation for 17 Residents. A later paragraph stated that the organisation is 'undenominational, and includes among its supporters men and women of most various shades of religious as well as political opinion'.[49]

The council attached great importance to the connection of the settlement with the universities and it was anticipated that the greater proportion of the residents would be university men. It was however recognised that there would be others from less academic backgrounds that would want to throw in their lot with the social work of the organisation.

The warden and the residents devoted themselves to a variety of projects in connection with public bodies as well as carrying out educational work in connection with University Hall. A library was set up with open access at set times but the number of borrowers was relatively small with only 350 volumes being taken out in the first three months.[50] The lecture list in 1898 was a large one and included a university extension course taught by G.C. Henderson of Balliol College who was well known in Canning Town. Among the lecturers listed for the year 1898 were Mr Leslie Stephen, Philip Wicksteed, Miss Jane Harrison, Dr Bosanquet and Charles Williams, the settlement's musical director. Among others who later gave lectures at the centre were George Bernard Shaw, Sidney Webb and Keir Hardie. In addition to the lectures, a wide range of other clubs and activities were organised, very similar in character to those put on by other settlements and missions. These included fortnightly social gatherings and smoking debates designed to capture the attention of working men and held on alternate weeks. There were clubs for men and women and one for boys and it was hoped to provide something equivalent for the girls. There was a strong emphasis on games and athletics. The settlement became a magnet and attracted ordinary people who came to enjoy the cultural and intellectual as well as the practical. There were a variety of interest groups including a factory girls club with 170 members, musical concerts and chess clubs. There was also much in the settlement programme that was practical including a coal club, a boot club, a poor man's legal service and a mothers' and toddlers' group. Mary Ward also initiated a strong campaign against the sweated trades. There was a poor man's lawyer who gave legal advice one evening every week to those who were unable to pay for it.[51] As was the case in other settlements, physical exercise was not neglected. There was a Passmore Edwards Cricket Club, which, besides matches, organised a number of social events for members. The Passmore Edwards Football Club played twenty matches in the 1898–9 season, winning nine, losing eight and drawing three.[52]

A Focus on Children

Children from the rougher surrounding neighbourhoods were a particular concern to Mary Ward,[53] for while middle-class children enjoyed toys and storybooks with their parents or nurses, most poor children were locked out until their parents returned from workplace. The most common reason for this was that open fires and improvised gas fittings were too dangerous for unsupervised children. Mary Ward therefore set out to provide these children with a warm environment, children's books and suitable toys. The aim was 'to provide through the Settlement, for the children of the neighbouring schools, such healthy recreation, amusement and intelligent occupation outside school hours, as come naturally to those who are brought up in well-to-do homes'.[54] Mrs Ward's conviction was that the children of the capable artisan were just as quick, keen and well endowed with artistic ability as children from richer homes. In consequence adult activities and classes did not begin until eight o'clock. Mary's endeavours marked the start of the evening play-centre movement.[55] The number of children on the registers in the autumn term of 1898 were about 500 but in the October of the following year the figure rose to 'close upon 800', and the entries for classes reached nearly 1,100.[56]

The older children particularly enjoyed the illustrated history and geography classes. The history of the colonies which was taught with 'beautiful slides' in the spring of 1899 by Mr A.W. Andrews was 'a great success' with 'very great keenness for tickets' and a weekly attendance of about 110.[57] Janet Ward, Mary's youngest daughter, gave seven lessons in the summer term of 1899 on Charles I illustrated with slides prepared from the pictures in Mr Green's *Illustrated History*. Some of the children in the class were taken to Whitehall and Westminster Abbey.[58] In the spring term of 1900 the children's classes were held for the neighbouring board schools that included history and geography, drama, reading and storytelling, gardening, singing and drill. The average weekly attendance was 850. By 1904 there were 1,700 attendances at the Passmore Edwards' Children's Recreational School and by 1907 Mary Edwards and her daughter, Janet, were promoting school play centres at which attendances numbered 418,113.[59] She saw these play schemes and centres as helping to curb hooliganism and disorderly behaviour.[60] In another development Mary read to schoolboys on Friday evenings. Eighty boys were selected by local headmasters to go to the settlement and hear her read from Kipling, Scott and other writers. Janet Ward helped with the children's work assisting initially with storytelling on Monday evenings to a hundred children aged between three and ten.[61]

The summer school holidays were a particular problem for many children in the area since there were very few safe or pleasant open spaces where they could play, the gardens in the great squares being closed to all but the children of the privileged few. The only open space to which the settlement had access was the garden at the rear of the premises, which they rented on an annual basis for the nominal sum of £10. When therefore Mary received a £100 donation from Lord Northcliffe she immediately used it to plant new turf and shrubs. From the beginning of the twentieth century the settlement was open to children throughout the August holiday period with 750 children in two sessions. On one occasion Mary put on a lantern presentation to 136 children, squashed together on only 76 chairs.[62] Assistance with the children was received from the students of Maria Grey College where her sister was the Principal and also from the Froebel Institute. Particular attention was paid to creating a safe play environment where bullying could be contained. From these beginnings Mary Ward went on to pioneer the development of children's play centres and playgrounds during the early years of the twentieth century. This activity, combined with taking large numbers of children away from central London in connection with *The Children's Country Holiday Fund*, was major aspect of the Settlement's work.[63]

Concern for Invalid Children

An early and influential innovation was the settlement's focus on children with disabilities who lived in the local community. Nationwide their numbers had been increasing because many more were surviving to school age and beyond. The 1889 Royal Commission on the Blind, Deaf and Dumb required that when the welfare of a handicapped child was under consideration, there should be no discrimination. Four years later the London School Board was aware of over eight hundred children who were unable on account of their physical disabilities to obtain the education which was their legal right under the terms of the 1870 Act. Mary Ward needed no convincing that she should open a school for cripples within the locality and quickly set about the task of identifying them. This was done in conjunction with local hospitals, schools' attendance officers and voluntary visitors from The Invalid Children's Aid Association. Mrs Ward took strong exception to the practice of putting cripples into the same classrooms as the 'mentally deficient' and was doubtless gratified when in 1900 the London School Board ruled 'that children of normal intelligence be not taught with the 'mentally deficient'. The Passmore Edwards School for Invalid Children was opened on 28 February 1899 and was placed under the management of the School Board. It had the first fully equipped classrooms for children with disabilities and provided tailor-made courses, physical therapies and meals. The children were brought to the settlement by horse-drawn ambulance and at one point there were as many as forty between the ages of five and fourteen. In addition, there was a play centre for children, which had begun in Marchmont Hall under the direction of Mary Neal. Mary Ward recognised that this was an aspect that needed development and from the time the new premises were opened great efforts were made to expand and develop this side of the work. In the years that followed Mary Ward campaigned strongly for greater state commitment to the needs and welfare of crippled children. The impact of the Invalid Children's School was considerable, resulting in the government opening two similar such schools in London in October 1900, one in Bethnal Green and one in Paddington. Others followed shortly in Deptford and Battersea and in other towns and cities including Liverpool, Bristol, Glasgow, Edinburgh, Manchester and Birmingham.[64]

Social and Philanthropic Work

A brochure about the Passmore Edwards Settlement prepared jointly by Mary Edwards and R.G. Tatton was published in 1897 giving full details of the proposed activities.[65] Section 5 entitled Local Government and Social Work referred to the opportunities for social activity available to intending residents. These included work as school managers, membership of the committees of local charities and more specific local government involvement serving on the Board of Guardians, the vestry and the County

Council.[66] Inspired partly by the precedent set in this area by Toynbee Hall, both the Council and the residents did all in their power to further good government in the local area and worked hard in a campaign against the unsanitary conditions in St Pancras and the shortage of adequate housing. Mr Norman Franks, one of the residents, was reported to have been a very active member of the St Pancras Vestry during the year 1898–9. Another resident, Mr H.J. Tozer, was heavily involved in the local committee of *The Charity Organisation Society* and Dorothy Ward was busy in her work as a School Manager.[67] A conference was organised during the winter of 1900 to consider 'The Causes of Sickness among the Wage Earners'. Following the example of Toynbee Hall, the Passmore residents became actively involved in the struggle to persuade the ratepayers of St Pancras to adopt The Public Libraries Act and thus have the benefits of their own local library. They made their first attempt in 1894 when members of the settlement actively campaigned in the local area but lost the poll by a majority of 1,674.[68] Then in 1898 they tried again and organised a public meeting and invited 400 leading parishioners, including county councillors, vestrymen, guardians, ministers of religion and many others. A four-page circular was drawn up and later 30,000 copies were printed off and put in envelopes, which were addressed by hand by a band of willing helpers. Despite all this effort, the battle was lost largely because the local newspapers informed the ratepayers that the parish was £500,000 in debt, but omitting to say that this expenditure was on profitable public works such as the electric lighting plant.[69] H.J. Tozer closed his report noting that they had achieved an increase of 274 more supporters than previously and resolving to 'fight again till the people have gained wisdom enough to rout the foes who have so long deluded them'.[70]

The Second Annual Report of the Passmore Edwards Settlement stated that 'there has been much steady expansion: some disappointments and delays' and that there had been a good deal of fresh help from outside. Of particular encouragement was the fact that the number of 'Associates' had now reached 319 of whom 142 were men and 177 women. 'Associates' dated back to the old Marchmont Hall days and had to be 'workmen and workwomen' of the neighbourhood.[71] In his report for the year the warden stated that the management of a mixed club of some 300 to 350 members 'has been the one most important part of the work of Residents in the past year'. He was convinced that the great need was for more lady helpers who could give a substantial amount of time to the work. It had to be borne in mind that a majority of the Associates were women and girls so he hoped that they might have more ladies among the resident helpers.

In an address given shortly after the opening of the Passmore Edwards premises, Mrs Ward stressed her great hope that 'before long we expect to have four hundred working men and women of St Pancras, in close organic connection with the settlement'.[72] Such had always been an initial core objective of all the London settlements but inevitably it was going to be an increasingly uphill task, given the circle of helpers and the cultural levels of the educational and interest classes that were being offered. It was clear that it was very largely the upwardly mobile semi-skilled artisans, clerks and shop managers who were going to be drawn into the community. In his report for 1898 the warden was clearly aware of the problem and remarked that fears had been expressed that the character of the club might easily change if the genuinely working-class men and women were allowed to be replaced by clerks and shopmen.[73] Tatton evidently shared this concern for he wrote that 'something no doubt may be done by making the advantages and opportunities of the Settlement more widely known and understood among working men'. But he felt that this alone would be no long-term solution to the problem. As he saw it, the only way forward was for 'those who are near the class to be reached' to take an increasingly active role in all the activities and at the same time make them as widely known as possible.[74]

The Importance of Music

Particular importance was attached to music and Mr Charles Williams was appointed as the first musical director shortly after the settlement opened. He resigned in the spring of 1899 and was succeeded by Dr Madeley Richardson. Among other musical activities there was a ladies' string orchestra whose performances 'are always looked forward to with keen interest' and a choral class with 80 members. Popular music concerts were held on Saturday evenings with audiences of 350 or 400 that 'consist mainly of our working class neighbours'.[75] Musical drill was a particular favourite among both the younger girls and boys with 160 names entered on the lists in October 1898. The settlement report noted that the high standard of music could not have been maintained without the generous help of many professional musicians who gave their services at nominal fees. It was clear to all concerned that the popularity of these evenings was 'one more proof – if proof is still needed – that the best forms of recreation have only to be offered to the people to be gladly accepted by them'.[76]

An Unrealised Dream

In all of this it is clear that the Passmore Edwards Settlement was gradually moving away from Mrs Ward's religious aspirations. Perhaps the most obvious reason for this was her own determination in the name of tolerance not to push any particular religious agenda or conviction and that included her own. A further difficulty was that often when she did give vent to her own views, they appeared to be complex and unappealing to those who were looking for a more domestic and less intellectual spirituality. Thus for example, in an address at Manchester she spoke as follows:

> The sense of a new discipleship to Christ, and the new conceptions of God and the world which may be reached through it, have still to be expressed in poetical and yet practical forms, closely akin to it – yet different from – those which the first Christian imagination, drawing upon the stories about it, Roman, Jewish, Greek, found and adapted for itself with so much eagerness and simplicity. It is surely in this strengthening first of our Christian knowledge, the clarifying of our Christian ideas giving these ideas the most positive, and yet the most poetical and enthusiastic forms that we can, that our future lies. I would fain hope with all my heart that these new churches we are thinking of today, might largely help it forward. The Religious Tradition of our race is really made and re-made perpetually, by experience, by constant experiments of the religious mind.[77]

In her advocacy of higher biblical criticism, Mary Ward was of the view that 'the more certain new doctrine grows'; the more it was inevitable that some religious traditions might have to be 'thrown aside'.[78] Her great hope was that the national Church of England might broaden its base until 'it includes within its boundary, on terms of equal right, the simpler and more complex Christianity side by side'.[79] The difficulty she faced was that few of the residents appeared to share her convictions and any that did had neither the time nor the energy to make them an integral part of settlement life. Thus the focus of activity became centred on education and the needs of women and children in particular. Indeed, Mary herself came increasingly to speak of the work in terms of its educational agenda. For instance, in the address that she gave, probably in 1898, she recounted the first year's activity in the new buildings as follows:

> There was no religious propaganda of any sort ... and there was great insistence upon the importance of good citizenship, upon the better

and higher pleasures ... upon music and art and reading, and above all, upon the need of a truer and wiser fellowship between class and class, and on the power of friendship and sympathy to lighten the inequalities and privations of life even under existing conditions.[80]

It was therefore no surprise that the warden, R.G. Tatton, writing in the first edition of *The Associate,* also referred to the settlement 'as a place of education and self-improvement as well as recreation and sociability'.[81] At this same point in time Philip Wicksteed, the first warden but now President of the Settlement, was aware of Mrs Ward's great disappointment that the residents were not keen on giving any specific religious colour to their activities. He wrote of her 'rare magnanimity' in her recognition that the settlement could not be made to embody her full ideal and of her throwing all her powers into the development of all the other branches of her original purpose.[82]

Initially Samuel Barnett had his doubts as to whether or not Mary's new project would ever succeed. In a letter to his brother in 1890 he wrote:

On Thursday I saw Mrs Humphry Ward about her Settlement. I don't think it will go. Why should it? It has neither the force of a sectarian movement nor the charm of a free movement. A few people are caught by the phantom beauty of Elsmere's character, but it cannot be grasped. She is a sweet tender woman, full of anxieties, too great anxieties, to serve others. She was meant to be religious and is fitted for the Mary service rather than the Martha busyness of this age. We have had some good talks, and notably one on the possibility of religion for the crassly ignorant.[83]

Some years afterwards Barnett came to revise his opinion writing in 1909 that 'Mrs Humphry Ward's vacation school is a great institution and must soon come into vogue'.[84] Later when Mrs Barnett wrote her husband's biography she commented: 'Everyone knows how, under Mrs Humphry Ward's inspiring energy, there now exists, in all parts of London, a great network of play centres, with their troops of salaried and volunteer workers'.[85]

So Mrs Humphry Ward, or Mary Ward as she was more commonly known in the Settlement Movement, was a woman of great vision and dogged determination. One of her most obvious talents was an ability to attract others to the work and inspire them to share and carry forward her ideas, as well as to raise large sums of money to make them a reality. All this she achieved alongside her family concerns and an active social life. Her diaries, now in the possession of University College, London, reveal a constant stream of dinner, social and speaking engagements both in the city and in the vicinity of Tring where the family had a summer residence. One of Mary's great and significant qualities which served her well in all of this was her steady perseverance which showed itself in the fact that she wrote her later novels with her hands in great pain and finding it a real effort even to hold a pen. Mary Ward was clearly one of the most remarkable women of the Victorian and Edwardian eras, a great organiser, an innovator, an outstanding and popular novelist, a pioneer of women's work in the professional sphere and a distinguished figure in the educational world of young children.

9

WHAT THE SQUIRES ACHIEVED

A number of criticisms of those who gave part of their lives to work in the missions and settlements in the late Victorian years were made both by their contemporaries and subsequently. Some of them have more validity than others. Undoubtedly the missions were very largely run by 'Squires', almost all of them being staffed by public school Old Boys and Old Girls and Oxbridge graduates supported by undergraduates. It is clear that the great majority who gave their time and energy to serve the poor in education, local government and clubs and recreational activities were inspired by the changing mood in the country that had been prompted by *The Bitter Cry* and other similar social surveys. These, together with the resurgence of Christian Socialism and a growing sense of duty towards the poor, challenged college heads and undergraduates alike to take practical action and to go and live in London's poorest parishes in an attempt to bridge the gap between privilege and poverty.

Foremost among contemporary critics was George Lansbury (1859–1940) who later became the leader of the Labour Party. Lansbury, a teetotal Anglican, was elected to the Poplar Board of Guardians in 1892 and later appointed a member of the Royal Commission on Poor Laws in 1905. He regarded Toynbee Hall as a base for the privileged to do their social work in East London.[1] In *My Life* he wrote that 'my sixty years' experience in East London leaves me quite unable to discover what permanent social influence Toynbee Hall[2] or any other Settlement has had on the life and labour of the people'.[3] Lansbury in fact raised four criticisms against settlements. First he felt that their supporters and staff separated themselves from the people of their surrounding districts, their lifestyle and dress further increasing the gap between them. Second, he felt that some of the young men and women from 'good schools' who went down to the East End used the experience as a means of future advancement as they went on to gain good positions in Government and the Social Services. Third, Lansbury was of the opinion that many of the settlers who professed to want to lessen the gap between rich and poor in fact contented themselves with a much more conservative agenda such as 'the business of making the present conditions more tolerable'.[4] Lansbury's fourth and perhaps more significant criticism was that the residents of Bow, Poplar and Whitechapel might work in serving capacities in East End settlements and missions cleaning and cooking and they might even benefit from the education programmes but they did not exercise ownership or control. These were roles that remained firmly in the hands of the middle classes and professionals who dominated their management committees.

Whilst it is now more widely accepted that social services should be controlled and organised locally, the fact was that the settlements and missions were privately owned by schools and colleges who were not in a position to relinquish them or the opportunities they gave to their students. Furthermore, it should be noted that for all his liberal views Samuel Barnett strove for social harmony but he never set out to work for social equality. Rather his vision was to achieve social justice through education, sanitary legislation, relief work, caring for children, garden suburbs and old-age pensions. These programmes would help to create right relationships between classes but not eradicate the differences between them. This fact is clear in the following lines taken from his volume *Towards Social Reform*:

> A body in which every member is a hand could do no work, and a city of one class would have no life. The classes in our great cities are many, but terms such as 'rich' and 'poor', if not exact definitions, represent clearly enough the two great classes of society. Their unity means strength, their division means ruin.[5]

Like many of his predecessors Barnett recognised that poverty is a relative term. Indeed at times he came close to endorsing the celebrated views of the Evangelical, Archbishop Sumner, who at the beginning of the century drew a contrast between 'honourable poverty' which he saw as the lot of many in a well-ordered society and 'indigence' or extreme poverty, the latter being largely self-inflicted. Barnett wrote: 'The citizen whose cottage home, with its bright housewife and happy children, is a light in our land, is poor in comparison with some stately mansion. But his poverty is not an evil to be cured'.[6] For Barnett, as for Sumner before him, this was merely a fact of human existence in which both those in 'different circumstances' could nevertheless experience a full and satisfying life. That said, Barnett was adamant that 'the poverty which has to be cured is the poverty which degrades human nature, and makes impossible for the ordinary man his enjoyments of the powers and the tastes with which he was endowed at his birth'.[7] As Barnett saw it, this kind of poverty was the result of human selfishness, neglect and social injustice. The settlers could help to alleviate such poverty by serving the poor and seeking to raise their quality of life to a level at which they too 'could feel the joy of their being, and, living together in peace and goodwill, make a society to be a blessing to all nations'.[8] For men of socialist convictions such as George Lansbury, the Barnetts' whole approach was insufficient and served only to maintain the status quo of Benjamin Disraeli's *Two Nations*. Sir Walter Besant when visiting Mansfield House in 1897 remarked that 'the new teaching concerning relations of the cultured and uncultured classes, which has taken shape and expression in the University Settlements, is very peculiarly the creation and growth of our time ... of the later Victorian age'.[9] The reality of this was that college missions and settlements, together with other philanthropic work of the period, remained rooted in a fixed social hierarchy and there was no ultimate or stated intent to raise the poor of London to a more equitable level with the rest of society.

Culture and Condescension

One problem from which most settlements and missions suffered was that many of their lectures and educational classes were well-above the level of the very poor. Typical of most settlement programmes the 'Popular Lectures' so called put on by the Caius Mission must have been well above the cultural understanding of the Battersea locals with lectures on 'Shakespeare and His Plays' by the Revd Canon Daniel and 'Ancient Schools of Philosophy' by Mr T.M. Taylor, Scholar of Caius College.[10] In places *The Battersea Caian and Yelverton Magazine* subtitled 'A monthly record of the work in connection with Gonville and Caius College, Cambridge' reads more like that of the parish magazine of the Oxford University Church of St Mary the Virgin than that of a Battersea Mission. The front page of the February 1892 issue for example, advertised 'Sacred Music on Sunday Evenings' and 'A Course of Four Lectures on Political Economy' by 'Mr H. Holman B.A., (Exhibitioner of Caius College and University Extension Lecturer)'. It was this kind of sophisticated and academic environment that caused one kindly American visitor to Toynbee Hall to write that

it is essentially a transplant of university life in Whitechapel. The quadrangle, the gables, the diamond-paned windows, the large general rooms, especially the dining room with its brilliant frieze of college shields, all make the place seem not too distant from the

dreamy walks by the Isis or the Cam. But these things are not so
much for the sake of the university men as their neighbours, so that
they may breathe a little of the charmed atmosphere.[11]

His comments should have caused no surprise since Elijah Hoole, the
London architect of Toynbee Hall, wanted it to appear in the style of 'a
manorial residence' and his design was clearly influenced by Oxford and
Cambridge colleges. Despite being constructed of red brick the quadrangle
and ecclesiastical doors with dog tooth patterns and mullions were
deliberately chosen to create a home from home for the young Oxbridge
squires who would come to take up residence there.[12] Whilst it was the case
that some settlements, such as the first Browning Hall premises and St
John's mission building were modest affairs in comparison with Toynbee,
the fact was that many were replaced with larger and often quite grandiose
ecclesiastical gothic style buildings. This was particularly so in the case of
public school missions where it was felt to be necessary to promote and
uphold the image of the school.

Another later visitor to Toynbee, Stephen Hobhouse, found it to be a
comfortable academic enclave cut off from the abject poverty and gloom of
the surrounding district. 'It was', he wrote, 'the same with two or three
other Settlements I visited – Oxford House, the Cambridge and Eton
Missions, and the Browning Settlements'.[13] A certain Ernest Bramwell
described an early visit to Oxford House: 'My first impressions were, what
a nice house, what splendid clubs etc. for working men ... In the House
were Oxford and many Cambridge men, and they all had different jobs
assigned to them; they were full of the Head's enthusiasm, and there was a
delightful spirit of friendship and welcome'.[14] The measure of The House's
public school Oxbridge atmosphere was that it even boasted a fives court!
This was a sport in which Winnington-Ingram excelled.[15] There is no
doubt that many of the settlements and missions breathed an air of
condescension, which was for the most part unspoken but was from time
to time verbalised. It was apparent for example in Oxford House's two
men's clubs, 'The Oxford House Club for Clerks and Skilled Artisans' and
'The University Club for Unskilled Working Men', the latter in James
Adderley's own words, giving the settlers every opportunity to interact with
'typical specimens of the upper grade of the East End Society'.[16]

Accomplishments

Notwithstanding these criticisms the fact remains that the settlements and
missions made a number of significant contributions to the life and worship

of many poorer communities in South and East London. They also
impacted the thinking of many within the churches and beyond. The
settlements kept alive the link between socialism and the churches. Indeed
a number of the settlements were part of the resurgence of later Christian
Socialism. Whilst it may be the case that the isolated attempt on the part of
one mission or settlement to influence its particular locality was small, the
aggregate of their separate efforts was more significant both in terms of its
impact on the poor but also on the wider public. The Church and the
national and local presses reported settlement work quite widely and the
general public recognised that there was an ongoing genuine Christian care
and concern for the poor on the part of the churches.

Education

A major contribution made by the settlements and missions was in the field
of education. In this, as in other aspects of their work, the Barnetts and
others were influenced by the earlier thought and action of F.D. Maurice
and his circle. After the failure of their co-operative schemes, Maurice's
circle had reached the conviction that it was only the education of the
working man that would in the end bring about social justice. Virtually all
the settlements and missions considered in this book made education a part
of their work. For some, such as Toynbee Hall, Oxford House and the
Bermondsey Settlement, this was a major priority. Indeed for Barnett,
education was not simply a means of training, it was a way of life and for
this reason he had organised adult classes in arithmetic, composition,
drawing and languages at St Jude's Whitechapel, well before the founding
of Toynbee. When later Mrs Barnet came to write her husband's biography
she marvelled at his faith in attempting to provide such courses in the light
of 'the degradation of the majority of the population of our parish in
1873'.[17] In 1881 he had organised the first of what later became annual art
exhibitions and in 1884 he had welcomed the University Extension Society
into Toynbee Hall. The following year he wrote that the University
Extension Society had carried on its classes in Toynbee Hall and 'the
number of students has risen to 455' and a library of 2,500 volumes has
been formed'.[18] Oxford House, Browning Hall and the Bermondsey
Settlement were among other institutions that became significant and
active centres of university extension teaching.

When Toynbee Hall was established it also provided a very wide range of
courses including subjects at elementary level for men in arithmetic,
composition, citizenship and chemistry. There were a variety of afternoon
classes for girls and practical subjects such as first aid, ambulance work, life

saving and photography. There were also a whole range of advanced courses of a more academic nature which included Latin, Greek, Hebrew, Italian, German and French literature, history, botany, geology and anatomy. In addition, there were art exhibitions, Sunday concerts, discussions and educational visits to places of interest. Some settlements copied Toynbee's art exhibitions though on a smaller scale. Oxford House similarly offered a great range of courses such that by the mid-1890s there were more than sixty lecturers offering courses on its premises. Clearly the settlers anticipated the need for adult education and were its pioneers often working with limited resources and in very inadequate surroundings.

As was noted earlier in chapter 2 of this book, Toynbee had been instrumental in campaigning for the establishment of Whitechapel Public Library, which was finally opened in 1892. As a result of Barnett's endeavours, the library movement spread rapidly in East London. In fact it was recognised that it was his publicly expressed opinion that librarians should have formal training that significantly influenced the development of professional librarianship. All missions and settlements recognised the need for books and started libraries almost as soon as their premises were opened. Both the Clare and St John's College Missions gave particular attention to their libraries and were constantly on the look out to increase their book stocks.

Barnett and other settlement wardens and missioners recognised that there were problems associated with the adult education that they offered, not least that in some cases the fees for university extension courses were too high and that there was a need for individual personal tutorial help. No settlement quite equalled the extent of courses put on by Toynbee but they all regarded education as crucial and in varying degrees followed Toynbee's lead. It is clear that the residents of the settlements were pioneers of adult education in an age when the opportunities for it were not widely available. Thomas Kelly in his monumental study of adult education in Great Britain noted that Toynbee in particular had 'anticipated the later work of the Workers' Educational Association'.[19] R.H. Tawney wrote the following assessment of Barnett's contribution to education.

In the eventful chapter of English Education that was unfolded between 1870 and 1913 Canon Barnett had played a considerable, if self-effacing part. His special interest lay, however, in an aspect of education which, till a few years before his death, had hardly begun to receive serious attention. The importance of Adult Education is to-day a common-place. It is assisted by organised labour, by the universities, by the Board of Education, and by an increasing number of Education Authorities .... Working-class students, by their demands for classes and by their enthusiasm in supporting them, showed that Canon Barnett has guaged a living need.[20]

The educational work of the settlements included providing support for local teachers and pupil teachers in particular. Toynbee and several other settlements and missions offered hospitality, social activities and courses for pupil teachers. Among them were the Southwark Women's Settlement, the Lady Margaret Hall Settlement and the Bermondsey Settlement, which even provided accommodation for a number of pupil teachers in their local areas. Other settlements such as Passmore Edwards offered schooling for the handicapped and crippled. The picture exhibitions put on by a number of settlements drew very large numbers of visitors and gave many local residents their first taste of 'high' culture It was this experience that in many cases created an appreciation and a thirst for the aesthetic which led on to a desire for further courses in art, literature and history.

There is no doubt that the settlements and missions that were established in East and South London touched many lives. Not only were the people of the local districts given care, practical help and the opportunity of a rudimentary education and cultural enrichment, many of them were also brought within the Christian community. Amos and Hough, for example, in their assessment of Cambridge College Missions noted that they had charge of districts in South London containing from 40,000 to 50,000 inhabitants. This meant that on a conservative estimate some 5,000–6,000 children were receiving church teaching at their hands.[21] Amos and Hough also calculated that the Cambridge College Missions had some 2,000–3,000 communicants attached to them and that the whole of this large group of people looked to Cambridge and its Colleges 'as the source under God of their spiritual health and strength'.[22] Almost all the London settlements were active in supporting the work of The Children's Country Holiday Fund. Through their work many thousands of children were enabled to spend a small part of their holidays in the countryside, an experience that widened their horizons and improved their health. Besides providing additional basic education for thousands of young children who left school at a young age and had little or no home support, three settlements in particular pioneered the education of the physically handicapped. Mary Ward's University Hall Settlement was the first institution ever to provide a fully equipped learning environment for the physically handicapped at Marchmont Hall. Almost immediately after

The Lady Margaret Hall Settlement was opened, they began to provide education for invalid children and made themselves responsible for running the North Lambeth branch of The Invalid Children's Aid Association. The Bermondsey Settlement also made a significant contribution to the theory and practice of bringing up young children.

A New Generation of Muscular Christians

There is no doubt that the settlements produced several generations of 'muscular Christians' of the Kingsley Hughes variety. A large number of clergy with a practical social concern were inspired by the example of their wardens and missioners and in consequence went on to train for the church's ministry. S. Mayor observed that in the first 10 years of Toynbee's existence 16 out of just over 80 residents went into the church's ministry or were already clergymen.[23] Others such as Frank Weston from the Trinity Oxford Mission and Edith Langridge, the first warden of the Lady Margaret Hall Settlement, went out to serve on the foreign mission fields. Hundreds, indeed thousands of public schoolboys, were prompted by their clerical Headmasters, chaplains and school missioners to a sense of duty and a desire to join one of the caring professions.

There seems little doubt that the great majority of the wardens and missioners who were almost all drawn from the ranks of the clergy had been impacted by the earlier thinking and practical schemes of Frederick Denison Maurice and the early Christian Socialists. Maurice's stress on a practical kingdom theology and the notion of brotherhood were particularly strong in the teaching and leadership of men such as Lidgett,[24] Alden and Stead. Henry Scott Holland, Charles Gore and others endorsed Maurice's emphasis on the doctrine of the incarnation and applied it to the issues of Christian citizenship and the importance of dealing with social problems. Indeed, it was Scott Holland who famously remarked, 'You cannot believe in the incarnation and not be concerned about drains'. Winnington-Ingram was one of many who were influenced by a combination of Maurice and Kingsley's 'hands-on' Christianity and the principles of the later Tractarians of Keble College from which he came. St Margaret's House, the women's arm of Oxford House, was clearly influenced by Christian social thinking and established its own branch of the Christian Social Union. The public schools gave little overt credence to socialism. It therefore seems more likely that most of their missions were founded out of a sense of duty, a concern that their pupils should be acquainted with poverty, and a desire to see more stable Christian communities established in London's poorest urban boroughs.

Clearly the great majority of Victorian settlements and missions were Anglican foundations the majority being identified with the Tractarian principles of the Oxford Movement. Oxford House stood for a gospel that was sacramental but also involved bringing people to personal Christian faith in a way that was not dissimilar from the Evangelicals. Both Christ Church and Trinity, Oxford, acknowledged that they were influenced by the ethos and principles of Oxford House. Indeed during Tupper-Carey's wardenship, Christ Church's mission engaged in advanced forms of ritualism. The Trinity College Cambridge Mission also indicated their Tractarian sympathies when the Sisters of St James Holme, Kilkhampton in Cornwall were invited to take part in the work. In contrast, the Free church communities at Bermondsey, Canning Town and Walworth were all strong advocates of the settlement principle but also motivated by a more overtly Protestant form of evangelicalism. The first wardens appointed by each of them were ordained ministers who saw their role as both applying the teachings of Christ to public life while at the same time urging those who came to their clubs and activities to enter into a personal relationship with Christ.

Youth and Clubs

The way in which muscular Christianity was most apparent in the settlements and missions was in the proliferation of clubs, particularly those designed to meet the needs of teenage boys and young men. Through these clubs young undergraduates were able to test out their leadership potential and, at the same time, many poor lads were introduced to the sports of soccer, cricket and boxing. Of these, football was by far the most popular. It was both a team game and a game which could be played almost anywhere and with minimal resources. It has been shown by Colm Kerrigan that it was the public school influence that caused so many missions and settlements to take up football.[25] Indeed Kerrigan wrote, 'This debt to the public schools has been acknowledged by historians'.[26] He went on to consider 'the "Muscular Christianity"' which 'was in evidence in the public school missions to working-class areas in the 1880s and 1890s' and noted that 'football was the most popular activity at the boys clubs they established and teams were often trained by missioners who had been prominent in teams in their public schools'.[27] Famous ex-public schoolboy players often visited the schools' missions to talk to the boys as was the case when the internationals G.O. Smith and C. Wresford-Brown visited the Charterhouse Mission.[28] Winnington-Ingram was once asked about starting a boys' club and his reply was that the first thing to do was to start a football club. His house's monthly journal *The Oxford House Chronicle* played an important part in promoting club enthusiasm by giving reports of the various mission matches and printing full league tables. In order 'to appeal especially to the clubs' the journal was enlarged with increased coverage starting in January 1894.[29] There can be little doubt that the settlers had a significant impact on the development of secular youth and religious youth work. Their philosophy, as William Reason of Mansfield House pointed out, was not 'to attempt to force religion on the lads' as 'there will be ample opportunity to bring whatever form of Christianity the promoters may favour to bear upon their lives in a natural way'.[30] The worst possible scenario, as Reason saw it, was to make religion compulsory. The best course in his view was to run a Bible class in conjunction with the club. This seems to have been the preferred option adopted by most of the wardens and missioners.

Support for Trade Unions

Whilst it was the case that a good deal of the social action was ambulance work that involved providing cheap meals, opening lodging houses and loaning blankets, it was by no means exclusively so. Settlements such as Toynbee, Bermondsey, Mansfield and Browning in particular became active centres of trades unions that even in some cases helped to organise and back strike action. The great dock strike drew the sympathy and support of most missions and settlements. Toynbee in particular was to the fore in the emergence of the New Unionism, which began to emerge in the 1880s, and it became the home base for many trade union meetings and debates on labour issues. The Nonconformist settlements also proved remarkably strong in support of trade unionism. Lidgett in particular was totally convinced that only by backing unionism could the problem of the unskilled casual workers be solved. Browning Hall of which Keir Hardie was a resident, worked tirelessly to give Christian input to the Labour Movement. The settlements were one of the few sections of the denominational churches that gave active support to the trade unions in the late Victorian years. M.D. Stocks has shown that it was the personal encounters between the Oxford settlers and the sweated workers in East London that generated the sweated industries campaign that later led to statutory wage regulation in 1909.[31] The active support and work which a number of the settlements gave to the trade unions certainly needs to be set against the harsh criticisms of men such as George Lansbury.

Closely associated with the trades unions was the issue of women's rights and here Barnett and some of the settlements were unequivocal. In an era when the Established Church eschewed radical politics, Toynbee loaned strong support to female trades union activities. They encouraged the formation of trade unions in support of women's work such as the tailoresses and gave their support to the Match Girls in their dispute with Bryant and May in 1888. Barnett was committed to the removal of all restrictions on the occupations of women even within the church. In summary, it was the case that in the activities of the settlements the churches' stand for women and women's rights was at its most visible. The women's settlements also pioneered opportunities for women at a time when many of the professions were still closed to them. In particular, they provided openings for nursing, teaching, family welfare, local government, public health and youth and club work. In some respects the settlements offered the first formal training courses in social work. Such was the case at Browning Hall which offered various classes in aspects of social work. Women such as Henrietta Barnett, Dorothea Beale and Mary Ward were actively concerned to open up new horizons for the first generation of female students who were graduating from Oxford and Cambridge and the newly established London-based women's colleges.

Social Work and Local Government

Residents from every settlement and mission were active in social work, visiting the destitute, the sick and the unemployed in their homes. Most provided practical courses in basic hygiene, sanitation and home medicine. They also became concerned about the state of housing, the lack of clean water and adequate heating. In all of this they anticipated the emergence of the twentieth century social services. Indeed it was individuals such as Octavia Hill who pioneered the need for habitable dwellings and Herbert Stead of Browning Hall who began formal training for social workers.

Settlements made a significant contribution to the Boards of Guardians and the administration of the Poor Law. The residents of St Margaret's House, for example, regularly visited the infirm wards of the local workhouses. The Women's University Settlement under the wardenship of Margaret Sewell worked in conjunction with St Saviour's Board of Guardians on a variety of charitable enterprises. Miss Kerrison of Mansfield House was a member of the West Ham Board of Guardians and Miss Cheetham of the Women's Settlement in Canning Town was both a Guardian for a number of years as well as being chairman of Plaistow House, a branch of the West Ham Workhouse. Scott Lidgett, as has been noted, was a Poor Law Guardian in St Olave's Union. There is no doubt that by their practical involvement and their writing on the subject that the settlements helped to make churches and the Christian public more aware of the desperate plight of many poor and elderly people in the nation's capital. It was for these reasons that the anonymous author of a history of Lady Margaret Hall asserted that Settlements had made significant contribution to social work.[32]

Involvement with Poor Law administration was inevitably intertwined with local government and in this area many of the graduate residents provided a very useful service in their local areas serving as public health inspectors, reporting on unhealthy dwellings and impure water supply. Others held positions on local vestries and parish councils where they were able to raise issues of noise, hooliganism, drunkenness and petty criminal activity. Those in more permanent positions as wardens or missioners were able to take on greater responsibilities. The Barnetts played prominent roles on major local committees and Scott-Lidgett served for many years on the Greater London Council while Percy Alden of Mansfield eventually became a Liberal MP for Tottenham. Keir Hardie (1856–1915) was elected as the Independent Labour MP for South West Ham in 1886 and later became leader of the Labour Party in Parliament. In these ways the settlers were setting a pattern of involvement in local government or, in Herbert Stead's words, seeking to 'crown him [Jesus] Lord of our public life'! M.D. Stocks in his study of the impact of Settlement work wrote:

> There is indeed scarcely any field of social legislation or any statutory instrument of social service which does not owe something to the inception or direction to the recorded observations or voluntary experiments of settlers, who year by year followed the call of Samuel Barnett to those mean streets where their fellow-citizens led anxious, meagre lives.[33]

Old Age Pensions and Legal Aid

One major social contribution which must go down to the inspiration of the settlements was the successful campaign for old-age pensions. As early as 1883 Barnett had written an article in *The Nineteenth Century* advocating universal old age pensions that would secure freedom from anxiety for every person in their old age.[34] Other institutions endorsed his views but it was left to Browning Hall to launch the public campaign in 1898, which finally, through the lectures of Charles Booth, resulted in the Pensions Act becoming law in 1909. This success caused Herbert Samuel[35] to pay tribute to 'the splendid educational work which the settlement had done'.[36]

Another significant aspect of settlement activity was that of the poor man's lawyer which provided free legal aid for the poor. The scheme was first

begun by Mansfield House but was copied and found effective by a number
of other settlements. Both Mansfield and Bermondsey found that they had
several thousand clients each year taking up their offer of free legal advice.
Thus long before the era of free legal aid the settlements had led the way in
bringing justice to those who otherwise would have been unable to afford it.

Decline of Settlements

Despite these obviously positive outcomes from the work of the Settlements
and missions, by 1900 there were already signs that the initial energy and
enthusiasm was beginning to wane. There were a number of reasons for
this. By the beginning of the twentieth century the supply of
undergraduates was not as forthcoming as it had been a decade or so earlier.
A report in the Corpus Christi College magazine of 1900 bemoaned the
falling interest in their mission in the Old Kent Road: The writer urged
more Corpus men to visit the Mission or better still to offer help even for
a few days.[37] R.J. Millwood, Andrews' successor at Pembroke, reported that
he was unable to maintain the College interest on the same scale. He had
been at Pembroke but had spent a number of years away in a northern
parish and lacked Andrews' personal influence among the students.[38] The
Annual Report of Oxford House for 1900 was proud that three of their
intending residents had gone out to the battle front in South Africa instead
of to Bethnal Green but went on to state that 'practically, the Oxford supply
failed us in October. Two recruits, instead of the usual eight or more, came
into residence in the autumn, and we have, therefore, to start the new year
with sadly diminished forces'.[39] The report went on to say that the House
needed a minimum of 20 residents to pay its way and that they were having
to begin the year with only 16. There was a distinct possibility that 'unless
some further volunteers come quickly to the rescue, it is difficult to see how
we can maintain efficiently the several Institutions for which the House has
become responsible'.[40] Another related problem was that many of the best
workers began to move out of the poorer inner-city areas to take up
residence in the new estates that were springing up along the suburban
railway lines of Essex, Kent and Surrey. As early as 1894 Scott Lidgett wrote
in dispirited mood of the changing atmosphere in South London,'because
members and money have removed' resulting in a steadily growing spirit of
distrust and defiance 'of which Independent Labour Parties and the like
phenomena are the manifestations'.[41]

Another factor was that by the 1890s Socialism of a more radical kind
than that of the settlers was beginning to make its presence felt in the
poorer areas of London. Men such as George Lansbury, Ben Tillett and Keir

Hardie, who had himself been a member of the Browning Hall Settlement, began to propose state intervention to deal with the issues of employment, wages, sanitation, public health and housing. Their complaint against the settlers was their belief that the rich were as necessary as the poor and that the lot of the poor could not be improved without the help of the rich.

Prompted by the growing democracy of local government, many of the activities and educational enterprises which the settlers had established gradually became municipalized. As J.W. Dickie observed, 'Missions and Settlements had to decide their role within a Welfare State'.[42] Even by 1900 some of their activities began to be replicated by local colleges and polytechnics. This was particularly true of some of their educational and practical courses. In the 1880s residents of the settlements campaigned against the slums and unsanitary conditions but even by 1902 Charles Booth noted that the worst London slums had gone.[43] That said, many of the public schools and university missions continued on until the late 1930s. Only in the wake of wartime bombing, the Butler Education Act and the expanding brief of the Welfare State did a significant number begin to bow out. Some of course have survived to the present time but those that have, are changed in their character and objectives.

As early as 1905 Samuel Barnett observed that 'Settlements had been inclined to become too much like the parish they were designed to supplement'.[44] On another occasion he stated that 'Settlements are too few, and they have often yielded to the temptation to rival other organisations with a show of their works'.[45] Charles Masterman in 1901 was of the view that the creative impulse of the movement was at an end: 'The wave of enthusiasm which created the modern settlement has ceased to advance; the buildings remain and a few energetic toilers, and the memory of a great hope'.[46] Even though it was the case that the settlements and missions barely survived the generation that created them the fact remains that they proclaimed a Christianity that was compassionate and social and which served the local communities. As Charles Booth once said, 'London would have been poorer without the Settlements'.

NOTES AND REFERENCES

Chapter 1: London's Desperate Need

1 A.F. Winnington-Ingram was Bishop of London from 1901–39.
2 Winnington-Ingram, A.F., *Work in Great Cities* (London, 1896), p. 21.
3 'A Rambler in London', *Speaker*, 7 June 1890.
4 Booth, W., *In Darkest England and the Way Out* (London, Salvation Army, 1890), p. 21.
5 Ibid., p. 23.
6 Ibid., p. 22.
7 Kelly, T., *A History of Adult Education in Great Britain* (Liverpool, Liverpool University Press, 1992), p. 239.
8 *The Record*, 6 January 1882.
9 Inglis, K.S., *Churches and the Working Classes in Victorian England* (Routledge and Kegan Paul, 1963), p. 25.
10 Tait, A.C., *A Charge to the Clergy at His Visitation in December*, 1866, p. 72.
11 See John Charles Ryle.
12 *Ecclesiatical Gazette*, 16 August 1880, p. 26 cited by Inglis, K.S., op. cit., p. 25.
13 Inglis, K.S., op. cit., p. 26.
14 Ibid., p. 27.
15 Ibid., p. 27.
16 Tait, A., *A Charge to the Clergy of the Diocese of London at His Visitation in December* (1866), pp. 69–70.
17 Chadwick, O., *The Victorian Church* (London, A and C Black, 1970), Part 1, p. 366.
18 Rowsell, T.J.,'Deficiency of the Means of Spiritual Instruction', Select Committee, House of Lords, Appendix S, p. 634 in *Parliamentary Papers*, 1857–8, IX cited by Inglis, K.S., op. cit., p. 52.
19 Inglis, K.S., op. cit., p. 50.
20 It was for this reason that Bishop John Sumner sent for a locksmith during a church service and had a pew made available to the poor. See Balleine, G.R., *History of the Evangelical Party in the Church of England* (London, Longmans, Green and Co., 1933), pp. 195–6.
21 Booth, C., *Life and Labour of the London People* (MacMillan and Co., 1892), vol. 1, Table XIX East London and Hackney Attendances at Churches and Chapels on Sunday, 24 October 1886.

22 Ensor, R.C.K., *England 1870–1914* (Oxford, OUP, 1936), p. 308.
23 Anon., 'Dwellings of the Poor in Bethnal Green, *The Illustrated London News*, 24 October 1863.
24 Ibid., p. 1.
25 Ibid., p. 1.
26 Kinglsey, C., *His Letters and Memories of His Life* (London, Macmillan and Co. Limited, 1908), p. 86.
27 Davidson, R.T., *Life of Archibald Campbell Tait* (Macmillan and Co., 1891) vol. 1, p. 470.
28 Ibid., p. 471.
29 Tait, A.C. *A Charge... 1866*, p. 74.
30 In *Contemporary Review*, December 1883, p. 933 Mearns stated: 'I ought to explain that I have no wish to be described as the author of *The Bitter Cry of Outcast London*, but having seen printed statements to the effect that two others who acted as my assistants are credited with the pamphlet, it seems necessary that I should say that the inception was entirely mine, the investigation was carried out under my direction, and the pamphlet was prepared according to my instructions and subject to my revision. I was greatly helped by the Rev James Munro, formerly of Limerick, and in the literary work by the Rev W.C. Preston, formerly of Hull, and acknowledge my indebtedness to both'. Cited from Inglis, K.S., op. cit., note 1, p. 67.
31 Inglis, K.S., op. cit., p. 69.
32 Mearns, A., *The Bitter Cry of Outcast London* (James Clarke & Co., 1883), p. 1.
33 For a discussion of this, see Kelly, T., *A History of Adult Education in Britain* (Liverpool University Press, 1992), p. 239.
34 Ibid., pp. 1–2.
35 Ibid., p. 57.
36 Ibid., p. 57.
37 Ibid., p. 4.
38 Ibid., p. 4
39 Ibid., p. 4.
40 Ibid., p. 5.
41 See Brock, M.G. and Curthoys, M.C., *The History of the University of Oxford. VII. Nineteenth-Century Oxford,* Part 2 (Oxford, Clarendon Press, 2000), p. 670.
42 Sims, G.R., *How the Poor Live* (London, Chatto and Windus, 1883), p. 39.
43 Ibid., p. 39.
44 Ibid., p. 64.
45 Ibid., p. 64.
46 Ibid., p. 7.
47 Ibid., p. 7.
48 Ibid., p. 9.
49 Ibid., p. 8.
50 Ibid., p. 11.
51 Ibid., p. 15.
52 Ibid., p. 17.
53 Ibid., p. 16.
54 Thompson, R.B., *Peter Thompson* (1910), p. 33 cited Inglis, K.S., op. cit., p. 68.
55 *Wesleyan Conference Minutes* (1884), p. 310.

56 Hughes, D., *The Life of Hugh Price Hughes* (Hodder and Stoughton, 1907), pp. 193–4.
57 *Contemporary Review*, December 1883.
58 Ibid., p. 917.
59 Ibid., p. 924.
60 Ibid., p. 919.
61 Ibid., p. 920.
62 Ibid., p. 918.
63 Ibid,. p. 923.
64 Barnett, H.O., *Canon Barnett, His Life, Work and Friends* (1921), p. 305.
65 *Ninth Report of the Universities' Settlement in East London*, 1893 (Penny and Hull, 1895). See also Barnett S.A., *Settlements of University Men in the Great Towns* (Oxford, 1884) p. 1.
66 Ibid., p. 1.
67 Ockwell, A. and Pollins, H., in Brock, M.G. and Curthoys, M.C., *The History of the University of Oxford, VII, Nineteenth-Century Oxford*, Part 2, p. 670.
68 Gell, P., The Work of Toynbee Hall' in *Arnold Toynbee* (John Hopkins University Studies in Political Science, 1889) cited Brock, M.G., and Curthoys, M.C., op. cit., p. 671.
69 'Artisans Life in East London', *The Oxford Magazine*, 31 October 1883.
70 Ibid., 5 December 1883, p. 432.
71 Ibid., 7 March 1884, p. 150 cited Inglis, K.S., ibid., p. 148.
72 See *The Oxford Magazine*, 30 January 1884, pp. 21–3, 'Oxford and East London'; 23 April pp. 171–2, 'Oxford and East London' and p. 172 'Oxford in Bethnal Green'; 14 May, p. 226, 'Oxford House in Bethnal Green' and 'University Settlement in East London'; 11 June, p. 297, 'Oxford House Movement'; 29 October p. 355, 'Oxford House in Bethnal Green'; 26 November, pp. 431–2, 'Oxford House in Bethnal Green'.
73 See Mayor, S., *The Churches and the Labour Movement* (Independent Press Ltd, 1967), p. 57 and Inglis, K.S., op. cit., pp. 147–8.
74 Barnett, S., *Practical Socialism* (London, Longmans, Green and Co., 1894), p. 166.
75 Ibid., p. 168.
76 Barnett, S., *Settlements of University Men in Great Towns*, a paper read at St John's College, Oxford (Oxford, 1884).
77 Barnett, S.A., 'A Democratic Church', *Contemporary Review* vol. XLVI, November 1884, p. 675.
78 Barnett, S., *Practical Socialism* (London, Longmans, Green and Co., 1894), p. 174.
79 Anon., *Handbook of Settlements in Great Britain (The Federation of Residential Settlements and Educational Settlements*, 1922), p. 5.
80 Ibid., p. 6.
81 *The Oxford Magazine*, 21 November 1883, p. 397.
82 Anon., *The Harrow Mission A Story of Fifty Years* (published as a Supplement to the Harrovian 1933), p. 4.
83 *Work for University Men among the London Poor: speeches* (1884), p. 10, cited Inglis, K.S, op. cit., p. 157.
84 *The Times*, 21 January 1891, cited ibid., p. 157.

85 Henson, H., 'The University Settlements in the East End' in *Some Urgent Questions in Christian Lights* (1889), p. 259 in ibid., p. 157.
86 Lockhart, J.G., Cosmo Gordon Lang (1949), cited ibid., p. 157.
87 Winnington-Ingram, A.F., 'The Classes and the Masses', in *The Church of the People* (1894), p. 180 cited ibid., p. 158.
88 Barnett, H.O., *Canon Barnett, His Life, Work and Friends*, p. 421.
89 Legge, H., *Trinity College Mission in Stratford 1888–1889* (Pamphlet 1899), p. 3, Trinity Mission Archives.
90 Lang, C., *Tupper A Memoir of the Life and work of a very human parish Priest by His Friend* (London, Constable and Co, Ltd, undated), pp. 12–13.
91 *The Eagle*, vol. XIII, May 1884, p. 82.
92 Amos, H., and Hough, W.W., *The Cambridge Mission* (Cambridge, undated, Trinity College), p. 123.
93 *The Official Church of England Year-Book 1900* (London, SPCK, 1900), p. 52.
94 Pembroke College Mission – Missioner's Report, 1886.
95 *The Official Church of England Year-Book 1900* (London, SPCK, 1900), p. 52. See also *The Caian* vol. 1, p. 170.
96 Dickie, J.W., *College Missions and Settlements in South London 1870–1920* (B.Litt. thesis, Oxford University, 1976), p. 7.
97 Chadwick, O., *The Victorian Church* (A and C Black, 1970), Part 2, pp. 345–6.
98 How, F.D., *Bishop Walsham How A Memoir* (London, Isbister and Company Ltd, 1899), p. 154.
99 Chadwick, op. cit., p. 155.
100 How, F.D., op. cit., p. 157.
101 *The Worker*, July 1890, cited How, F.D., op. cit., p. 155.
102 How, F.D., op.cit., p. 156.
103 Ibid., p. 156.
104 Simpkinson, C.H., *The Life and Work of Bishop Thorold* (London, Isbister and Company Ltd, 1896), p. 147.
105 Ibid., p. 151.
106 Ibid, p. 153.
107 Ibid., p. 156.
108 The Revd Charles Hare Simpkinson BA Oxford 1877, was Curate St Mark Kennington 1878–80, Vicar of Holy Trinity, Greenwich 1881–7, Vicar of St Paul, Walworth 1887–1894 and Examining Chaplain to the Bishop of Winchester 1894–97.
109 Ibid., p. 318.
110 *The Official Church of England Yearbook* for 1900 listed the following: Cheltenham College at Nunhead, Charterhouse at St George the Martyr in Southwark in 1885, Christ's Hospital at St John's Islington in 1892, Dulwich College at Walworth in 1885, Eton College at Hackney Wick in 1885, Felstead at St Michael's Bromley, Haileybury at St Giles in the Field, East London in 1894, Harrow at St Helen, North Kensington in 1888, Highgate at St Mark's Dalston in 1894, Malvern at All Saints, Haggerston in 1881 and later in Canning Town, Marlborough in Tottenham in 1882, Merchant Taylors at Shackwell in 1889, Radley at St Peter's London Docks, Wapping Rossall at All Saints, Newton Heath, Tonbridge at King's Cross in 1883, Uppingham in Poplar in 1869, Wellington College in Walworth in 1884,

Westminster School in the Seven Dials area in 1888, Winchester in South
Bromley in 1877 and Cheltenham Ladies College in Bethnal Green in 1886.
Cranleigh gave support to the St John's College Mission in Walworth and
Berkhamsted supported the costs of a dormitory in the Webbe at Institute of
Oxford House.

111 Edward Thring, Addresses (London, 1887), sermon 83, cited Tozer, M., 'The
Readiest hand and the most open heart: Uppingham's first mission to the
poor', History of Education, 1989, vol. 18, no. 4, pp. 323–32.

112 The Berkhamstedian, March 1887.

113 For Green see entry in New Dictionary of National Biography. His most
important work, Prolegomena to Ethics was published the year after his death.

114 Inglis, K.S., op. cit., p. 152.

115 Dickie, J.W., College Missions and Settlements in South London 1870–1920 (B.
Lit. thesis, Oxford University, 1976), p. i.

116 Davies, R. (editor), John Scott Lidgett (London, Epworth Press, 1957), p. 53.

117 Ibid., p. 54.

118 Ibid., p. 54.

119 Ibid., p. 55.

120 The Congregational Year Book, 1903, cited Mayor, S., The Churches and the
Labour Movement (Independent Press Ltd., 1967), p. 65.

121 British Weekly, 28 October 1895, p. 89, cited Mayor, S., op. cit., p. 159.

122 Mansfield House Settlement in East London (Canning Town, 1892), cited
Inglis, K.S., op. cit., p. 160.

123 British Weekly, 28 October 1895 p. 89, cited Mayor, S., op. cit., p. 159.

124 Ibid., p. 159.

125 Gleeson, D., 'The Decade of an East End Settlement', Month, December
1904, cited Inglis, K.S., op. cit., p. 160

126 See chapter 6.

127 Inglis, K.S., op. cit., p. 161.

128 Trevelyan, J.P., The Life of Mrs Humphry Ward (1923), cited Mayor, S., op.
cit., p. 282.

Chapter 2: Samuel Barnett and the Founding of Toynbee Hall

1 William Reason, University and Social Settlements (London, Methuen, 1896),
p. 52.

2 Charles Herbert Grinling – Hertford College 1878–83.

3 Barnett, H.O., Canon Barnett, His Life, Work, and Friends (London, John
Murray, 1921), p. 405.

4 Ibid., p. 406.

5 Briggs,A., and Macartney, A., Toynbee Hall (Routledge and Kegan Paul,
1984), p. 22.

6 Barnett Papers, London Metropolitan Archives, Ms F/BAR/461.

7 Ibid., Ms F/BAR/462.

8 The Revd the Hon William Henry Freemantle was rector of St Mary's
Bryanston Square 1865–83, chaplain to Bishop Tait of London 1861–83 and
when he was Archbishop of Canterbury 1868–82. Canon of Canterbury 1882.

9 Barnett, H.O., Canon Barnett His Life, Work and Friends (London, John
Murray, 1921), pp. 26–35.

10 Ibid., p. 29.
11 *Barnett Papers*, Letter from Bishop of London, 27 November 1872, Ms F/BAR/464/1.
12 Ibid., Ms F/BAR/465.
13 Octavia Hill to Mrs Harris, 27 November 1870, *Barnett Papers*, London Metropolitan Archives, F/BAR/460.
14 Apprenticed to a jeweller and became active in the Shop Assistants Union, joined the Labour Party and Fabian Society in 1903, Warden of Toynbee Hall, 1919–54.
15 Note by J.J. Mallon, cited by Briggs, A., and Macartney, A., op. cit., p. 27.
16 Barnett, H.O., op. cit., 1921, p. 74.
17 Ibid., p. 75.
18 Ibid., p. 75.
19 Ibid., p. 82.
20 Edward Denison (1840–70) built an endowed school in Mile End Road in 1867, was MP for Newark 1868 and died at Melbourne where he had gone for the sake of his health to study the working s of colonisation.
21 Barnett, H.O., op. cit., p. 306.
22 *Jowett Papers*, vol. 1, Ms H63f.
23 Letter to his uncle, 11 August 1878 *Toynbee Correspondence*, Balliol College, Oxford.
24 Toynbee, G., *Reminiscences and Letters of Joseph and Arnold Toynbee* (undated), p. 105 cited Inglis, K.S., *Churches and the Working Classes in Victorian England* (Routledge and Kegan Paul, 1963), p. 150.
25 Barnett, H.O., op. cit., p. 314.
26 Bolton King (1860–1903), Eton and Balliol, chairman of the Warwickshire Technical Education Committee 1893–1903 and Director of Education for Warwickshire from 1904.
28 *Memorandum of Association* printed in *First Annual Report of the Universities' Settlement in East London* (Oxford, 1885).
29 Briggs,A., and Macartney, A., op. cit., p. 5.
30 Ibid., p. 7.
31 Ibid., p. 11.
32 Barnett, H.O, op. cit., p. 308.
33 *Second Annual Report of the Universities Settlement in East London* (Oxford, 1886).
34 Barnett, H.O., op. cit., p. 414.
35 Ibid., p. 415.
36 *The Star*, October 1889.
37 Briggs, A., and Macartney, A., Toynbee Hall (Routledge and Kegan Paul, 1984), p. 47.
38 Probably James Bonar, Balliol, 1873–7.
39 Toynbee Memorial Fund Minute Book, Minutes of 27 June 1885, Ms A/Toy 1/1London Metropolitan Archives.
40 Barnett, H.O., op. cit., p. 457.
41 Briggs, A., and Macartney, A., op. cit., p. 45.
42 Arthur George Liddon Rogers, Balliol 1884–7.
43 Ibid., p. 46.

44 Mayor, S., op. cit., p. 59.
45 Smith, L., *Religion and the Rise of Labour* (Keele University Press, 1993), p. 65.
46 *The Toynbee Record*, vol. 2, no. 1, October 1889. See also Briggs, A., and Macartney, A., Toynbee Hall (Routledge and Kegan Paul, 1984), p. 48.
47 *The Toynbee Record*, vol. 2, no. 1, October 1889, p. 8.
48 *Daily Chronicle*, 2 November 1889.
49 Ibid., 2 November,1889.
50 Ibid., 2 November 1889.
51 Barnett, S. to Frank, 16 November 1889, *Barnett Papers* Ms F/BAR/101.
52 Ibid., p. 48.
53 Ibid., p. 65.
54 *The Manchester Guardian*, 1 April 1890.
55 *The Times*, 31 March 1891.
56 Probably Arthur Hamilton Peppin of Worcester College, 1884–7.
57 *Daily Chronicle*, 18 March 1891.
58 *Sixth Annual Report of the Universities Settlement in East London* (London, 1890), p. 28.
59 *The Times*, 31 March 1890.
60 *Annual Report of Toynbee Hall*, 1890. See also Briggs, A., and Macartney, A., op. cit., p. 49.
61 *Annual Report of the Universities Settlement in East London* (London, Penny and Hill, 1891), p. 43.
62 Ibid., p. 29.
63 Briggs, A., and Macartney, A., op. cit., p. 38.
64 Barnett, H.O., op. cit., p. 459.
65 Ibid., p. 611.
66 See for example the report in *The Women's Gazette*, 14 June 1890.
67 *The Women's Gazette*, 14 June 1890.
68 'Notes on a Visit to Toynbee Hall – 1890', *Jowett Papers*, Ms 1H 76.
69 Briggs, A., and Macartney, A., op. cit., p. 7.
70 Briggs, A., and Macartney, A., op. cit., p. 38.
71 *Sixth Annual Report of the Universities' Settlement in East London* (London, 1890), p. 7.
72 Barnett, H.O., op. cit., p. 667.
73 *Eighth Annual Report of the Univerities' Settlement in East London 1895* (London, Penny and Hill, 1895), p. 35.
74 Barnett, H.O., op. cit., p. 671.
75 Ibid., p. 675.
76 Carpenter, S.C., *Church and People*, p. 334.
77 *The Toynbee Record*, March 1894.
78 *The Toynbee Record*, vol. X, no. 2, November 1897.
79 *The Toynbee Record*, vol. VIII, no. 1, October 1895.
80 Barnett, S.A., *Settlements of University Men in Great Towns* (Oxford, 1884), p. 10.
81 *The Times* 3 August 1896.
82 Barnett, H.O., op. cit., p. 697.
83 *The Christian Union*, 18 September 1890.
84 *Minute Book of House Committee, Wadham House*, Minutes 13 February 1901.
85 Barnett, H.O., op. cit., p. 457.

86 *Daily News*, 6 April 1891.
87 Reason, W., *University and Social Settlements* (London, Methuen, 1896), p. 22.
88 Ibid., p. 24.
89 Ibid., p. 24.
90 Alden, P., 'Settlements in Relation to Local Government', ibid., p. 32.
91 Barnett, H.O., op. cit., p. 334.
92 *The Scottish Leader*, 7 December 1891.
93 Pimlott, J.A.R., *Toynbee Hall* (1935), p. 60. See also Barnett, H.O., op.cit., 1922, p. 327.
94 Barnett, H.O., op. cit., p. 335.
95 Ibid., p. 336.
96 Robert Ernest Sperling Hart, b. 1872, Merton, 1890–1992.
97 Kelly, T., *A History of Adult Education in Great Britain* (Liverpool University Press, 1992), pp. 241–2.
98 Briggs, A., and Macartney, A., op. cit., p. 29.
99 Ibid., p. 242.
100 Reason, W., op. cit., p. 29.
101 Barnett, H.O., op. cit., pp. 330–1.
102 *The Scottish Leader*, 7 December 1891.
103 *The Christian Union*, 18 September 1890.
104 George Lewis Bruce, Balliol, 1881–6.
105 *Eighth Annual Report of the Universities' Settlement in East London* (London, Penny and Hill, 1892), p. 24.
106 Barnett, H.O., op. cit., p. 342.
107 Ibid., p. 344.
108 Ibid., p. 345.
109 *The Bristol Mercury*, June 1894, cited Barnett, H.O., op. cit., p. 443.
110 Ibid., pp. 344–8.
111 Barnett, H.O., op. cit., p. 683.
112 Ibid., p. 62.
113 Barnett, S., to Frank, 11 April 1885 *Barnett Papers*, London Metropolitan Archives, Ms F/BAR/24.
114 *The Times*, 26 March 1890.
115 Barnett, H.O., op. cit., p. 553.
116 Mayor, S., op. cit., p. 64.
117 Briggs, A., and Macartney, A., op. cit., p. 55.
118 Anon., *Handbook of Settlements in Great Britain* (The Federation of Residential Settlements and Educational Settlements in Great Britain, 1922), p. 8.
119 Barnett, op. cit., p. 491.
120 Ibid., p. 495.
121 Ibid., p. 495.
122 Ibid., p. 395.
123 See for Example the report in *The Manchester Examiner*, 7 December 1889.
124 *Christian Herald*, 20 March 1890.
125 Kelly, T., *A History of Adult Education in Great Britain* (Liverpool University Press, 1992), p. 241. For further details see Pimlott, J.A.R., *Toynbee Hall* (1935), chapters 4, 9 and 11.
126 *Daily Chronicle*, 1892, cited by Barnett, H.O., op. cit., p. 398.

127 Barnett, H.O., op. cit., p. 403.
128 Mayor, S., *The Churches and the Labour Movement* (The Independent Press, 1972), p. 58.
129 *The Toynbee Record*, April 1898, vol. X, no. 7.
130 Barnett, H.O., op. cit., pp. 360– 3.
131 Ibid., p. 361.
132 Ibid., p. 365.
133 Reason, W., *University and Social Settlements* (1898), p. 45.
134 *Toynbee Record*, April 1898, vol. X, no. 7.
135 *Fifth Annual Report of the Universities' Settlement in East London*, 1889, p. 14.
136 Ibid., vol. X, no. 7.
137 Barnett, H.O., op. cit., p. 489.
138 Ibid., p. 490.
139 Barnett Correspondence, Ms F/BAR/161.
140 Barnett, S., *Settlements of University Men in Great Towns* (Oxford, 1884), p. 10.
141 *Fifth Annual Report of the Universities' Settlement in East Londo*n (London, 1890), p. 8.
142 Ibid., p. 9.
143 Ibid., p. 9.
144 *New York Herald*, 23 March 1890.
145 Barnett, H.O., op. cit., p. 490.
146 Ibid., p. 420.
147 Ibid., p. 421.
148 Ibid., p. 421.
149 Ibid., p. 63.
150 Barnett, H.O., *Canon Barnett, His Life and His Friends* (1918), p. 45.
151 Briggs, A., and Macartney, A., *Toynbee Hall* (Routledge and Kegan Paul, 1984), p. 25.
152 S. Barnett to Frank, 9 May 1885, Barnett Correspondence, Ms F/BAR/25, London Metropolitan Archives.
153 B. Jowett to Florence Nightingale, 6 December 1887, *Jowett Papers*, Ms III, 608.
154 B. Jowett to Florence Nightingale, 6 September 1893, *Jowett Papers*, Ms III, 670.
155 Briggs, A., and Macartney, A., op. cit., p. 55.
156 *New York Herald*, 23 March 1890.
157 Barnett, H.O., op. cit., p. 434.
158 *The Westminster Gazette*, 18 June 1913 cited ibid., p. 777.
159 Ibid., p. 421.

Chapter 3: Oxford Colleges in the East End

1 Colson, P., *Life of the Bishop of London An Autobiography* (Skeffington & Son Ltd., 1936), p. 27.
2 *The Oxford House Chronicle*, vol. VIII, no. 2, 1894, p. 5.
3 Reason, W., *University and Social Settlements* (London, 1898), section on Oxford House.
4 Ibid., p. 5.
5 *Oxford House Annual Report*, 1897, p. 7.
6 *Oxford House Annual Report*, 1888, p. 6.

220SQUIRES IN THE SLUMS

7 Ashworth, M., *The Oxford House in Bethnal Green* (London, Oxford House, undated), p. 5.
8 Winnington-Ingram, A.F., *Fifty Years Work in London 1889–1939* (Longmans, Green and Co., 1940), p. 2.
9 Ibid., p. 8.
10 Ibid., p. 5.
11 *The Oxford House Chronicle*, vol. VIII, no. 1, January 1894.
12 Ibid., p. 9.
13 Ibid., p. 9.
14 *Oxford House Magazine*, 1894, cited Ashworth, M., *The Oxford House in Bethnal Green* (London, Oxford House, undated), p. 4.
15 *Oxford House Annual Report*, 1886, p. 5.
16 Hensley Henson, H., 'The University Settlements in the East End', cited Briggs, A., and Macartney, A., *Toynbee Hall The First Hundred Years* (Routledge and Kegan Paul, 1984), p. 9.
17 *Oxford House Annual Report*, 1889, p. 1.
18 *The Oxford House Chronicle*, vol. VIII, no. 8, 1894, p. 3.
19 Ibid., vol. IX, no. 1, January 1895.
20 *The Oxford House Chronicle*, vol. VIII, no. 1, January 1894 p. 1.
21 Ibid., p. 2.
22 Ibid., p. 3.
23 Ibid., vol. VIII, no. 4, April 1894, p. 4.
24 Bradley, I., *Oxford House in Bethnal Green 1884–1984* (London, Robert Stockwell Ltd, 1984), p. 3.
25 Coulton, P., *Life of the Bishop of London* (London, Skeffington & Son Ltd. 1936), p. 22.
26 Adderley, J., *In Slums and Society Reminiscences of Old Friends* (London, T. Fisher Unwin Ltd, 1916), p. 61.
27 Ashworth, M., op. cit., p. 9.
28 Ibid., p. 4.
29 Ibid, p. 4.
30 Mace, J.H.B., *Henry Bodley Bromby* (Longmans, Green, and Co., 1913), p. 100.
31 Ibid., p. 102.
32 Ibid., p. 106.
33 Ibid., p. 11.
34 *Oxford House Annual Report*, 1890, p. 8.
35 Ibid., 1892, p. 33.
36 Ibid., 1890, p. 8.
37 Ibid., 1891, p. 4.
38 Ibid., p. 5.
39 Ibid., p. 8.
40 Ibid., p. 9.
41 Ibid., p. 10.
42 Ibid., pp. 10–11.
43 *The Oxford House Chronicle*, vol. VIII, no. 2, February 1894.
44 Ibid., p. 10.
45 *Oxford House Annual Report*, 1897, p. 10.
46 Ibid., p. 10.

47 Ibid., p. 9.
48 Winnington-Ingam, A.F., *Fifty Years*, p. 8.
49 Colson, P., op. cit., p. 32.
50 Ibid., p. 9.
51 Ibid., p. 11.
52 *Oxford House Annual Report*, 1886, p. 22.
53 Ibid., p. 34.
54 Ibid., p. 34.
55 *Oxford House Chronicle*, vol. IX, no. 8, August 1895.
56 Winnington-Ingram, A.F., op. cit., p. 14.
57 *Oxford House Annual Report*, 1897, p. 41.
58 Colson, P., op. cit., p. 39.
59 Oxford House Annual Report, 1898, p. 9.
60 Bernard Wilson (b. 1876), Keble College 1876–1880, BA 1880 and MA 1885.
61 *Oxford House Annual Report*, 1897, p. 12.
62 Ibid., 1899, p. 49.
63 *Oxford House Annual Report*, p. 11.
64 *Oxford House Annual Report*, 1889, p. 28.
65 Ibid., 1889, p. 28.
66 Ibid., p. 5.
67 *Oxford House* Annual Report, 1886, p. 5.
68 Ibid., p. 13.
69 Winnington-Ingram, A.F., *Fifty Years Work in London 1889–1939* (Longmans, Green and Co., 1940), p. 6.
70 Ibid., p. 12.
71 *Oxford House Annual Report*, 1888, p. 25.
72 Ibid., p. 5.
73 *Oxford House Annual Report*, 1886, p. 5.
74 Ibid., 1895, p. 12.
75 Ibid., p. 15
76 Ibid, p. 15.
77 Harold Hodge (b. 1862) Pembroke College 1881–5, BA 1886 and MA 1888.
78 Ibid., 1887, p. 22.
79 Ibid., 1887, 23.
80 *Oxford House Chronicle*, vol. VIII, No, 2, February 1894, p. 3.
81 Ibid., vol. VIII, no. 3, 1894.
82 *The Guardian*, 12 June 1895.
83 *Oxford House Annual Report*, 1887, p. 19.
84 Ibid., p. 29.
85 For a detailed account of the Oxford House Co-operative see *Oxford House Annual Report*, 1889, p. 23.
86 Ibid., 1891, p. 22.
87 *Oxford House Annual Report*, 1891, p. 22.
88 See *Oxford House Annual Report*, 1889, p. 25.
89 Ibid., p. 25.
90 Ibid., p. 10.
91 Colson, P., op. cit., p. 27.
92 Ibid., p. 79.

93 Ibid., p. 78.
94 *Oxford House Annual Report*, 1895 p. 10.
95 *The East End News*, 18 July 1890.
96 Evans, J., *The Parish of St Frideswide of Oxford Poplar Our First Fifty Years 1881–1931* (no publisher, 1931), p. 11.
97 Clarke, C.P.S., *Poplar* (Unpublished Manuscript, Christ Church Archives), p. 1. See also Lang, C., *Tupper Carey* (London, Constable & Co., undated), p. 13.
98 Lang, C., op. cit., p. 12.
99 Henry Luke Paget was the son of Sir James Paget, Bt., Serjeant-Surgeon to Queen Victoria. A younger brother, the Revd Francis Paget was senior student at Christ Church and later Bishop of Oxford.
100 Evans, J. (editor), *The Parish of St Frideswide of Oxford Poplar Our First Fifty Years 1881–1931* (no publisher, 1931), p. 3.
101 Ibid., p. 3.
102 Adderley, J., op. cit., p. 69.
103 Ibid., p. 5.
104 Lord Victor Seymour was later Vicar of St Stephen's Gloucester for many years.
105 Ibid., p. 6.
106 Ibid., p. 14.
107 Ibid., p. 16.
108 Ibid., p. 14.
109 Legge, H., *Trinity College Mission in Stratford 1888–1899* (Trinity College Archives, undated) p. 11.
110 *Trinity College Oxford Mission Report 1897–1898*, p. 5.
111 Ibid., p. 5.
112 Ibid., p. 11.
113 Ibid., p. 11.
114 Darell Tupper-Carey was at Christ Church 1884–7.
115 Clarke, C.P.S., op. cit., p. 5.
116 Ibid., p. 5.
117 Ibid., p. 5.
118 Ibid., pp. 5–6.
119 Ibid., p. 6.
120 Charles Philip Stewart Clarke (b. 1872).
121 Ibid., p. 12.
122 *Church Review*, 22 January 1891.
123 *Letter from H.G. Woods, President of Trinity*, December 1887 (Trinity College Mission Archives).
124 Revd C.H.Baumgarten (b. 1862) was at Merton 1880–4.
125 Ibid.
126 *Trinity College Mission Report*, 1897–8, p. 3.
127 Ibid., 1889–99, p. 6.
128 For details of the building see *The Builder*, 25 February 1893.
129 Lang, C., op. cit., p. 13.
130 *The East End News*, 18 July 1890.
131 For a full description of the opening of St Frideswide Mission House, see *East End News*, 17 February 1893.

132 William Alexander Carroll graduated BA (third class theol.) 1885, MA 1894, deacon 1886, priest 1887, curate of Holy Trinity Dalston 1886–91, Secretary of the Church of England White Cross League 1891–3 and Christ Church Missioner 1893–8, Vicar of Bickley 1898–1922, Hon. Canon of Rochester 1916.

133 *East End News*, 7 March 1893.

134 Clarke, C.P.S., op. cit., p. 3.

135 *The Oxford House Chronicle*, vol. VII, no. 2, February 1893.

136 Legge, H., op. cit., p. 13.

137 Baumgarten,C., *Letter to the President of Trinity* 24 July,1890 (Trinity Mission Archives, folder 9). Baumgarten later went out to work in the parish of St Mary, Johannesberg. See Foster, J., *Oxford Men and Their Colleges 1880–1892* (James Parker & Co., 1893), p. 39.

138 *Trinity College Mission Brochure*, December 1887.

139 Letter from G. Williams to the President of Trinity, 23 September 1891, Trinity College Mission Papers, folder 9.

140 *Trinity College Oxford Mission Report*, 1889–1900, p. 6.

141 Clarke, C.P.S., op. cit., p. 4.

142 Lang, C., op. cit., p. 15.

143 Ibid., p. 15.

144 *Trinity College Oxford Mission Report*, 1899–1900, p. 5.

145 Letter from Stevens to President Woods, 12 February 1894, Trinity Mission Papers, folder 9.

146 *The Oxford House Chronicle*, July 1893, vol. VII, no. 7, p. 8.

Chapter 4: Cambridge South of the Thames

1 A settlement was established by Queen's College in Peckham in October 1901 but this falls just outside the age of Victoria.

2 *The Eagle*, vol. XII, 1883, p. 380.

3 Ibid., p. 380.

4 Ibid, p. 380.

5 Ibid., vol. XIII, May 1884, p. 82.

6 Ibid., vol. XIV, December 1885, p. 62.

7 Ibid., p. 62.

8 Ibid., vol. XIV, March 1886.

9 See a report of the Trinity College Mission in *The Cambridge Review*, 10 May 1885.

10 The Revd Charles Henry Grundy, St Edmund Hall BA 1867, MA 1871, was organising Secretary for the Rochester Diocesan Society 1878–83, Wilberforce Missionary 1883–7, Vicar of St Peter's Greenwich from 1887 and Rural Dean of Greenwich from 1895.

11 Ibid., 10 May 1885.

12 *Daily News*, 25 April 1890.

13 Anon., *Pembroke College Mission* (Printed Pamphlet), p. 7.

14 Amos, A., and Hough, W.W., *The Cambridge Mission to South London A Twenty Years' Survey* (Cambridge, Mac Millan and Bowes, 1904), p. 83.

15 Ibid., p. 84.

16 *Caius House Battersea Report of London Committee*, 1889 (Gonville and Caius Mission Papers).

17 *Circular Mission Letter*, August 1888.

18 Amos, A., and Hough, W.W., op. cit., p. 121.

19 Ibid., p. 122.

20 Frank Francis (1862–1929), assistant missioner.

21 *The Eagle*, vol. XV, December 1887, p. 64.

22 *Clare College Annual Mission Report*, 1885, p. 5.

23 *Trinity College Mission Annual Mission in St George's Camberwell*, South London (printed pamphlet, 1888), p. 1.

24 'The Trinity Mission', *Cambridge Review*, 10 May 1885.

25 Ibid., 10 May 1885.

26 Anon., *Pembroke College Mission*, p. 12.

27 Revd Charles Andrews (b. 1871). Missioner in Newington 1896–9. Later joined the Cambridge University Mission and worked in Delhi.

28 Andrews, C.F., *What I Owe to Christ* (London, Hodder and Stoughton, 1933), p. 68.

29 Ibid., p. 65.

30 Ibid., p. 65.

31 Ibid., p. 65.

32 Amos, H., and Hough, W.W., op. cit., p. 84.

33 Ibid., p. 94.

34 *Gonville and Caius College Mission and Settlement at Battersea, S.W.* (printed pamphlet, 1888).

35 *The Trinian*, June 1891, p. 24.

36 *The Eagle*, vol. XVI, 1889, p. 101.

37 Ibid., p. 101.

38 *Clare College Annual Mission Report*, 1887, p. 2.

39 Rules for the Clare Mission in *Clare College Mission 4th Annual Report*, 1888, p. 2.

40 *Clare College Mission 10th Annual Report*, 1884, p. 9.

41 Ibid., p. 6.

42 *Trinity College Mission Minute Book*, Minutes 23 January 1886, section 3(b).

43 Ibid., section 4.

44 John Tetley Rowe (b. 1860), Curate of St George's Trinity College Mission 1886–95. He later became a Residentiary Canon at Rochester Cathedral.

45 Ibid., Executive Committee Minutes, 31 January 1888.

46 Amos, A., and Hough, W.W., *The Cambridge Mission*, p. 121.

47 Ibid., p. 125.

48 Anon., *Pembroke College Mission*, p. 9.

49 Ibid., p. 9.

50 *Pembroke College Mission Third Annual Report*, 1888–9, p. 20.

51 *Corpus Christi College (Cambridge) Mission*, Corpus Mission Papers, Box 3, Ms OA5B.

52 *Gonville and Caius Mission and Settlement Annual report October 1895–September 1896*.

53 *The Caian*, vol. 3, no. 1, 1893.

54 Ibid., vol. 10, no. 3, 1901.

55 *The Eagle*, vol. XX, 1899, p. 618.

56 Ibid., vol. XIV, December 1887.

57 The Revd Frank H. Francis was Assistant Missionary at St John's Mission 1889–94.

58 Ibid.,vol. XX, 1899, p. 255.

59 Ibid., vol. XX, 1899, p. 255.

60 Ibid., vol. XX, 1899, p. 618.

61 *Clare College Mission 1st Annual Report*, 1885, p. 5.

62 Ibid., *2nd Annual Report*, 1886, p. 3.

63 *Minute Book of the Clare College Mission*, Minute 6 November 1886, Ms CCAD/5/1/2/2/1

64 *Clare College Mission 5th Annual Report 1889*, p. 4.

65 Ibid., *10th Annual Report, 1893*, p. 10.

66 Ibid., *10th Annual Report 1894*, p. 9.

67 Ibid., *12th Annual Report*, 1896, p. 9.

68 Ibid., *14th Annual Report*, 1898, p. 3.

69 Ibid., *11th Annual Report*, 1895, p. 9.

70 Ibid., *12th Annual Report*, 1896, p. 4.

71 *Trinity College Mission Minute Book*, Minutes 23 January 1886.

72 Ibid., 23 January 1886.

73 Ibid., General Committee Minutes, 11 November 1886.

74 Ibid., Executive Committee Minutes, 31 January 1888.

75 Copy of a letter from Sister Clara Maria to J. Tetley Rowe dated 22 January 1888 and attached to ibid., Executive Minutes 31 January 1888.

76 Letter from Norman Campbell to the Mater of Trinity, 18 April 1894, Ms 103/32 Trinity College Mission Archives.

77 Letter from J Tetley Rowe to Parry, 26 October 1895, Ms 103/32, Trinity College Mission Archives.

78 James, E., 'Trinity in Camberwell', *Trinity Review*, Michaelmas, 1959, pp. 26–7.

79 *Trinity College Mission Minute Book*, General Committee minutes 3 June,1890.

80 Revd M.C. Sturges (1859–1939) was Pembroke Missioner from 1886–90.

81 An account of the Pembroke Mission attached *Pembroke Mission Annual Report*, 1896.

82 Anon., *Pembroke College Mission*, p. 11.

83 Ibid., p. 13.

84 *Pembroke College Mission Second Annual Report*, 1887–8, p. 6.

85 Charles Freer Andrews (b. 1871) was Vice-Principal of Westcott House 1899–1902 and with the Cambridge University Mission I Delhi 1904–15.

86 Andrews, C.F., *What I Owe to Christ* (London, Hodder and Stoughton, 1933).

87 Ibid., p. 40.

88 Ibid., p. 66.

89 Ibid., p. 67.

90 Ibid., p. 70.

91 Ibid., p. 73.

92 Hough was 'Curate of Corpus Christi Mission' 1887–1900. He later became Archdeacon of Kingston-on-Thames 1916–19 and Bishop Suffragan of Woolwich 1918–19.

93 Amos, A., and Hough, W.W., op. cit., p. 85.
94 *The Benedict*, no. 3, 1898.
95 *The Benedict*, no. 1, 1898.
96 He later became Rector of Lavenham.
97 The Revd Arthur Shillito (1873–1947) was Warden of Caius Mission 1899–1905.
98 *The Caian*, vol. 9, no. 2, 1899
99 *The Caian*, vol. 7, no. 2, 1897.
100 Ibid., vol. 10, no. 3, 1901, p. 97.
101 *The Caian*, vol. 3, no. 2,1893 p. 134.
102 Ibid., p. 135.
103 *The Eagle*, vol. XIII, May 1884, p. 85.
104 *Clare College Mission 8th Annual Report*, 1892, p. 10.
105 *Clare College Mission 13th Annual Report*, 1897, p. 7.
106 *Clare College Mission 3rd Annual Report*, 1887, p. 7.
107 *The Caian*, vol. 1, 1892, p. 71.
108 *The Eagle*, vol. XIV, March 1886, p. 136.
109 Ibid., vol. XIV, 1887, p. 338.
110 Ibid., vol. XY, March 1888, p. 133.
111 *Pembroke College Mission First Annual Report*, 1886–7, p. 6.
112 Ibid., Second Annual Report, 1887–8, p. 9.
113 Ibid., p. 11.
114 Amos, A., and Hough, W.W., op. cit., p. 94.
115 *Trinity College Mission Minute Book*, Executive Committee Minutes, 20 January 1887.
116 *Clare College Mission Parish Magazine*, no. 16, October 1887, Ms CCAD/5/1/2/3/3.
117 *The Caian*, vol. 10, no. 1, 1900.
118 *The Trinian,* June 1891, p. 352.
119 Ibid., p. 352.
120 James, E., 'Trinity in Camberwell', *Trinity Review,* Michaelmas, 1959, p. 27.
121 Ibid., p. 27.
122 *Clare College Mission 8th Annual Report,* 1892, p. 10.
123 Amos, A., and Hough,W.W., op. cit., p13.
124 Amos, A., and Hough, W.W., op. cit., p. 94.
125 Andrews, C.F., op. cit., p. 67.
126 *The Caian*, vol. 9, no. 1, 1899, p. 96.
127 *The Eagle*, vol. XIII, December 1884, pp. 243–4.
128 Ibid., vol. XIV, March 1886, p. 134.
129 *Trinity College Mission Minute Book*, Executive Minutes 16 November 1886.
130 *The Cambridge Review*, 2 February 1887.
131 Thorold, A., *The Church Congress*, 1886 attached to *Pembroke College Mission Report* 1886–7.
132 James, E., 'Trinity at Camberwell', *Trinity Review*, Michaelmas 1959, p. 26.
133 *Trinity College Mission Appeal Document*, 1888, p. 4.
134 Ibid., p. 85.
135 *Clare College Mission 2nd Annual Report*, 1886, p. 4.
136 Ibid., *4th Annual Report*, 1888, p. 4.

137 *The Eagle*, vol. XII, 1883, p. 380.

138 Ibid., vol. XIV, December 1885, pp. 66–7.

139 Ibid., vol. XV, December 1887,p. 416.

140 *Pembroke College Mission First Annual Report*, 1886–7.

141 *Pembroke College Mission third Annual Report*, 1888–9, p. 19.

142 Ibid., *Fifth Annual Report*, 1890, p. 27.

143 *The Eagle*, vol. XIV, December 1885, pp. 66–7.

144 *Clare College Mission 9th Annual Report*, 1893 p. 10.

145 Ibid., *14th Annual Report*, 1898, p. 7.

146 Ibid., *16th Annual Report*, 1900, p. 7.

Chapter 5: Public School Missions

1 See Newsome, D., *Godliness and Good Learning: Four Studies on a Victorian Ideal* (John Murray, 1961), Vance, N., 'The Ideal of Manliness', in Simon, B. and Bradley, I., *The Victorian Public School: Studies in the Development of an Educational Institution* (Gill and MacMillan, 1971), Tozer, M., *Physical Education at Thring's Uppingham* (Uppingham School, 1976).

2 Hughes, T., *Tom Brown's School Days* (Wordsworth Classics, 1993) chapter 3, p. 57.

3 Ibid., preface, p. xvi.

4 Mack, E.C., *Public Schools and British Opinion Since 1800: The Relationship between Ideas and Evolution of an English Instituion* (Columbia University Press, 1941), p. 130.

5 Blackie, J., *Bradfield 1850–1915* (The Warden and Council of St Andrew's College Bradfield, 1976), p. 96.

6 Kerrigan, C., '"Thoroughly good football": teachers and the origins of elementary school football', *History of Education*, 2000, vol. 29, no. 6, p. 521.

7 Evors, C.A., *The Story of Highgate School* (London, Forbes Robertson Ltd, 1938), p. 23. The Revd Arthur Edmund Allcock (d. 1925) was Headmaster of Highgate from 1893–1908.

8 Kingsley and others of his circle had spent time in Bermondsey during the cholera epidemic of 1848 instructing the poor on the importance of pure water. Kingsley had also publicised the evils of sweated labour in his celebrated tract, *Cheap Clothes and Nasty* as well as in his best known novel, *Alton Locke*.

9 Graham, E., *The Harrow Life of Henry Montagu Butler, D.D.* (Longmans, Green and Co., 1920), pp. 251–2.

10 *The Marlburian*, November 1881, p. 180.

11 Ibid., March 1882, p. 52.

12 Ibid., December 1884, p. 198.

13 Ibid., 1886, p. 59.

14 *The Tonbridgian*, June 1883, p. 605.

15 Fletcher, C.R.L., *Edmond Warre* (John Murray, 1922), p. 137.

16 David Livingstone (1813–75) made many journeys into the interior of Africa, commanded the expedition to explore eastern and Central Africa in 1858 and discovered the source of the Nile in 1872.

17 Parkin, G., Edward Thring Life, Diary and Letter (London, MacMillan and Co. Limited, 1898), vol. 1, pp. 310–11.

18 Edward Tufnell was Bishop of Brisbane 1859–75.

19 See 'Uppingham School Mission Work', *Uppingham School Mission*, 1872, p. 268.

20 Ibid., p. 310.

21 Ibid., p. 312.

22 'School Missions', *The Elizabethan*, 1885, vol. IV, no. 21, pp. 213–14.

23 *The Bradfield College Chronicle*, vol. VI, no. 1, March 1896, p. 8.

24 Ibid., vol. V, no. 14, December 1893.

25 Hinde, T., *Highgate School: A History* (London, James and James, 1993), p. 210.

26 Ibid., p. 210.

27 *The Wellingtonian*, December 1884, p. 261.

28 Ibid., December 1884, p. 261

29 Ibid., March 1885, p. 18.

30 *The Carthusian*, December 1881.

31 The Revd Dr J Merriman (1835–1905) MA, BD, DD, of St John's College, Cambridge, was the first Headmaster of Cranleigh 1865–91 and Rector of Freshwater, Isle of Wight 1891–1905.

32 The Revd Peter Green (b. 1871) was curate of Lady Margaret Chapel, Walworth 1894–8.

33 *Letter from Herbert Sutton to Rev Dr J Merriman*, 24 September 1894, Cranleigh School Mission Papers.

34 Letter from Herbert Sutton to W. Gardener Esq., 1 October 1894, Cranleigh School Mission Papers.

35 Graham, E.C., *The Harrow Life*, pp. 253–4.

36 *The Marlburian*, October 1880, p. 158.

37 Ibid., p. 158.

38 Ibid., December 1880, p. 205.

39 Ibid., March 1882, p. 51. F.W. Farrar was Canon of Westminster (1876–95) and Dean of Canterbury (1895–1903).

40 Ibid., p. 52.

41 Ibid., February 1884, p. 29.

42 See Simpkinson, C.H., *The Life and Work of Bishop Thorold Rochester 1877–91, Winchester 1891–95* (London, Isbister & Company Ltd, 1896), p. 107.

43 Ibid., p. 155.

44 *Eton College Chronicle*, no. 312, May 1880.

45 *Minute Book of the Eton College Mission 1880–1895*, Minutes 23 June 1880.

46 *Eton College Chronicle*, no. 341, 3 February 1882, p. 1365.

47 Ibid., 3 Febraury, 1882, p. 1366.

48 *The Malvernian*, June 1894, p. 239.

49 *The Marlburian*, February 1881, p. 15.

50 Ibid., p. 15.

51 Ibid., vol. XIX, no. 317, 20 December 1884, p. 197.

52 Ibid., 20 December 1884, p. 198.

53 Ibid., 20 December 1884, p. 199.

54 Corke, S., *Charterhouse in Southwark 1884–2000* (Charterhouse, Charterhouse Press, 2001), p. 9.

55 Simpkinson, C.H., *The Life and Work of Bishop Thorold* (Isbister and Company Ltd, 1896), pp. 318–19.

56 *The Cheltonian*, 1890, p. 56.
57 *The Malvernian*, December 1894, p. 508.
58 See Cooper, A.B., *Public School Missions*, chapter 11, Haileybury College Mission, p. 614.
59 The Revd Gresham Francis Gillet (1867–1940) was Priest in Charge of Malvern College Mission 1894–1904. He later went out as a missionary to East Africa 1904–17 and was Archdeacon of Inhambane.
60 Watherston, P., *A Different Kind of Church* (London, Marshall Pickering, 1994), citing the Old Malvernian, 1898, p. 27.
61 Hinde, T., *Highgate School: A History* (London, James and James, 1993), pp. 77–8.
62 *Printed Circular from H. Montagu Butler to Old Harrovians*, 31 May 1881, Harrow Mission Archives Ms HAS/ 11C/1877–85.
63 *Harrow Notes*, 24 Febraury 1883.
64 Trotter, H.S.S., *Harrow Mission A Story of Fifty Years 1883–1933* (published as a supplement to the Harrovian, 1933), p. 5.
65 *The Marlburian*, December 1888, p. 204.
66 *The Wellingtonian*, December 1884, p. 261.
67 Ibid., April 1885, p. 43.
68 Ibid., July 1887, p. 102.
69 *The Cheltonian*, 1890, p. 56.
70 Ibid., pp. 108–9.
71 See, for example, *Oxford House Annual Report*, 1895, p. 10.
72 Ibid., p. 12.
73 *The Wykehamist*, no. 106, February 1877, p. 46.
74 Corke, S., op. cit., p. 9.
75 *Charterhouse Mission Annual Report*, 1884, p. 5.
76 Ibid., 1886, p. 12.
77 Booth, C., *Life and Labour of the London Poor*, cited in Notes on Dulwich College Mission, Dulwich College Mission Papers.
78 Whetlor, S., *The Story of Notting Dale From Potteries and Piggeries to Present Times* (Kensington and Chelsea History Group, 1998), p. 9.
79 *Harrow Notes*, 24 February 1883, p. 10.
80 *The Harrowvian*, 22 September 1967.
81 Anon., *Harrow in London* (London, 1909), p. 2.
82 Anon., *Harrow Mission*, p. 11.
83 *The Cholmeleian*, July 1990, p. 209.
84 *The Malvernian*, October 1884, p. 484.
85 Ibid., p. 485.
86 *The Marlburian* November 1881, p. 164.
87 Ibid., July 1881, p. 121.
88 The Revd Herbert Lucas was Wellington Missioner 1885–7.
89 *The Wellingtonian*, February 1886, p. 162.
90 *The Tonbridgian*, June 1883, p. 605.
91 *Cheltenham College Mission Committee Report and History of the Mission at Nunhead, S.E. from 1890* (no publisher, undated), p. 4.
92 *Harrow Notes*, 3 March 1885,p. 14.
93 Ibid., p. 14.

94 During Thring's first decade at Uppingham the number of boys attending rose from 25 (a number cited by Thring but denied by supporters of his predecessor, Dr Holden) to about 300. See Leinster-Mackay, D., *The Educational World of Edward Thring* (Falmer Press, 1987). Venn, J.A., in *Alumni Cantabrigienses* (Cambridge, CUP,1954), p. 183: 'He raised it to a foremost position among public schools with 30 masters and 11 boarding houses'.

95 *Uppingham School Magazine*, 1869, p. 238.

96 Parkin, G.R., *Life of Edward Thring*, vol. 1, p. 312.

97 See, for example, Trotter, H.S.S., *Harrow Mission*, p. 4.

98 Ibid., vol. 1, p. 313.

99 Ibid., vol. 1. pp. 313–14. For a full account, see also *St Mark's Victoria Docks Parish Magazine*, October 1872, no CVL (Uppingham Archives) and *The Uppingham School Magazine*,1872, pp. 274–9.

100 Ibid., vol. 1, p. 314.

101 Ibid., vol. 1, p. 316.

102 For Linklater see Marr, P., *Robert Linklater SSC: A Life- with Memories of Father Lowder* (published by the Anglo-Catholic History Society).

103 *The Wykehamist*, no. 90, December 1875, p. 6. See also Sabben-Clare, J., *Winchester College* (Winchester, P. and G. Wells, 1988), pp. 164–5.

104 George Ridding became Bishop of Southwell in 1884 and died in 1904.

105 *The Wykehamist*, no. 147, October 1880, p. 380.

106 *The Alleynian*, vol. L, October 1922, p. 246.

107 The Revd George C. Allen (1855–1921) was assistant master at Dulwich 1881–92.

108 *Dulwich College Mission Visitors' Book 1888–1921*, Dulwich College Mission Archives.

109 *The Alleynian*, vol. L, October 1922, p. 249.

110 Fletcher, C.R.L., *Edmond Warre* (John Murray, 1922), pp. 136–7.

111 Ibid., p. 87.

112 Graham, E., *The Harrow Life of Henry Montagu Butler D.D.* (London, Longmans, Green, and Co., 1920), pp. 253–4.

113 Trotter, H.S.S., op. cit., p. 5.

114 Graham, E., op. cit., pp. 254–5.

115 Ibid., pp. 255–6.

116 Trotter, H.S.S., op. cit., p. 3. James Edward Cowell Welldon (1854–1937) was successively Headmaster of Dulwich 1883–5 and Harrow 1885–98, Bishop of Calcutta 1898–1902, Dean of Manchester 1906–18 and Dean of Durham 1918–33.

117 Hinde, T., op. cit., p. 211.

118 *The Cholmeleian*, July 1897, p. 308.

119 *The Malvernian*, October 1894.

120 *The Marlburian*, February 1884, p. 27.

121 Ibid., April 1887, p. 68.

122 *The Radleian*, May 1881, p. 469.

123 Ibid., June 1899, p. 20.

124 Orchard, B., *A Look at the Head and the Fifty A History of Tonbridge School* (Tonbridge), p. 46. See also *The Tonbridgian*, October 1883, p. 659.

125 Blackie, J., *Bradfield 1850–1915* (Bradfield, The Warden and Council of St Andrew's College Bradfield, 1976), p. 96

126 See Consecration of the Marlborough College Mission Church at Tottenham in *The Marlburian*, April 1887, p. 66.

127 Sabben-Clare, J., Winchester College, pp. 164–5.

128 *The Wykehamist*, no. 147, October, p. 380.

129 *Eton College Chronicle*, no. 312, 20 May 1880.

130 *The Marlburian*, February 1881, p. 15.

131 Ibid., March 1882, p. 51.

132 *Printed Circular Old Harrovians* from H. Montagu Butler to 31 May 1883.

133 Graham, E., *The Harrow Life of Henry Montagu Butler*, p. 255.

134 *Harrow Notes*, 25 July 1885, p. 97.

135 *The Wellingtonian*, November 1884, p. 244.

136 Ibid., February 1885, p. 10.

137 *The Bradfield College Chronicle*, vol. V, no. 14, December 1893.

138 Cranleigh School Magazine, June 1894, p. 68.

139 Letter from Herbert Sutton to Dr J Merriman, 28 September 1894, Cranleigh School Mission Archives.

140 *The Alleynian*, May 1891, pp. 91–2.

141 Hinde, T., op. cit., p. 77.

142 *The Malvernian*, June 1894, p. 443.

143 *The Radleian*, 12 October 1900, p. 129.

144 *The Wykehamist*, February 1879, p. 230.

145 *Charterhouse Mission Annual Report*, 1884, p. 4.

146 See *Cranleigh School Magazine*, June 1894, p. 68 and April 1895, p. 121.

147 Parkin, G., *Edward Thring*, vol. 1, p. 313.

148 Ibid., vol. 1, p. 313.

149 Card, T., *Eton Renewed* (John Murray, 1994), p. 78.

150 *Circular to Old Harrovians*, May 1883, Ms HSA/11C/1877–85.

151 *Harrow Notes*, 24 February, 1883.

152 Graham, E., *The Harrow Life of Henry Montagu Butler*, pp. 253–5.

153 Revd Arthur Gordon (1858–1912), missioner 1890–2.

154 Trotter, H.S.S., op. cit., p. 10.

155 Ibid., p. 11.

156 Ibid., p. 11.

157 *The Cholmeleian*, July 1897, p. 307.

158 *The Marlburian*, February 1881, p. 15.

159 Ibid., p. 15.

160 Ibid., March 1882.

161 Ibid., March 1882

162 Ibid., March 1882.

163 *The Wellingtonian*, vol. IX, no. 11, February 1886, p. 161.

164 *The Wellingtonian*, February 1896, p. 128.

165 *The Cholmeleian*, April 1899, p. 225.

166 Parkin, G.R., *Edward Thring*, vol. 1, p. 315.

167 *The Wykehamist*, no. 141, February 1880.

168 *The Marlburian*, March 1882.

169 Ibid., March 1883.

170   Ibid., February 1885, p. 21.
171   Ibid., 1885, p. 21.
172   See obituary Edward Floyer Noel Smith (1850–1908), Marlborough College 1863–8, Marlborough Missioner 1882–1908, *The Marlburian*, vol. XLIII, no. 651, 2 April 1908.
173   Evors, C.A., *The Story of Highgate School*, p. 78.
174   Ibid., p. 78.
175   See *The Hollington Club for Young People*, Dulwich College Mission Papers.
176   The Revd St Clair Donaldson (1863–1935) was later Bishop of Brisbane, Australia 1904–5 and Archbishop of Queensland 1905–21 and Bishop of Salisbury 1921–35.
177   *Minute Book of Eton Mission*, 1896, Minutes 8 May 1896, Ms Misc / Miss/ 1/3.
178   *The Malvernian*, December 1894, p. 508.
179   *The Radleian*, 7 June 1899.
180   *The Eagle*, vol. XIV, December 1885, p. 65.
181   *The Wellingtonian*, July 1888, p. 229.
182   *The Carthusian*, October 1886.
183   *Charterhouse Mission Annual Report*, 1894, p. 7.
184   *The Blue*, April 1893, pp. 50–3.
185   Stogden, E., *Harrow in London* (Harrow Mission, 1909), pp. 3–5.
186   *The Cholmeleian*, July 1900, pp. 209–10.
187   *The Malvernian*, March 1895, p. 526.
188   *The Marlburian*, December 1884, p. 200.
189   *The Wellington Year Book*, 1891, p. 31.
190   *Charterhouse Mission Annual Report*, 1894, p. 8.
191   Ibid.,1886, p. 7.
192   *Cheltenham College Mission Committee Report and History of the Mission at Nunhead, S.E.* (no publisher, undated), p. 4.
193   Ibid., p. 7.
194   *Minute Book of Eton Mission*, Minutes 19 March 1899.
195   Stogdon, E., *Harrow in London*, p. 2.
196   See for example, Kerrigan, C., '"Thoroughly good football": teachers and the origins of elementary school football', *History of Education*, 2000, vol. 29, no. 6, pp. 520–3.
197   Ibid., p. 520.
198   *The Marlburian*, March 1883.

Chapter 6: Nonconformist Settlements

1   A copy of *The Bitter Cry* had been sent to Cardinal Manning while he was in Rome and he had been deeply impressed by it.
2   Turbefield, A., *John Scott Lidgett Archbishop of Methodism?* (Epworth, 2003), p. 31.
3   Ibid., p. 31.
4   Ibid., p. 31.
5   Davis, R., *John Scott Lidgett* (London, Epworth, 1957), p. 46.
6   Ibid., p. 48.
7   Lidgett, J.S, op. cit., p. 63.
8   *Report of the Bermondsey Settlement*, 1891, p. 7.

9 Ibid., p. 8. See also *Wesleyan Methodist Magazine*, 1900, p. 760.
10 Ibid., p. 51.
11 *Primitive Methodist Magazine*, 1894, p. 290.
12 *The Methodist Times*, 19 June 1890.
13 Ibid., 19 June 1890.
14 *Pall Mall Gazette*, 9 December 1891.
15 Ibid., 9 December 1891.
16 Lidgett, J.S., *My Guided Life* (London, Methuen, 1936), p. 118.
17 *Report of the Bermondsey Settlement*, 1892, p. 9.
18 *Wesleyan Methodist Magazine*, 1890, p. 338.
19 Ibid., 1891, p. 34.
20 Ibid., 1891, p. 34.
21 *Report of the Bermondsey Settlement*, 1891, p6.
22 *Daily News*, 13 November 1891.
23 See Tuberfield, A., op. cit., p. 38.
24 *Report of the Bermondsey Settlement*, 1891, p. 12.
25 Ibid., 1891, p. 6.
26 See Lidgett, J.S., *My Guided Life* (1936), p. 59.
27 *Report of the Bermondsey Settlement*, 1892, p. 10.
28 Ibid., 1897, p. 7.
29 *Pall Mall Gazette*, 9 December 1891.
30 *Report of the Bermondsey Settlement*, 1892, p. 12.
31 Ibid., p. 14.
32 Cox., J., *The English Church in A secular Society 1870–1930* (Oxford, University Press, 1982), p. 169.
33 Davies, R., op. cit., p. 60.
34 *Report of the Bermondsey Settlement*, September 1897, pp. 16–17.
35 Ibid., September 1895, p. 17.
36 Ibid., p. 17.
37 Ibid., September 1899, p. 10.
38 *Daily News*, 13 January 1891.
39 *Report of the Bermondsey Settlement*, September 1900, p. 17.
40 See for example, Cox, J., *The English Churches in a Secular Society: Lambeth 1870–1930* (Oxford, OUP., 1982), p. 170 and Davies, R., (editor) *John Scott Lidgett*, p. 64.
41 Alden, P., in Reason, W. (editor), *University and Social Settlements*, p. 39.
42 *Report of the Bermondsey Settlement*, September 1892, p. 18 and September 1893, p. 21f.
43 Ibid., September 1893, p. 9.
44 Ibid., September 1892, p. 17.
45 Scott Lidget, J., 'Settlements and Poor Law', in Reason, W., *University and Social Settlements*, p. 68.
46 Ibid., p. 70.
47 Ibid., September 1892, p. 11.
48 Ibid., September 1893, p. 9.
49 Ibid., September 1893 p. 21.
50 *Wesleyan Methodist Magazine*, 1891, p. 34.

51   Ibid., 1900, p. 575. See also *Report of the Bermondsey Settlement*, September 1899, p. 43.

52   Ibid., September 1899, p. 43.

53   *Report of the Bermondsey Settlement*, September 1892, p. 9.

54   See *Bermondsey Settlement Minute Book*, Minutes, March 1896: 'Resolved that the meeting gives its hearty support to the principles of the Sunday Closing Bill to be read a second time in the House of Commons on May 6th and requests the chairman to forward the resolution to the member of the Borough'. (Borough Road Local Studies Library).

55   *Report of the Bermondsey Settlement*, September 1893, p. 12.

56   Ibid., September 1894, p. 8.

57   Ibid., September 1900, p. 7.

58   Ibid, September 1898, p. 11.

59   Ibid., September 1901, p. 11.

60   Ibid., September 1901, p. 11.

61   When Hugh Price Hughes died Lidgett took on his editorial chair of *The Methodist Times*. Lidgett also edited *Contemporary Review* with Sir Percy Bunting and G.P. Gooch. See, for example, Davies, R., *John Scott Lidgett*, p. 65

62   Ibid., September,1893, pp. 9–11.

63   *Mansfield House Magazine*, vol. III, no. 1, January 1896, p. 5.

64   *Report of the Council of Mansfield College*, 1890–1, pp. 8–9.

65   See *Minute Book of the Executive Committee of Mansfield House*, Canning Town, Stratford Library.

66   See Smith, L., *Religion and the Rise of Labour*, p. 65.

67   *Mansfield College Report*, 1890–1, p. 9.

68   Alden, P., in *The Christian Commonwealth*, 29 March 1894.

69   *Mansfield House Magazine*, 1884, p. 49.

70   Anon., *A Record and an Appeal for Mansfield House University Settlement* (London, Mansfield House University Settlement, 1925), p. 26.

71   See *Mansfield College Magazine*, 14 June 1899, p. 92 in which Alden quotes from F.D. Maurice.

72   Anon., *Life at Mansfield House by Residents* (London, Hazell, Watson and Viney Limited, 1892), p. 7.

73   *Mansfield House Magazine* 1897, pp. 87–8.

74   *The Quintinian*, November 1892 issued as a supplement to *The Polytechnic Magazine* 3 November 1892.

75   See *Congregational Year Book*, 1929, p. 231.

76   *Weekly Times and Echo*, 13 November 1891. Browning's mother and father were both members of the church. His mother before marriage and his father after. The poet was baptised on 14 June 1812 followed two years later by his sister. The church books showed that Mrs Browning kept a missionary box until two years before her death. See Stead, F.H., *Eighteen Years in the Central City Swarm* (London, W.A. Hammond, 1913), p. 13.

77   See Cleal, E., *The Story of Congregationalism in Surrey* (James Clarke and Co., 1980) pp. 68–9.

78   Stead, F.H., *Eighteen Years*, p. 19.

79   Ibid., p. 19.

80   *Mansfield House Magazine*, vol. IV, 1897, p. 123.

81 Ibid., p. 19.
82 Anon., *A Record and an Appeal for Mansfield House*, p. 20.
83 Inglis, K.S., *Churches and the Working Classes in Victorian England* (London, Routledge and Kegan Paul, 1963), p. 159.
84 *Mansfield House Magazine*, vol. IV, 1897, p. 5.
85 Ibid., vol. IV, 1897, p. 4.
86 Ibid., vol. IV, p. 5.
87 Fairbairn, A.M., *Studies in Religion and Theology* (London, 1910), p. 160.
88 *The Christian World*, 9 November 1893.
89 For Reason see *Congregational Year Book*, 1927, pp. 150–1. Reason married Alden's sister and worked in the Settlement for seven years.
90 *Report of the Council of Mansfield College Oxford*, 1897–8, p. 14 noted the resignation of W. Reason who had been sub-warden for six years.
91 Reason, W., *A Week at Mansfield House* (1893), cited Inglis, K.S., op. cit., pp. 165–6.
92 Anon., *Mansfield House University Settlement in East London* (no publisher, 1892), p. 1. Bodleian Library Ms 24724e19.
93 Anon., *Life at Mansfield House by Residents* (London, Hazell, Watson and Viney Ltd., 1892), p. 5.
94 *Mansfield House Settlement Directory*, 1894, p. viii.
95 *The British Weekly*, 28 October 1895, p. 89.
96 Stead, F.H., *Eighteen Years in the Central City Swarm*, p. 15.
97 *Congregational Year Book*, 1929, p. 232.
98 Reason, W., op. cit., p. 181.
99 Stead, F.H., op. cit., p. 36.
100 Anon., *Life at Mansfield by Residents*, p. 9.
101 *Cambridge University Nonconformist Union Hand Book*, 1910, p. 12. See also *The Ilfracombe Gazette*, 18 April 1891, 'The Browning Mission consists of Cambridge students of the Congregational persuasion'.
102 Stead, F.H., op. cit., p. 39.
103 Stead, F.H., op. cit., p. 40.
104 Ibid., p. 37.
105 Anon., *Life at Mansfield House by Residents*, p. 7.
106 Stead, F.H., op. cit., p. 41.
107 Anon., *A Record and an Appeal Mansfield House University Settlement*, p. 16.
108 Ibid., p. 13.
109 *Life at Mansfield House by Residents*, pp. 12–13.
110 Anon., *A Record and an Appeal Mansfield House University Settlement*, p. 26.
111 Stead, F.H., op. cit., p. 74.
112 Ibid., p. 75.
113 *Mansfield House Magazine*, vol. I, 1894, p. 1.
114 *Mansfield House Report*, 1897.
115 Reason, W., 'The poor Man's Lawyer' in Reason, W. (editor), *University and Social Settlements* (Methuen, 1898), p. 153 f.
116 Ibid., p. 153.
117 Ibid., p. 153.
118 Ibid., p. 154.
119 Ibid., p. 157.

120 Ibid., p. 157.
121 Stead, F.H., *Eighteen Years*, p. 79.
122 Stead, F.H., *Eighteen Years in the Central City Swarm*, p. 93.
123 *Life at Mansfield House by Residents*, p. 28.
124 Anon., *Mansfield House University Settlement*, p. 2.
125 *A Record and an Appeal*, p. 18.
126 Stead, F.H., op. cit., pp. 141–3.
127 Smith, L., *Religion and the Rise of Labour* (Keele University Press, 1993), p. 65.
128 *Life at Mansfield House by Residents*, p. 11.
129 Ibid., p. 15.
130 *The Quintinian*, November 1892, supplement to *The Polytechnic Magazine*, 3 November 1892.
131 *Mansfield House Magazine*, vol. IV, no. 12, December 1897.
132 Stead, F.H., *Eighteen Years in the Central City Swarm*, p. 83.
133 Ibid., pp. 86–7.
134 *Mansfield House Magazine*, vol. 111, no. 1, January 1896, p. 35.
135 Cox, J., op. cit., p. 202.
136 *Mansfield House Magazine*, vol. 1, 1894, p. 77.
137 Stead, F.H., op. cit., pp. 18–19.
138 Ibid., p. 177.
139 Anon., *A Record of An Appeal*, p. 20.
140 *The Quintinian*, November 1892.
141 *Mansfield House Magazine*, October 1896, vol. III, no. 10, p. 205.
142 *The British Weekly*, 3 February 1898, p. 320.
143 Stead, F.H., op. cit., p. 51.
144 *A Memorial to the Cardinal Archbishop and Bishops of England on the Matter of Catholic Education* (printed pamphlet, undated, Westminster Archdiocesan Archives, Vaughan Papers). It is likely to be dated in the early 1890s since it related to the time when Vaughan was Archbishop.
145 O'Neil, R., *Cardinal Herbert Vaughan* (Burns and Oates, 1995), p. 411.
146 See 'Newman House The Pioneer Catholic Settlement', in *The Month*, March 1933, p. 211.
147 Barnett, H.O., *Canon Barnett*, pp. 148–9.
148 Ibid., p. 688. See also pp. 217, 225, 306, 308,370, 440 and 455.
149 *The Tablet*, 10 October 1891.
150 Ibid., 10 October 1891.
151 Ibid., 31 October 1891.
152 See for example *Report of the Council of Mansfield College, Oxford*, 1894–5, p. 13 'Over a hundred members of the House visited the College…'. *Mansfield College Magazine*, vol. 2, March 1900, p. 167, 'We have had, as in former years, a Whit Monday party from Mansfield House, and entertained them in the usual way. The number, something under 40 – was smaller than of late…'.

Chapter 7: Women's Settlements

1 Besant, W., *East London* (London, Chatto and Windus, 1901), p. 115.
2 See Bell, E., *Octavia Hill: A Biography* (London, Constable & Co Ltd), pp. 218–19 and Smith, M.J., *Professional Training for Social Work in Britain: An Historical Account* (1965), pp. 69–78.

3 Guild of Cheltenham Ladies College, autumn 1897, p. 335.
4 Barnett, G., *Blackfriars Settlement a Short History 1887–1987* (1987), p. 2.
5 *Women's University Settlement, First Annual Report*, p. 11, Ms GB/106/5/WUS/R/1.
6 Ibid., pp. 6–7.
7 Ibid., p. 2.
8 Brodie, D.M., *Women's University Settlement* (London, Women's University Settlement, 1937), p. 8.
9 Barnett, G., op. cit., pp. 3–4.
10 Ibid., p. 4.
11 *Lady Margaret Hall Old Students Association Report*, 1894, p. 11. The same report p. 13 noted that present students of the hall were good enough to get up a Christmas entertainment in the vacation which they performed before 'appreciative and enthusiastic audiences' of factory girls and tenants of Miss Octavia Hill.
12 *Women's University Settlement Twelfth Annual Report*, June 1899, p. 10.
13 Brodie, D.M., op. cit., p. 11.
14 Barnett, G., *Blackfriars*, p. 7.
15 Ibid., p. 9.
16 *Women's University Settlement Fifth Annual Report*, 1892, p. 7.
17 See Bodie, D.M., op. cit., p. 19.
18 Article in *The Birmingham Gazette*, 29 April 1890.
19 *Women's University Settlement Annual Report*, June 1896, p. 20.
20 *The Birmingham Gazette*, 29 April 1890.
21 *Women's University Settlement, Annual Report*, June 1893 p. 19.
22 Lewis, J., *Women and Social Action* (Edward Elgar, 1991), p. 68.
23 Ibid., p. 69.
24 Octavia Hill's close relationship with Margaret Sewell was well illustrated in 1890 when Margaret asked her to serve the WUS and come over and live in Southwark. Octavia was quite tempted but decided that her home and her sisters were rooted in Marylebone.
25 Sewell, M.A., 'Method and Education in Charitable Work', *Charity Organisation Review*, December 1900, p. 379, cited ibid., p. 256.
26 Avery, G., *Cheltenham Ladies* (James and James Publishers Ltd, 2003), p. 107.
27 Ibid., p. 107.
28 *Guild of Cheltenham Ladies College*, autumn 1889, p. 180.
29 Ibid., p. 182.
30 Ibid., p. 187.
31 See *Letter* from Flora E. Kerr to the Secretary of the Guild of Cheltenham Ladies College, 11 November (no year stated), letter 7538.
32 *The Cheltenham Ladies College Magazine*, no. XX, autumn 1889, p. 184.
33 Ibid., p. 186.
34 Cath E. Newman to Miss Anson, 22 May 1889, Letter 7502.
35 Cath E. Newman to Miss Anson, Letter 7516.
36 *Cheltenham Ladies College Magazine*, no. XXIX, spring 1894, p. 158.
37 Ibid., p. 158.
38 *The Oxford House Chronicle*, vol. VIII, no. 1, January 1894, p. 5.
39 Ibid., p. 5.

40 See Steadman, F. C., *In the Days of Miss Beale A Study of her Work and Influence* (London, Ed. J. Burrow & Co. Ltd., 1931), p. 5.
41 Mace, J.H.B., *Henry Bodley Bromby A Memoir* (Longmans, Green, and Co., 1913) pp. 14–15. For his ritualism see p. 106 and p. 111.
42 *Papers relating to the Appointment of Dorothea Beale as Principal of Cheltenham Ladies College*, Cheltenham Ladies College Archives, Ms 514–517.
43 *Guild of Cheltenham Ladies College*, spring 1892, Report for October 1890–October 1891, p. 154.
44 Ibid., spring 1894, p. 151.
45 Ibid., spring 1893, p. 100.
46 *The Oxford House Chronicle*, vol. IX, no. 6, June 1895, p. 4.
47 Ibid., vol. IX, no. 1, January 1895, p. 6.
48 *The Oxford House Chronicle*, vol. ix, no. 2, February 1895, p. 5.
49 Ibid., spring 1897, p. 176.
50 *Letter* Catherine E. Newman to Miss Anson, 30 August 1889, letter 7509.
51 *Letter* Catherine E. Newman to Miss Anson, 13 April 1898, letter 7519.
52 *Guild of Cheltenham Ladies College*, spring 1893, p. 102.
53 *Guild of Cheltenham Ladies College*, spring 1893, pp. 102–3.
54 Avery, G., *Cheltenham Ladies*, p. 107.
55 Ibid., p. 108.
56 Ibid., p. 109.
57 *The Cheltenham Ladies College Magazine*, no. XXXVII, spring 1898.
58 Ibid., no. XCI, spring 1900, p. 82.
59 *The Oxford House Chronicle*, vol. IX, no. 5, May 1895, p. 4.
60 *Guild of Cheltenham Ladies College*, spring 1892, p. 260.
61 *The Oxford House Chronicle*, vol. VIII, no. 7, July 1894, p. 4.
62 Ibid., vol. VIII, no. 11, November 1894, p. 6.
63 Ibid., vol. IX, no. 1, January 1895, p. 1.
64 *Oxford House Chronicle*, vol. VIII, no. 1, January 1894, p. 5.
65 Ibid., vol. VIII, no. 8, August 1894.
66 Ibid., vol. VIII, no. 9, September 1894, p. 6.
67 Ibid., vol. VIII, no. 11, November 1894.
68 Ibid., vol. IX, no. 2, February 1895, p. 5.
69 See Pennar-Lewis, W.T., *Mansfield College, Oxford* (London, Independent Press, 1947), pp. 23–4.
70 *Report of the Council of Mansfield College, 1891–2*, p. 11.
71 Mansfield House Magazine, vol. 1, 1894, p. 119.
72 Ibid., 1894, p. 119.
73 Ibid., p. 160.
74 Ibid., p. 160
75 Ibid., p. 161.
76 Anon., *A Week at Mansfield House* (Plaistow, W.S. Caines, 1893), p. 14.
77 Sewell, M.A., and Powell, E.G., Women's Settlements in England' in Reason, W., *University Settlements* (London, Methuen, 1896), p. 93.
78 *Mansfield House Magazine*, vol. 1, 1894, p. 19.
79 Ibid., vol. 1, 1894, p. 40.
80 Ibid., vol. 1, 1894, p. 116.
81 Ibid., vol. 1, 1894, p. 119.

82 *Annual Report of the Bermondsey Settlement*, 1892, p. 9.
83 See *Wesleyan Methodist Magazine*, 1900, p. 762.
84 Ibid., p. 9.
85 Turberfield, A., *John Scott Lidgett* (Epworth Press, 2003), p. 37.
86 *Report of the Bermondsey Settlement*, September 1892, p. 15.
87 Ibid., p. 16.
88 Ibid., p. 93.
89 Ibid., September,1893, p. 21.
90 *Report of the Bermondsey Settlement*, 1895, p. 25.
91 Ibid., 1895, p. 16.
92 Ibid., 1896, p. 7.
93 Anon., *Lady Margaret Hall A Short History* (Oxford, OUP, 1923), p. 110.
94 See Ibid., p. 111.
95 Ibid., pp. 119–120.
96 *Women's University Settlement, Tenth Annual Report*, p. 19, Ms GB/ 106 / 5 / WUS / R / 9.
97 *First Minute Book of the Lady Margaret Settlement*, 1896, Ms A / LMH / 1
98 Ibid., minutes for 16 October 1896.
99 *Lady Margaret Hall Old Students' Association Report*, 1896, p. 19.
100 Ibid., p. 19.
101 Ibid., p. 20.
102 Ibid., p. 23.
103 Ibid., Minutes of Extra-ordinary meeting, 13 November 1896.
104 Battiscombe, G., *Reluctant Pioneer A Life of Elizabeth Wordsworth* (London, Constable, 1978), p. 23.
105 Ibid., p. 19.
106 *Lady Margaret Hall Old Students Association Report*, 1896, p. 16.
107 Anon., *Lady Margaret Hall A Short History* (Oxford, OUP, 1924), p. 110.
108 Ibid., Minutes of the Provisional Committee, 4 December 1896.
109 *Lady Margaret Hall Old Students Association Report*, 1897, p. 11.
110 Anon., *Lady Margaret Hall A Short History* (Oxford, OUP, 1924), p. 112.
111 *Lady Margaret Hall Old Students Association Report*, 1898, p. 13.
112 Ibid., p. 121.
113 Ibid., p. 122.
114 *Second Minute Book of the Lady Margaret Settlement*, 1897, Minutes of 11 October 1897.
115 Ibid., Minutes 11 January 1897.
116 Ibid., Minutes 3 July 1899.
117 *Lady Margaret Hall Old Students Association Report*, 1901, p. 15. The Report of the Lady Margaret Hall, 1899–1900, p. 11 noted that 'the students of the Hall continue zealously to support the Lady Margaret Hall Settlement...and also continue to interest themselves in the Women's University Settlement at 44 Nelson Square', Blackfriars Road and in the Universities Mission to Central Africa, meetings of which are terminally held at one or the other women's colleges in Oxford'.
118 Reason, W., op. cit., p. 185.
119 See Reason, W., op. cit., p. 91.

120 United Girls' School Mission Annual Report 1897, p. 1 and p. 11, cited Dickie, J.W., op. cit., p. 110.

121 Information derived from *The Report of St Luke's Women's Guild of Aid of Work Done During 1910* (Leighton Buzzard, Faith Press, 1911), pp. 1–2, London Metropolitan Archives, Ms P73/LUK/71–79.

122 Ibid., p. 3.

123 *The Presbyterian Settlement in Poplar Report*, 1899, p. 6.

124 Ibid., p. 5.

125 Ibid., p. 15.

126 Ibid., p. 8.

127 Ibid., p. 10.

128 Ibid., p. 7.

129 *The Tablet*, 16 December 1893.

130 Ibid., 16 December 1893.

131 Ibid., 16 December 1893.

132 For other details of the House see Anon., *Jubilee of the Church of Guardian Angels* (undated), p. 2 in Mile End Parish Records, Westminster Archdiocesan Records.

133 Maynard, J.O., *History of the Parish of Guardian Angels, Mile End 1868–1903* (undated), chapter 21.

134 Much of this information has been derived from anonymous notes in *The Guardian Angels Parish files*, Westminster Archdiocesan Archives.

135 See *The Tablet*, 27 October 1894 for a brief description of St Anthony's House and its activities.

136 See entry for St Cecilia's House, *Catholic Directory*, 1895.

137 *The Oxford House Chronicle*, vol. VIII, no. 4, p. 4.

138 Reason, W., *University Settlements* (Methuen and Co., 1898), pp. 90–1.

139 Reason, W., op. cit., p. 93.

Chapter 8: University Hall, a Non-Sectarian Settlement

1 *The Freeman*, 7 March 1890.

2 *University Hall*, printed appeal document, March 1890, p. 2, Mary Ward Papers (Letter Box).

3 Information taken from Brehoney, A.J., 'A Socially Civilising Influence? Play and the Urban "degenerate"', paper presented at Birmingham University, July 2001).

4 Lewis, J., *Women and Social Action in Victorian and Edwardian England* (Edward Elgar, 1991), p. 200.

5 See Ward, H., *Robert Elsmere*, chapter 38.

6 *Printed Circular* explaining the aims of the Settlement at University Hall, 1890 (Mary Ward Papers).

7 Card entitled *Marchmont Hall Association Our Beliefs and Aims*, Mary Ward Papers.

8 Ibid., p. 2.

9 See press cutting from *The Cambridge Independent*, dated in ink November 1898, Mary Ward Papers.

10 *Untitled Address* possibly given at the Manchester University Settlement about 1899, Mary Ward papers. (Box containing her talks and addresses.)

11 Ibid., November 1898.
12 Cited by Lewis, J., op. cit., p. 206.
13 *The Times*, 11 February 1898, p. 5.
14 *Second Report of the Universal Hall Settlement*, 1894.
15 *University Hall, Marchmont Hall Scheme*, p. 1, printed pamphlet, Mary Ward Papers.
16 Ibid., p. 2.
17 *Marchmont Hall Workers' Curriculum*, October 1891, Mary Ward Papers (Letter Box).
18 *Notes on Marchmont Hall*, for the six months ending 30 June 1892 (W. Speaight and Sons, 1892), printed leaflet, Mary Ward Papers.
19 *Marchmont Hall Holiday Fund*, 1895, p. 1.
20 Wicksteed to Mrs Humphry Ward, Letter dated 18 February 1891 (Letter Box), Mary Ward Papers.
21 Ibid., p. 2.
22 Wicksteed to Mrs Humphry Ward, Letter dated 1 March 1891 (Letter Box), Mary Ward Papers.
23 W. Blake Odgers to Mrs Humphry Ward, Letter dated 12 April 1891 (Letter Box), Mary Ward Papers.
24 *University Hall Minute Book 1890–1895*, Minutes 21 March 1893, Mary Ward Papers.
25 Ibid., 21 March 1893.
26 Wicksteed to Mrs Humphry Ward, letter attached to ibid., 21 March 1893.
27 Rogers, J., *Mary Ward Settlement A History 1891–1931* (Passmore Edwards Research Series, 1931) no. 1, p. 5.
28 Ibid., p. 5.
29 *University Hall Minute Book 1890–1891*, Minutes 26 June 1891.
30 Ibid., Minutes 30 May and 27 June 1893.
31 Ward, M., *Address* circa 1898 or 1899 possibly at Manchester, p. 11, Mary Ward Papers.
32 Ibid., p. 11. The term 'Associates' was the name given to paying members of the hall.
33 *Passmore Edwards Settlement First Annual Report for the year 1897*, p. 4.
34 John Passmore Edwards (1823–1911) began life as a lawyer's clerk and later engaged in various publishing ventures. He supported the Chartist agenda and the Anti-Corn Law League. He was Liberal MP. for Salisbury 1880–5 and founded some seventy free libraries, hospitals and convalescent homes in the United Kingdom.
35 Passmore Edwards, J. to Mrs Humphry Ward, 30 May 1894 attached to the Minutes of 5 June 1894, *University Hall Minute Book, 1890–1895*, Mary Ward Papers.
36 Passmore Edwards, J., to Mrs Humphry Ward, 20 January 1895, *University Hall Minute Book*, attached to minutes of 22 January 1895.
37 Evans, D., *Passmore Edwards Settlement* (31 December 2003), p. 2.
38 *Mansfield House Magazine*, vol. V, no. 2, February 1898, p. 12.
39 See 'The New Settlement' in *Daily News,* 12 February 1898.
40 Tatton, R.G., and Ward, M., *The Passmore Edwards Settlement* (no publisher, undated), p. 5.

41 *The Times*, 11 February 1898.
42 *Plans for the Passmore Edwards Settlement*, London Metropolitan Archives, Ms GLC/AR /BR/19/0/249.
43 See *Robert Elsmere*.
44 *The Times*, 11 February 1898.
45 *Manchester Guardian*, 11 October 1897.
46 Ibid., 11 October 1897.
47 *Memorandum and Articles of Association of the Passmore Edwards Settlement* (Jordan and Sons Limited, 1895), Mary Ward Papers.
48 After her death the Settlement was re-named 'The Mary Ward Centre'.
49 *Passmore Edwards Settlement*, a printed prospectus, dated September 1900, Mary Ward Papers.
50 Jones, E.H., *Mrs Humphry Ward* (Heinemann, 1973), p. 119.
51 *Passmore Edwards Settlement*, a printed prospectus, dated September 1900, Mary Ward Papers.
52 See *The Associate*, April 1899 for full reports of the cricket and football clubs.
53 This point was particularly made in an article in *The Times* of 11 February 1898.
54 *Passmore Edwards Settlement Second Annual Report, 1898–1899*, p. 14.
55 Jones, E.H., *Mrs Humphry Ward* p. 123.
56 *Passmore Edwards Settlement Second Annual Report, 1898–1899*, p. 14.
57 Ibid., p. 15.
58 Ibid., p. 15.
59 Lewis. J, op. cit., p. 216.
60 Ibid., p. 216.
61 Jones, E.H., op. cit., p. 124.
62 Ibid., p. 124.
63 Ibid., p. 125.
64 *Passmore Edwards Settlement, Fourth Annual Report 1900–1901*, pp. 27–8.
65 Tatton, R.G., and Edwards, M., *The Passmore Edwards Settlement* (no publisher, 1897).
66 Ibid., p. 7.
67 *The Associate*, October 1898, no. 1, p. 5.
68 *The Associate*, 1898, no. 1, p. 15.
69 Ibid., p. 17.
70 Ibid., p. 17.
71 *Passmore Edwards Settlement Second Annual Report, 1898–9*, p. 10.
72 Ward, M., *Type-written Address*, untitled and undated but shortly after 1898, p. 11a, Mary Ward Papers. (Box of Addresses by Mrs Humphry Ward.)
73 Ibid., p. 11.
74 Ibid., p. 11.
75 Ibid., pp. 8–9.
76 Ibid., p. 9.
77 *Speech at Manchester*, type-written, undated, p. 4, Mary Ward Papers. (Box of Addresses.)
78 Ibid., p. 3.
79 Ibid., p. 1.
80 *Speech*, undated probably 1898, p. 10, Mary Ward Papers. (Box of Addresses.)

81   *The Associate*, October 1898, no. 1, p. 3.
82   See unpublished paper entitled, *'The Origins of the Mary Ward Settlement written at the time of the Settlement Jubilee,* autumn 1947.
83   Barnett, S.O., *Life of Canon Barnett*, p. 389.
84   Ibid., p. 722.
85   Ibid., p. 288.

Chapter 9: What the Squires Achieved

1   Holman, B., *Good Old George* (Lion, 1990), p. 196.
2   It is perhaps of interest that Toynbee Hall became more radical after Lansbury's time.
3   Lansbury, G., *My Life* (Constable, 1928), cited Holman, B., ibid., p. 196.
4   Lansbury, G., *Your Part in Poverty* (The Herald, 1917), p. 91, cited Holman, B., op. cit., p. 197.
5   Barnett, S.A., and Barnett, H.O., *Practicable Socialism*, p. 143, cited Inglis, K.S., op. cit., p. 171.
6   Barnett, S.A. and Barnett, H.O., *Practicable Socialism*, p. 143, cited Inglis, K.S., op. cit., p. 171.
7   Ibid., p. 171.
8   Ibid., p. 171.
9   Reason, W., *A Week at Mansfield House* (1893), p. 4.
10   *The Battersea Caian and Yelverton Magazine*, February 1892, p. 51.
11   Woods, R.A., 'The Social Awakening of London' in Woods, R.A. (Editor), *The Poor in the Great Cities* (1896), pp. 19–29, cited by Inglis, K.S., *Churches and the Working Classes in Victorian England* (London, Routledge and Kegan Paul, 1963), p. 170.
12   Briggs, A., and McCartney, A., *Toynbee Hall*, p. 22.
13   Hobhouse, S., *Forty Years and an Epilogue* (1951), p. 133, cited Inglis, K.S., op. cit., p. 170.
14   Ashworth, M., *The Oxford House in Bethnal Green* (Oxford House, 1984), p. 10.
15   Ibid., p. 10.
16   Oxford House, *Annual Report*, 1886, p. 5.
17   Barnett, S.O., *Canon Barnett*, p. 326.
18   Ibid., p. 334.
19   Kelly, T., *A History of Adult Education in Great Britain* (Liverpool University Press, 1992), p. 242.
20   Barnett, H.O., op. cit., p. 499 and p. 506.
21   Amos., H., and Hough, W.W., *The Cambridge Mission to South London* (undated), p. 132.
22   Ibid., p. 132.
23   Pimlott, J.A.R., *Toynbee Hall* (1935), p. 51, cited Mayor, S., *The Churches and The Labour Movement* (Independent Press Ltd., 1967), p. 63.
24   For the influence of Maurice on Lidgett, see Dickie, J.W., op. cit., p. 139.
25   Kerrigan, C., '"Thoroughly good football": teachers and the origins of elementary school football', *History of Education Bulletin*, 2000, vol. 29, no. 6, 517–541.
26   Ibid., p. 520.
27   Ibid., p. 521.

28 See *Boy's Own Annual*, XXXVIII, p. 437, cited ibid., p. 521.
29 See *The Oxford House Chronicle*, vol. VIII, no. 1, p. 2.
30 Reason, W., 'Settlements and Recreations' in Reason, W. (editor), *Universities and Social Settlements*, p. 76.
31 Stocks, M.D., op. cit., p. 2.
32 Anon., *Lady Margaret Hall A Short History* (Oxford, OUP, 1923), p. 117.
33 Stocks, M.D., *Fifty Years in Every Street: The Story of the Manchester University Settlement* (Manchester University Press, 1945), p. 2.
34 Barnett, H.O., *Canon Barnett His Life*, p. 675.
35 Herbert Louis Samuel (1870–1963), first Viscount Samuel, Liberal MP and later cabinet minister.
36 Stead, F.H., *How Old Age Pensions Began to Be* (1909), p. 316, cited Inglis, K.S., *Churches and the Working Classes in Victorian England* (Routledge and Kegan Paul, 1963), p. 165.
37 *The Benedict*, no. 9, 1900, p. 25.
38 *Pembroke Annual Mission Report*, 1900, p. 3.
39 *Oxford House Annual Report*, 1900, p.1.
40 Ibid., p. 1.
41 *Report of the Bermondsey Settlement*, 30 September 1894.
42 Dickie, J.W., op. cit., p. 175.
43 Davies, R. (editor), *John Scott Lidgett* (London, Epworth, 1957), p. 74.
44 Ellis, L.E., *Toynbee Hall and the University Settlements* (1948), p. 167.
45 Reason, W., *University Settlements*, p. 25.
46 Masterman, C.F.G., *The Heart of the Empire* (1901), p. 35, cited Inglis, K.S., op. cit., p. 173.

BIBLIOGRAPHY

Newspapers, Magazines and Journals

Boy's Own Annual, XXXVIII
British Weekly
Cambridge Review
Christian Herald
Church Review
Contemporary Review
Cranleigh School Magazine
Daily Chronicle
Daily News
Eton College Chronicle
Ecclesiatical Gazette
The East End News
Guild of Cheltenham Ladies College
Harrow Notes
Manchester Guardian
Mansfield House Magazine
New York Herald
Pall Mall Gazette
Primitive Methodist Magazine
St Mark's Victoria Docks Parish Magazine (Uppingham Archives)
Speaker
The Alleynian
The Associate
The Battersea Caian and Yelverton Magazine
The Benedict
The Berkhamstedian
The Birmingham Gazette
The Bradfield College Chronicle

The Builder
The Bristol Mercury
The British Weekly
The Caian
The Cambridge Independent
The Cambridge
The Carthusian
The Cheltenham Ladies College Magazine
The Cheltonian
The Cholmeleian
The Christian Commonwealth
The Christian World
The Congregational Year Book
The Eagle
The Elizabethan
The Freeman
The Guardian
The Harrowvian
The Illustrated London News
The Malvernian
The Manchester Examiner
The Marlburian
The Methodist Times
The Month
The Oxford House Chronicle
The Polytechnic Magazine
The Quintinian
The Radleian
The Record
The Scottish Leader
The Star
The Tablet
The Times
The Tonbridgian
The Trinian
The Toynbee Record
The Wellingtonian
The Westminster Gazette
The Women's Gazette
The Worker

The Wykehamist
Uppingham School Magazine
Weekly Times and Echo
Wesleyan Methodist Magazine

Primary Sources

A Memorial to the Cardinal Archbishop and Bishops of England on the Matter of Catholic Education (printed pamphlet, undated, Westminster Archdiocesan Archives, Vaughan Papers).

Adderley, J., *In Slums and Society Reminiscences of Old Friends* (London, T. Fisher Unwin Ltd, 1916).

Andrews, C.F., *What I Owe to Christ* (London, Hodder and Stoughton, 1933).

Amos, A., and Hough, W.W., *The Cambridge Mission to South London A Twenty Years' Survey* (Cambridge, MacMillan and Bowes, 1904).

Anon., *A Record and an Appeal for Mansfield House University Settlement* (London, Mansfield House University Settlement, 1925).

Anon., *Handbook of Settlements in Great Britain* (London, The Federation of Residential Settlements and Educational Settlements, 1922).

Anon., *Jubilee of the Church of Guardian Angels* (London, undated), Mile End Parish Records. Westminster Archdiocesan Records.

Anon., *A Week at Mansfield House* (Plaistow, W.S. Caines, 1893).

Anon., *Lady Margaret Hall: A Short History* (Oxford, OUP, 1923).

Anon., *Life at Mansfield House by Residents* (London, Hazell, Watson and Viney Limited, 1892).

Anon., *Mansfield House Settlement in East London* (Canning Town, 1892).

Anon., *Pembroke College Mission* (Cambridge, printed pamphlet, undated).

Anon., *The Harrow Mission: A Story of Fifty Years* (published as a supplement to the Harrovian, 1933).

Anon., *The Origins of the Mary Ward Settlement written at the time of the Settlement Jubilee* (London, no publisher, 1947).

Annual Reports of the Bermondsey Settlement.

Annual Report of the Universities Settlement in East London (London, Penny and Hill, 1891).

Ashworth, M., *The Oxford House in Bethnal Green* (Oxford House, 1984).

Avery, G., *Cheltenham Ladies* (James and James Publishers Ltd, 2003).

Barnett Papers, London Metropolitan Archives.

Barnett, G., *Blackfriars Settlement a Short History 1887–1987* (London, no publisher, 1987).

Barnett, H.O., *Canon Barnett, His Life, Work, and Friends* (London, John Murray, 1921).

Barnett, S.A., 'A Democratic Church', *Contemporary Review*, vol. XLVI, November 1884.

Barnett, S., *Practical Socialism* (London, Longmans, Green and Co., 1894).

Barnett S.A., *Settlements of University Men in the Great Towns* (Oxford, no publisher, 1884).

Bermondsey Settlement Minute Book Report of the Bermondsey Settlement.

Booth, C., *Life and Labour of the London People* (London, MacMillan and Co., 1892) vols. 1–9.

Booth, W., *In Darkest England and the Way Out* (London, Salvation Army, 1890).

Brooke Lambert Papers (University of Iowa).

Catholic Directory.

Cranleigh School Mission Papers.

Davidson, R.T., *Life of Archibald Campbell Tait* (Macmillan and Co., 1891), 2 vols.

Caius House Battersea Report of London Committee, 1889 (Gonville and Caius Mission Papers).

Cambridge University Nonconformist Union Hand Book.

Charterhouse Mission Annual Reports.

Clare College Mission Annual Reports.

Clare College Mission Parish Magazine, No. 16, October 1887.

Clarke, C.P.S., *Poplar* (London, unpublished manuscript, Christ Church Archives).

Congregational Year Book.

Corpus Christi College (Cambridge) Mission (Corpus Mission Papers).

Charterhouse Mission Annual Reports.

Dulwich College Mission Visitors' Book 1888–1921, Dulwich College Mission Archives.

Gonville and Caius Mission and Settlement Annual Reports.

Gonville and Caius College Mission and Settlement at Battersea, S.W. (printed pamphlet, 1888).

The Guardian Angels Parish files, Westminster Archdiocesan Archives.

Henson, H., 'The University Settlements in the East End' in *Some Urgent Questions in Christian Lights* (London, no publisher, 1889).

Jowett Papers, Balliol College, Oxford.

Kingsley, C., *His Letters and Memories of His Life* (London, Macmillan and Co., Limited, 1908).

Lady Margaret Hall Old Students Association Reports.

Lang, C., *Tupper A Memoir of the Life and work of a very human parish Priest by His Friend* (London, Constable and Co. Ltd, undated).

Legge, H., *Trinity College Mission in Stratford 1888–1899* (Trinity College Archives, undated).

Mansfield House Reports.

Mansfield House Settlement Directory.

Marchmont Hall Workers' Curriculum, October 1891, Mary Ward Papers.

Marchmont Hall Holiday Fund, 1895, Mary Ward Papers.

Marchmont Hall Association Our Beliefs and Aims, Mary Ward Papers.

Mearns, A., *The Bitter Cry of Outcast London* (James Clarke & Co., 1883).

Memorandum of Association printed in *First Annual Report of the Universities' Settlement in East London* (Oxford, 1885).

Memorandum and Articles of Association of the Passmore Edwards Settlement (Jordan and Sons Limited, 1895), Mary Ward Papers.

Minute Book of the Eton College Mission 1880–1895, Eton College Archives.

Minute Book of the Clare College Mission, Ms CCAD/5/1/2/2/1, Clare College Mission Archives.

Minute Book of Eton Mission, Eton College Archives.

Minute Book of House Committee, Wadham House, Toynbee Hall Papers.

Minute Book of the Executive Committee of Mansfield House, Canning Town, Stratford Library.

Minute Book of the Lady Margaret Settlement, 1896.

Minute Book of the Lady Margaret Settlement, 1897.

Notes on Marchmont Hall, for the six months ending 30 June 1892 (W. Speaight and Sons, 1892), printed leaflet, Mary Ward Papers.

Oxford House Annual Reports.

Parkin, G., *Edward Thring Life, Diary and Letters* (London, MacMillan and Co. Limited, 1898), 2 vols.

Passmore Edwards Settlement Annual Reports, Mary Ward Papers.

Passmore Edwards Settlement, a printed prospectus, dated September 1900, Mary Ward Papers.

Plans for the Passmore Edwards Settlement, London Metropolitan Archives.

Pembroke College Mission Annual Reports.

Printed Circular from H. Montagu Butler to Old Harrovians, May 1881, Harrow Mission Archives.

Reason, W., *A Week at Mansfield House* (London, no publisher, 1893).

Reason, W., *University and Social Settlements* (London, Methuen, 1896).

Reports of the Bermondsey Settlement.

Reports of the Council of Mansfield College.

Rowsell, T.J., 'Deficiency of the Means of Spiritual Instruction', Select Committee, House of Lords, Appendix S, p. 634 in *Parliamentary Papers*, 1857–8.

Rules for the Clare College Mission, attached to Fourth Annual Report, 1888.

Sewell, M.A., 'Method and Education in Charitable Work', *Charity Organisation Review,* December 1900.

Simpkinson, C.H., *The Life and Work of Bishop Thorold* (London, Isbister and Company Ltd, 1896).

Sims, G.R., *How the Poor Live* (London, Chatto and Windus, 1883).

Stead, F.H., *Eighteen Years in the Central City Swarm* (London, W.A. Hammond, 1913).

Stead, F.H., *How Old Age Pensions Began to Be* (London, no publisher, 1909).

The Official Church of England Year-Book, 1900.

The Report of St Luke's Women's Guild of Aid of Work Done During 1910 (Leighton Buzzard, Faith Press, 1911).

Tait, A.C., *A Charge to the Clergy of the Diocese of London at His Visitation in December,* 1866 (London, Rivingtons, 1866).

Tatton, R.G., and Edwards, M., *The Passmore Edwards Settlement* (London, no publisher, 1897).

The Hollington Club for Young People, Dulwich College Mission Papers.

The Wellington Year Book, 1891.

The Presbyterian Settlement in Poplar Report, 1899.

Thorold, A., *The Church Congress,* 1886 attached to *Pembroke College Mission Report,* 1886–7.

Toynbee Memorial Fund Minute Book, London Metropolitan Archives.

Hughes, T., *Tom Brown's School Days* (Wordsworth Classics, 1993).

Trinity College Mission in St George's Camberwell, South London (printed pamphlet, 1888).

Trinity College Mission Appeal Document, 1888.

Trinity College Mission Brochure, December 1887.

*Trinity College Mission Report*s.

Trinity College Oxford Mission Reports, Trinity College Mission Archives.

Trinity College Mission Minute Book, Trinity College, Oxford.

University Hall, printed appeal document, March 1890, Mary Ward Papers.

University Hall, Marchmont Hall Scheme, printed pamphlet, Mary Ward Papers.

University Hall Minute Book 1890–1895, Mary Ward Papers.

Ward, H., *Robert Elsmere* (Oxford, Oxford University Press, 1989)

Ward, M., *Address c.* 1898 or 1899, Mary Ward Papers.

Ward, M., *Type-written Address,* untitled and undated but shortly after 1898, Mary Ward Papers.

Ward Family Diaries, University College, London.

Winnington-Ingram, A.F., *Fifty Years Work in London 1889–1939* (Longmans, Green and Co., 1940).

Winnington-Ingram, A.F., 'The Classes and the Masses', in *The Church of the People* (1894).

Winnington-Ingram, A.F., *Work in Great Cities* (London, 1896)

Woods, R.A., (Editor), *The Poor in the Great Cities* (London, 1896).

Women's University Settlement Fifth Annual Reports.

Papers relating to the Appointment of Dorothea Beale as Principal of Cheltenham Ladies College, Cheltenham Ladies College Archives.

Books, Articles and Theses

Balleine, G.R., *A History of the Evangelical Party in the Church of England* (London, Longmans, Green and Co, 1933).

Battiscombe, G., *Reluctant Pioneer: A Life of Elizabeth Wordsworth* (London, Constable, 1978).

Besant, W., *East London* (London, Chatto and Windus, 1901).

Bell, E., *Octavia Hill: A Biography* (London, Constable & Co. Ltd,).

Blackie, J., *Bradfield 1850–1915* (The Warden and Council of St Andrew's College Bradfield, 1976).

Blomfield, A.A., *A Memoir of Charles James Blomfield* (London, John Murray, 1863), 2 vols.

Brehoney, A.J., 'A Socially Civilising Influence? Play and the Urban "degenerate"', paper presented at Birmingham University, July 2001.

Bradley, I., *Oxford House in Bethnal Green 1884–1984* (London, Robert Stockwell Ltd, 1984).

Briggs, A., and Macartney, A., *Toynbee Hall* (London, Routledge and Kegan Paul, 1984).

Brodie, D.M., *Women's University Settlement* (London, Women's University Settlement, 1937).

Card, T., *Eton Renewed* (London, John Murray, 1994).

Carpenter, S.C., *Church and People 1789–1889* (London, SPCK, 1933).

Chadwick, O., *The Victorian Church* (London, A and C Black, 1970), parts 1 and 2.

Cleal, E., *The Story of Congregationalism in Surrey* (Cambridge, James Clarke and Co., 1980).

Colson, P., *Life of the Bishop of London An Autobiography* (London, Skeffington & Son Ltd, 1936).

Corke, S., *Charterhouse in Southwark 1884–2000* (Charterhouse, Charterhouse Press, 2001).

Cornish, F.W., *A History of the Church in the Nineteenth Century* (London, MacMillan and Co, 1910), parts 1 and 2.

Coulton, P., *Life of the Bishop of London* (London, Skeffington & Son Ltd, 1936).

Cox, J., *The English Churches in A secular Society 1870–1930* (Oxford, Oxford, University Press, 1982).

Davidson, R.T., and Benham, W., *Life of Archibald Campbell Tait* (London, Macmillan, 1891), 2 vols.

Davies, R. (editor), *John Scott Lidgett* (London, Epworth Press, 1957).

Dickie, J.W., *College Missions and Settlements in South London 1870–1920* (B.Litt. thesis, Oxford University, 1976)

Ellis, L.E., *Toynbee Hall and the University Settlements* (London, 1948).

Ensor, R.C.K., *England 1870–1914* (Oxford, OUP, 1936).

Evans, D., *Passmore Edwards Settlement* (London, no publisher, 2003).

Evans, J., *The Parish of St Frideswide of Oxford: Our First Fifty Years 1881–1931* (no publisher, 1931).

Evors, C.A., *The Story of Highgate School* (London, Forbes Robertson Ltd, 1938).

Fairborrn, A.M., *Studies in Religion and Theology* (London, 1910).

Fletcher, C.R.L., *Edmond Warre* (London, John Murray, 1922).

Graham, E., *The Harrow Life of Henry Montagu Butler, D.D.* (London, Longmans, Green and Co., 1920).

Hinchcliff, P., *Frederick Temple Archbishop of Canterbury* (Oxford, Clarendon Press, 1998).

Hinde, T., *Highgate School: A History* (London, James and James, 1993).

Hobhouse, S., *Forty Years and an Epilogue* (London, 1951).

Holman, B., *Good Old George* (Tring, Lion, 1990).

How, F.D., *Bishop Walsham How A Memoir* (London, Isbister and Company Ltd, 1899).

Hughes, D., *The Life of Hugh Price Hughes* (London, Hodder and Stoughton, 1907).

Inglis, K.S., *Churches and the Working Classes in Victorian England* (London, Routledge and Kegan Paul, 1963).

James, E., 'Trinity in Camberwell', *Trinity Review,* Michaelmas, 1959.

Jones, E.H., *Mrs Humphry Ward* (London, Heinemann, 1973).

Kelly, T., *A History of Adult Education in Great Britain* (Liverpool, Liverpool University Press, 1992).

Kerrigan, C., '"Thoroughly good football": teachers and the origins of elementary school football', *History of Education*, 2000, vol. 29, no. 6, pp. 520–3.

Lansbury, G., *My Life* (London, Constable, 1928).

Lansbury, G., *Your Part in Poverty* (London, The Herald, 1917).

Leinster-Mackay, D., *The Educational World of Edward Thring* (Falmer Press, 1987).

Lewis, J., *Women and Social Action in Victorian and Edwardian England* (Edward Elgar, 1991).

Lidgett, J.S., *My Guided Life* (London, Methuen & Co., 1936).

Lockhart, J.G., *Cosmo Gordon Lang* (1949).

Mace, J.H.B., *Henry Bodley Bromby A Memoir* (Longmans, Green, and Co., 1913).

Mack, E.C., *Public Schools and British Opinion Since 1800: The Relationship between Ideas and Evolution of an English Instituion* (Columbia, Columbia University Press, 1941).

Newsome, D., *Godliness and Good Learning: Four Studies on a Victorian Ideal* (London, John Murray, 1961).

O'Neil, R., *Cardinal Herbert Vaughan* (London, Burns and Oates, 1995).

Orchard, B., *A Look at the Head and the Fifty A History of Tonbridge School* (Tonbridge).

Maynard, J.O., *History of the Parish of Guardian Angels, Mile End 1868–1903* (London, no publisher, undated).

Mayor, S., *The Churches and the Labour Movement* (London, Independent Press Ltd, 1967).

Payne, M., *A Short History of the First Centenary of The Cranleigh School Mission* (Cranleigh, 1987).

Pennar-Lewis, W.T., *Mansfield College, Oxford* (London, Independent Press, 1947).

Pimlott, J.A.R., *Toynbee Hall* (London, 1935).

Rogers, J., *Mary Ward Settlement A History 1891–1931* (Passmore Edwards Research Series, 1931).

Sabben-Clare, J., *Winchester College* (Winchester, P. and G. Wells, 1988).

Simon, B. and Bradley, I., *The Victorian Public School: Studies in the Development of an Educational Institution* (London, Gill and MacMillan, 1971).

Simpkinson, C.H., *The Life and Work of Bishop Thorold of Rochester 1877–1891, Winchester 1891–1895* (London, Isbister & Co., 1896).

Smith, L., *Religion and the Rise of Labour* (Keele University Press, 1993).

Smith, M.J., *Professional Training for Social Work in Britain: An Historical Account* (1965).

Soloway, R., *Prelates and People* (London, Routledge and Kegan Paul, 1967).

Steadman, F.C., *In the Days of Miss Beale A Study of her Work and Influence* (London, Ed. J. Burrow & Co. Ltd, 1931).

Stocks, M.D., *Fifty Years in Every Street: The Story of the Manchester University Settlement* (Manchester University Press, 1945).

Stogden, E., *Harrow in London* (London, Harrow Mission, 1909).

Tozer, M., *Physical Education at Thring's Uppingham* (Uppingham School, 1976).

Trevelyan, J.P., *The Life of Mrs Humphry Ward* (1923).

Trotter, H.S.S., *Harrow Mission A Story of Fifty Years 1883–1933* (published as a supplement to the *Harrovian*, 1933).

Turberfield, A., *John Scott Lidgett Archbishop of Methodism?* (London, Epworth, 2003).

Watherston, P., *A Different Kind of Church* (London, Marshall Pickering, 1994).

Whetlor, S., *The Story of Notting Dale: From Potteries and Piggeries to Present Times* (Kensington and Chelsea History Group, 1998).

INDEX

147, 148, 149, 150, 151, 154,
200, 201, 206, 207, 208, 210
Browning, Robert 52, 140
Bruce, George 42, 47
Bruce, Marion 163
Bryant and May 33, 207
Burrows, Winfred 56
Buss, Septimus 163
Butler, Montagu 12, 95, 98, 103,
115, 118, 119, 123

C

Caius House 50, 82, 92
Cambridge House 18, 50, 83, 86
Cambridge University
Nonconformist Union 143
Campbell, Norman 18, 89
Campion, William 56, 63
Canning Town 24, 25, 50, 109,
110, 119, 131, 138, 139, 145,
155, 164, 174, 187, 205, 207
Carroll, William Alexander 75
Carter, Bonham 63, 75
Carter, William 118, 123
Catholic Educational Summer
Schools 154
Catholic public schools 153
Charity Organisation Society
(COS) 28, 94, 158, 191
Charles, R.H. 182
Charterhouse Mission, Southwark
109, 113, 150, 205
Charterhouse School 106, 122,
126, 127, 128
Cheltenham College 109, 111,
114
Cheltenham College Mission,
Peckham Grove 109, 111, 128
Cheltenham Ladies College 60,
159, 173

Children's Country Holiday
Movement 48
Children's Holiday Fund 47, 48,
66, 94, 95, 161, 165, 174, 189,
203
Christ Church Camberwell 18,
81
Christ Church College 16, 18,
24, 59, 69, 70, 71, 72, 75, 76,
79, 205
Christ Church Mission 18, 69,
70, 71, 72, 73, 75, 76, 77, 78,
205
Christ's College 43
Christian Social Union 58, 78,
164, 204
Christian Socialist xiii, 4, 15, 29,
37, 41, 49, 101, 138, 140, 164,
204
Christian Year 90
Church Army 74
Church of England 2, 3, 4, 13,
30, 58, 85, 86, 103, 128, 150,
154, 168, 174, 193
Church of England Temperance
Society 77
Clare College 18, 80, 81, 83, 85,
87, 88, 93, 94, 95, 98, 99, 105,
202
Claughton, Thomas 74
Clayton, George 140
Clewer sisters 75
Co-operation 24, 33, 36, 47, 68,
103, 111, 133, 150
Co-operative Women's Guild 157,
159, 160, 161, 162, 163
Co-operatives, Co-operative
Society 33, 36, 47, 68, 69,
136, 140, 145, 183, 201